Quotas &
Affirmative
Action

Quotas & Affirmative Action

Edited by Lester A. Sobel

Contributing editors: Joseph Fickes, Raymond Hill

Indexer: Grace M. Ferrara

Facts On File
119 West 57th Street, New York, N.Y. 10019

Quotas & Affirmative Action

Published by Facts On File, Inc., 119 West 57th Street, New York, N.Y. 10019.

Library of Congress Cataloging in Publication Data

Main entry under title:

Quotas & affirmative action.

    Includes index.
      1. Affirmative action programs—United States.
2. Discrimination in employment—United States.
3. Discrimination in education—United States.
I. Sobel, Lester A.
HD4903.5.U58Q67   331.13'3'0973   79-26722
ISBN 0-87196-166-0

Contents

2079933

Conflict Over Ideas,
Actions & Motives

AFFIRMATIVE ACTION, QUOTAS, equal opportunity, reverse dis-crimination. These are among the disputed terms that added bitterness as well as hope to the troubled racial situation of the United States in the 1970s. The expressions in controversy also include racial balance, goals, timetables, guidelines, ratios, numeri-cal standards, under-representation. The dispute, of course, is over the ideas, actions and motives these words represent—or are said to represent.

"Affirmative action" is the expression that is the most "official." Perhaps appropriately, therefore, it seems to be the term about which there is most confusion.

"Affirmative action" entered the language of racial discourse at least as early as the mid-1960s. Following the passage of the Civil Rights Act of 1964, President Lyndon B. Johnson in 1965 issued Executive Order Number 11246, which required employers with federal contracts to "take affirmative action to ensure that appli-cants are employed and that employees are treated . . . without regard to their race, color, religion, or national origin." Affirmative action was ultimately required to bar discrimination against wom-en and minorities in education as well as employment and in a variety of other areas, including housing and military service.

Affirmative Action & Civil Rights Law

The Civil Rights Act of 1964 contains three titles that became closely involved in controversy over affirmative action: *Title IV* au-thorizes the U.S. Attorney General to file public-school desegrega-tion suits on written complaint (but does not cover busing of pupils

1

or other such steps to end "racial imbalance"). *Title VI* bars discrimination under any federally assisted activity. *Title VII* bars employment discrimination because of "race, color, religion, sex, or national origin."

In debate in the two houses of Congress before the Civil Rights Act of 1964 was passed, opponents of the proposals charged that the law would result in racial quotas for schools and jobs.

The late Sen. Hubert Humphrey (D, Minn.), a strong force in winning the measure's ultimate acceptance, rejected these warnings. He assured the Senate June 9, 1964 that "nothing in Title VII . . . tells any employer whom he may hire. What the bill does . . . is simply to make it an illegal practice to use race as a factor in denying employment. It provides that men and women shall be employed on the basis of their qualifications, not as Catholic citizens, not as Protestant citizens, not as Jewish citizens, not as colored citizens, but as citizens of the United States."

Humphrey emphasized that "[n]othing in the bill or in the amendments requires racial quotas. The bill does not provide that people shall be hired on the basis of being Polish or Scandinavian or German, or Negro, or members of a particular religious faith. It provides that employers shall seek and recruit employees on the basis of their talents, their merit, and their qualifications for the job. The employer will outline the qualifications to be met for the job. The employer, not the government, will establish the standards. This is an equal employment opportunity provision." Humphrey noted that "the proponents of the bill have carefully stated on numerous occasions that Title VII does not require an employer to achieve any sort of racial balance in his work force by giving preferential treatment to any individual or group."

It is also pointed out that Section 401 of the Civil Rights Act of 1964 specified: " 'Desegregation' means the assignment of students to public schools and within such schools without regard to their race, color, religion, sex, or national origin, but 'desegregation' shall not mean the assignment of students to public schools in order to overcome racial imbalance."

Dispute Over 'Affirmative' Actions & Motives

In practice, it is charged, the government misused the civil rights laws to impose racial and sexual quotas in employment and education.

Rep. Marie S. Holt (R, Md.) said in a statement in the Congressional Record Feb. 9, 1978 that Congress "spoke against discrimination by enacting the civil rights laws, but these laws have been increasingly perverted by the federal bureaucracy to require preferential treatment for one race over all others."

"The American people believe that the law should be color-blind," Rep. Holt continued, "but the civil rights bureaucracy believes that race quotas should govern employment in both public and private sectors, the assignment of pupils to public schools and the admission of students to institutions of higher learning. . . . Private employers having federally funded contracts are required by Executive order to meet quotas in their hiring and promotion practices. . . . The imposition of quotas has been rampant inside the federal bureaucracy for years. . . . The civil service merit system is no longer a system based on merit. . . . The special analysis of the [1979] budget [indicates] . . . that the federal government will increasingly be going to court to force massive transfers of students for racial balancing of school enrollments. . . ."

Sen. Jesse Helms (R, N.C.) charged in Senate debate July 20, 1979 that "proponents of discriminatory quotas and goals have been partially successful in blurring the distinction between non-discrimination and affirmative action." He said that "the Department of Labor characterized affirmative action as part of an employer's large obligation not to discriminate. This confusion between non-discrimination and affirmative action has promoted a system in which discrimination is being institutionalized under the guise of a nondiscrimination program. Under the present bureaucratic formulation, affirmative action is, in reality, affirmative discrimination. Within the academic community it has created a system of reverse discrimination. Affirmative action quotas and goals inescapably produce a situation where discrimination is commonplace."

Helms noted that former Attorney General Edward Levi, past president of the University of Chicago, had "rejected HEW's [Department of Health, Education & Welfare] claims that the goals it repeatedly imposes are different than numerical quotas." Helms quoted Levi as saying: "The country has been on a program where affirmative action, requiring the statement of goals, is said with great profoundness not to be the setting of quotas. But it is the setting of quotas."

Sen. Edward M. Kennedy (D, Mass.) the same day, however, described "affirmative action" as "a commitment to insure that minorities will be represented in every phase of American life." "At a minimum," he said, he supported authority to use "timetables, goals or ratios" and a policy that "would only prevent the use of quotas in admissions to academic institutions." This minimum policy "would not impede efforts to overcome the particularly harmful effects of past discrimination in employment," Kennedy held.

Rep. John M. Ashbrook (R, Ohio) asserted in a statement in the Congressional Record May 31, 1979 that "twenty-five years after the Supreme Court's school desegregation decision and fifteen years after the Civil Rights Act banned discrimination in employment, among other things, we are seeing racial distinctions made a focal point of national policy in education, employment, and even the appointment of federal judges."

According to Ashbrook, "the stated aim of the administration in all these fields is to prefer some racial and national origin minorities over others. . . . Private schools with no history of discrimination are to be forced to recruit a given quota of certain minorities or lose their tax exemption as educational institutions; employers of forty million workers are told to give preferential treatment in hiring, training and promotion to certain groups or lose their federal contracts; employers of millions more workers are told by the Federal Equal Employment Opportunity Commission to establish racial quotas or face expensive legal action. . . .

"[The Carter Administration] tries to mask racial quotas under the ambiguous and innocuous sounding term 'affirmative action.' As originally conceived, . . . the term meant simply the elimination of policies which discriminated on the basis of race, national origin, or (more recently) sex. But this laudable policy has undergone a striking change: Certain 'favored' minority groups (blacks, Chicanos, American Indians and Eskimos) and women are to be preferred in employment and every other conceivable way over every other minority group and men. . . ."

Not all those engaged in the controversy are opposed to quotas. Rep. Paren J. Mitchell (D, Md.) had conceded in the House of Representatives June 17, 1977 that "quotas and affirmative action programs were never designed to completely eliminate discriminatory practices." "But," he continued, "who would possibly be so naive as to believe that we could address discriminatory practices and policies both publicly and privately without some kind of mechanism? The removal or nonexistence of quotas would represent a severe setback to the minimal gains that have been made by minorities."

Mitchell added that "I find nothing to indicate that quotas have burdened the effectiveness of the democratic process. . . . The purpose of quotas is not to discriminate. They are rather a mechanism to enhance the effectiveness of legislation meant to address discrimination. . . . [A] system of quotas inadvertently discriminates against a certain class of Americans: those who are not disadvantaged economically and socially. If, in fact, an individual's qualifications for a job or admission to a university were based on his or her having equal accessibility to the ingredients that help to make us equal, . . . [an anti-quota] proposal would be timely. . . . [T]his is not the case, and until it becomes reality, . . . [anti-quota advocates] are out of line with the mandate of the Congress. The policies of . . . [federal agencies] cannot be implemented on a broad national level without some mechanism that checks discrimination. Undoubtedly, this is not merely an issue of numbers but a question of depriving those who have been historically deprived. It would be in the best interest of Americans if all could compete on an equal basis. . . . Since all Americans are not able to compete on an equal basis, the rules of the game must be altered where necessary. Thus, a system that guarantees a balance—between those who are automatically granted an advantage and those who are not—is in order."

Rep. Shirley Chisholm (D, N.Y.) said the same day that in the annual argument over proposals to restrict the spending of government funds, "whether the debate is over 'affirmative action' or 'goals' or 'equality of opportunity' or 'quotas,' the attempt is the same: to undo our government's commitment to protecting the civil rights of minorities and women. . . . [T]he history of our country is ladened with patterns of discrimination which are still being felt and, in many cases, are still in evidence. We need only to look at the statistics—in health care, in educational achievement, in employment—to realize that blacks, Hispanic Americans, and women have not yet achieved parity. . . ."

Mrs. Chisholm continued: "[T]he courts of this country have continually and consistently recognized that numerical goals based on race or sex are appropriate and valid ways of addressing the problem of discrimination. The courts have acknowledged that it is simply not enough to say, at this point in time, 'all persons should have equal opportunity'; given the fact that discrimination against women and minorities was a matter of national policy and common practice, that in essence racism has been much a part of our history in this country as the Declaration of Independence, the courts and the Congress have repeatedly confirmed that remedial action was necessary to undo and disrupt the devastating effects of discrimination.

"Any contention that the existing law encourages 'reverse discrimination' must be looked at in the context of the reality of our national situation. Minorities and women are still grossly underrepresented in our educational institutions, in the labor market, in virtually every aspect of American life. . . . I often hear the argument that [minority] students with lower academic scores are admitted to federally funded institutions over their [white] colleagues who perform better on those tests, and that this in itself constitutes a kind of reverse discrimination. I would like to emphasize, however, that academic achievement as measured on standardized tests has never been the sole criterion for admission to any of our institutions. Students whose families have influence, students with certain athletic abilities, applicants who have professors or counselors with pull at various schools, have a far better chance to get into our schools than others who do not. Academic performance on standardized tests—which in themselves have been shown to be discriminatory—have never been the only measure of determining admissions. Why cannot we, why should we not, include background and heritage in the admissions determination formulas?"

Sen. S. I. Hayakawa (R, Calif.) told the Senate July 20, 1979 that he had once requested a hold-up of funds for government "programs which give preferential treatment to minority groups." He explained that he "did not intend to destroy opportunities available to people who have suffered unfairly from discrimination in the past, but to keep those opportunities from becoming color-coded handouts." He asked, "What gives our government the right to decide which group is the most deserving of special treatment? And how do they make these decisions? Obviously, blacks have suffered in the past. . . . But how does one decide that blacks need more special consideration than the Jews, . . . or the Italians, the Irish or the Chinese? . . ."

Hayakawa reported hearing from "many small businessmen who have trouble adhering to our federal employment guidelines. They must hire so many of one group, so many of another type—and on and on." He cited the case of an owner of a small finance company in Washington who reported being required to "hire a certain number of minority employees. . . . But he says as soon as he tries to fire a minority employee who is incompetent and simply not doing the job, the EEOC [Equal Employment Opportunity Commission] starts an investigation."

Hayakawa agreed that the initial affirmative action plans were necessary—"if only to draw attention to a problem that existed and needed correction." But the time had come, he held, to "let people fend for themselves in this regard. Congress has done its duty. . . . But we have done enough, and to do any more would, I think, do harm to the intent of our original mandates."

The controversy also included allegations that the rights of some minorities are disregarded by those who police affirmative action.

Sen. Helms charged in Senate debate June 7, 1979 that the U.S. Civil Rights Commission ignores white males "who are discriminated against on a daily basis because of their national origin." He accused the commission of showing concern exclusively for groups that can be termed "governmentally approved minorities." The latter include "women, blacks, persons of Spanish origin, Native Americans, Asian Americans and other persons of non-Caucasian heritage." Although "there is both religious and ethnic discrimination on a wide scale," he said, "from the work of the commission one gets the impression that there . . . [has never] been discrimination against ethnic Americans, such as Polish-Americans, Hungarian-Americans or Italian-Americans."

Sen. Birch Bayh (D, Ind.) the same day argued against legislative proposals to deny the use of federal appropriations to support affirmative action timetables, goals, ratios, quotas or other numerical requirements. "Frankly," he admitted, "I am concerned about the arbitrary impact of some quota systems. But unless we are willing to say unalterably that we are going to cover up our eyes and stick our heads in a sandpile someplace, when you have an institution or an employer that just flat out refuses to hire people or educate them, and not let our government impose any sanctions or utilize any tool, . . . what we are saying is that we are not going to do anything to try to stop discrimination."

Busing a Center of Controversy

One of the disputed "tools" used to end or prevent racial segregation in the schools is busing. Many communities have been rent by controversy and violence in the conflict over government or court orders that "racial imbalance" be ended by busing black children to schools in white neighborhoods or white children to "black schools." Opponents of so-called "forced busing" denounce it on various grounds, among them assertions that busing for racial reasons is damaging to education, harmful to children and designed to institute racial quotas in violation of civil rights law.

Rep. Ronald M. Mottl (D, Ohio), author of a proposed Constitutional amendment designed to ban "forced busing" for racial balance, told the House of Representatives July 24, 1979 that such busing "is the use of government power against children solely on the basis of their race." He held that "under the principles of the Constitution and of fundamental fairness, a compelling and even overwhelming case must be made to support racial classifications by government officials. If children are to be classified by race, and then excluded from their neighborhood schools because of skin color and forced to travel elsewhere, the evidence must be clear and convincing that this racially based penalty is justified."

According to Mottl, "the case for court-ordered busing has never been proven. . . . Court-ordered busing has not worked. . . . It is a social policy imposed by an activist judiciary, and it is a mistaken social policy that is leading to the virtual destruction of public education at neighborhood schools in cities where it is used. . . ." Mottl said that opponents of his amendment "argue that court-ordered busing is really a temporary social irritation, unworthy of a constitutional response." His answer, Mottl said, was that "court-ordered busing is . . . the infliction of a penalty . . . on persons . . . solely because of their race." He charged that in ordering busing, "the federal judiciary . . . is routinely ordering discrimination on a massive scale."

Opposing Mottl's amendment, Rep. Cardiss Collins (D, Ill.), chairwoman of the Congressional Black Caucus, charged that the anti-busing proposal was "an attempt to turn back the clock on desegregation of the schools." She suggested that it was evidence "that some of my colleagues have forgotten the legacy of enforced segregation and slavery which still tells too many black children that they must have the worst school buildings, the worst textbooks, the worst school personnel and the worst learning opportunities." The anti-busing effort, she held, was evidence of a "desire to undercut desegregation—to undercut efforts to provide equal educational opportunity for all of America's schoolchildren."

Rep. Shirley Chisholm, also opposing a ban on "forced busing," called it "ironic . . . that in the 25th year of the celebration of the famous *Brown* decision [against segregation in public education] that we are gathered here . . . to prevent the courts from enforcing those measures which are necessary for the continual encouragement and promotion of the equitability of educational opportunities in this nation." She recalled that the *Brown* decision "was one of the decisions in which we said we had to use certain instruments . . . to move in the direction of equality and integrated education, and the reason we had to take this position is because we could not depend on the morality nor the conscience of those individuals who had the power to move into the direction of bringing about equitability of educational opportunity." Rep. Chisholm suggested that by defeating the proposed ban, she and her colleagues would "be able to go back to our constituents and explain that somehow . . . we are still moving in the direction of trying to bring about the equitability of opportunities on every level in this great country."

Rep. Paul Findley (R, Ill.), expressing a prevalent pro-busing viewpoint, held that the Mottl amendment and a proposed substitute were not anti-busing amendments. "Both are anti-desegregation amendments," he declared. "Only about three percent of the students who are now bused would be affected by either amendment," he continued. ". . . Ninety-seven percent . . . would be untouched. . . . Therefore, clearly, the issue is anti-school desegregation, plain and simple. . . ." "If you believe segregated schools are wrong," Findley held, "you are faced with the uncomfortable realization that busing is the only effective way to end it. . . ."

Rep. John M. Murphy (D, N.Y.) said in a statement opposing the anti-busing amendments that "busing is a remedy that is not applied without considerable proof of overt discrimination. The U.S. Supreme Court has held . . . that busing can only be imposed after proofs of 'purposely segregative practices' by a school district and only to the extent necessary to cure the particular constitutional violation established by the evidence."

Rep. Richardson Preyer (D, N.C.), opposing the anti-busing amendments, added that "to correct a past denial of equal rights on the basis of race, we must use race in formulating a remedy."

Rep. Carroll A. Campbell, Jr. (R, S.C.) held that "this issue is much more complex than those strongly on either side of the issue have suggested." Among the factors in the dispute, he said, "are considerations of the day-to-day lives of our children and the rightness or wrongness of becoming slaves to quotas—quotas dictating how many blacks or how many whites shall participate in our societal organizations, how many women or men, how many Puerto Ricans or Mexicans, how many Protestants or Catholics. . . ."

Rep. John H. Rousselot (R, Calif.) asserted that the anti-busing proposal "reaffirms the civil liberties guaranteed to all Americans by the Fourteenth Amendment as interpreted by the Supreme Court in its 1954 landmark desegregation decision, *Brown against the Board of Education.*"

Rousselot continued: "The arguments of the lawyers and justices associated with the *Brown* decision were based upon the proposition that the Constitution forbade any use of racial classification for governmental action. The NAACP Legal Defense Fund, in its briefs, in testimony introduced in the trial court in Topeka, Kan. and in the oral arguments before the U.S. Supreme Court, maintained unwaveringly that it was wrong to classify people on the basis of color and ancestry. Lawyers for the black plaintiffs urged the court again and again to remove from the states the power to use race in distinguishing among its citizenry. Robert Carter, chief counsel for Topeka's black plaintiffs, rested his case against school segregation on two grounds: First, that 'the state has no authority and no power to make any distinction or any classification among its citizenry based upon race and color alone'; and second, that 'the rights under the Fourteenth Amendment are individual rights' and not group rights—that each person should be treated as an individual, without regard for race, creed, or ancestry.

"In building the case against segregation, the Kansas NAACP lawyers stressed the individual rights of blacks to send their children to the nearest school. Segregation imposed on black children the handicap of spending extra time traveling to and from school, which, they argued, was detrimental to their development. . . . Oliver Brown, the lead plaintiff in the case, was spurred to action by what he considered to be an abridgement of the individual rights of his family. By no means an activist in the civil rights movement or a particular enthusiast of the NAACP, he was concerned primarily with the right of his daughter, Linda, to attend the neighborhood school. His action was motivated by his understandable parental concern over the inconvenience and lack of safety which resulted from busing Linda to the 'colored school' many miles away, instead of to the neighborhood school, only seven blocks from his home. It is this same 'parental concern,' not prejudice, that motivates the overwhelming public abhorrence of the forced busing programs mandated by the federal courts. . . ."

According to Rousselot, "the *Brown* decision was intended to remove from the states the power to use racial classification to restrict the opportunities of its citizens. That the Congress shared this understanding of the meaning of the *Brown* decision is reflected in the passage of the Civil Rights Act of 1964," which, he said "specifically disallow[ed] forced busing: 'Nothing herein shall empower any official or court of the U.S. to issue any order seeking to achieve a racial balance in any school by requiring the transportation of pupils or students from one school to another, or one school district to another, in order to achieve such racial balance. . . .'"

Rousselot said: "The 1954 *Brown* decision supposedly removed from the states the power to assign children to school on the basis of race. The federal court system has reversed that decision, using it instead as the authority for assigning children to school solely on the basis of race. . . . Today, 25 years after the *Brown* . . . decision, Linda Brown could still not attend the school nearest her home—she would have to be bused for racial balance. The individual rights her father had fought for and supposedly won in 1954 would still be denied to her."

RACIAL ANTAGONISM IS AN ENDEMIC American problem. It can be argued that its genesis is to be found in the initial arrival of Christopher Columbus in the Americas. This event is seen as the first in a long series of frequently bloody actions by which white people of European ancestry largely replaced dark-skinned non-Europeans on both of the American continents.

Or perhaps the basic racial struggle in the United States can be traced more directly to the landing of a Dutch ship in the British colony of Jamestown in 1619. The twenty Africans in its cargo were the first black people to be sold to white men in the land that was to become the United States. The events that followed include more than 200 years of black slavery, a fratricidal Civil War that ended legal slavery in the United States, long years thereafter of black suffering and discrimination and a brilliant but still incomplete civil rights struggle that in dedication and bitterness could be classified as another War Between the States.

The civil rights campaign's successes produced an apparent national consensus that racial discrimination must end and equal opportunity be assured for all. The resurgent feminist movement of more recent years has made the nation conscious of the injustices suffered by women too, and the consensus recognized the right of women also to equal treatment and opportunity.

The controversy over quotas and affirmative action, largely a phenomenon of the 1970s, is a result of the national effort to make the rights of women and minorities a reality. This book is intended to serve as a record of this phenomenon. The narrative that follows is based largely on the material compiled by FACTS ON FILE in its continuing chronicle of these times. Much of the story is highly controversial, but a conscientious effort was made to record all events without bias and to make this a useful and reliable reference tool.

LESTER A. SOBEL

New York, N.Y.
December, 1979

Integration Level Low in Early 1970s

Situation at Start of 1970s

Despite civil rights laws and affirmative action policies, serious lags were reported in the early 1970s in providing jobs on a non-discriminatory basis for women and minority members and in integrating American schools.

Clues from census. Indications of the employment and education situation of women and minorities as the 1970s started were provided Oct. 15, 1972 by the Census Bureau as it released its summary of general social and economic findings of the 1970 census. The report, based on sample data, included trends in employment, income, education, family patterns and ethnic background.

Employment—The census found that the increasing number of working women had swelled the nation's work force despite a trend of earlier retirement among men. In 1970, 39.6% of all women 14 years old and older were in the labor force, compared with 29% in 1950. Among white women, employment increased from 28.1% to 38.9% in the 20-year period, and among black women from 37.1% to 44.4%

Males aged 14 and over in the labor force declined from 79% in 1950 to 72.9% in 1970, largely because only 24.8% of men 65 years old and older were in the work force, compared with 41.4% in 1950.

Agriculture, forestry and fisheries occupied only 3.5% of the work force in 1970, a decline of nearly one half in one decade. Another sharp decline occurred among female domestics, whose numbers dropped to

1.1 million from 1.7 million 10 years before, including 500,000 black women, down from 900,000.

One of seven workers was employed by federal, state or local governments, totaling 12.3 million workers, up from 7.9 million in 1960. Self-employed men constituted 10.2% of working men, down from 15.7% in 1960, and 3.7% of working women, down from 5% in 1960.

Income—The census found 13.3% of all Americans in families with income below the poverty level, including one-fourth of those over 65, one-seventh of those under 18 and about one-third of all blacks. One of five families had incomes over $15,000 a year, while another fifth had annual incomes below $5,000.

Median family income for all Americans had risen to $9,590, a 70% increase from $5,660 in 1960. Proportionately, black family income had risen even more, nearly doubling from $3,161 to $6,067 in the decade, but still only 61% of the figure for whites—$9,961.

Families on welfare totaled 5.3% of all families—4% of white families and 17.6% of black families.

Education—In 1970, 59.5 million individuals attended schools at various levels, including 89.3% of all 16 and 17 year olds, up from 80.9% in 1960 and 68.7% in 1940; 21% of 19–25 year olds were in school in 1970, compared with 14.6% in 1960 and 6.6% in 1940.

Median school years attended by those over 24 had risen to 12.1 by 1970. Black men had attended an average of 9.7 years of school, and black women 10.2.

Of all 16–21-year-old males, 15.2% had not graduated from high school and were not enrolled in school, including 12.5% of urban whites, 25.1% of urban blacks and 25.4% of urban Spanish-heritage youths.

Family and sex patterns—Only 95 men were counted in the census for every 100 women, down from 97 in 1960 and 101 in 1940. Women's life expectancy was 74.6 years, men's was 67.1, and women outnumbered men in every age group over 20.

Of 51.2 million families, women headed 5.5%. Among blacks, 1.33 million of 4.8 million families had no male wage earner present.

Ethnic background—Some 9.6 million Americans were foreign born, and another 23.9 million had at least one foreign-born parent. About 7.8 million

Americans said their mother tongue was Spanish, 6.1 million cited German, 4.1 million Italian, 2.6 million French and 1.6 million Yiddish.

Blacks constituted 11.1% of the total population, and 21% of the population of central cities. Nine large cities had over 40% black populations, and four were over 50% black. Some 58% of all blacks lived in central cities, where only 28% of whites lived.

School integration low. The Department of Health, Education & Welfare reported Jan. 3, 1971 that a federal government-sponsored survey had indicated that 61% of the nation's black students and 65.6% of white students still attended largely segregated schools during 1968. Leon E. Panetta, director of HEW's Office of Civil Rights, said the figures "present what can be considered the basic nationwide picture today."

An HEW statement accompanying the figures said the survey of public schools "displayed a shockingly low desegregation ratio on a national basis." HEW Secretary Robert H. Finch said the survey "points up the extensiveness of the problem on a nationwide basis and the need to provide effectively for the educational rights and needs of the disadvantaged, no matter where they may be."

According to the survey, 61% of black students in elementary and secondary schools attended schools that had 95% black enrollment, with 39.7% in schools with no white students. Only 23.4% of black students attended schools where whites were in a majority. Only 2.1% of white students attended schools with 50% minority enrollment, according to the report. It said 65.6% of white students were in schools with 95 to 100% white enrollment.

Turnaround claimed—The Southern Regional Council asserted in a report made public March 24, 1971 that for the first time desegregation in the South's public schools was the rule rather than the exception. The turnabout occurred, the council said, despite the proliferation of all-white private academies and the continued operation of some all-black school systems.

In releasing the report from its headquarters in Atlanta, the council also ac-

cused the Nixon Administration of "playing a deceptive game of numbers" by using misleading figures about the extent of actual desegregation.

Despite the recent gains, the council said the South was "a far cry" from "the final dismantling of the dual [school] system." It added that desegregation in 1970 and so far in 1971 was less successful than the Administration asserted in its figures, but "more successful than policies of that government gave it any right to be."

The 35,000-word report, entitled "The South and Her Children: School Desegregation 1970-71," was prepared by the council's staff.

The report took issue with figures announced in 1970 by Elliot L. Richardson, who had replaced Robert Finch as health, education and welfare secretary, that 97% of Southern school districts were desegregated and 90.5% of all students enrolled in schools in those districts. The council said Richardson's figures "obscured the fact that the pattern of segregation within so-called desegregated areas was widespread."

Seven Nixon Administration officials had met March 6 with representatives of Southern school systems in Atlanta and praised their efforts to end school segregation as "a record of remarkable progress."

Following the closed door session, Richardson lauded the educators' desegregation achievements. He told newsmen that "as far as the actual achievement of desegregated school systems . . . the South now had proportionately more black people attending desegregated schools than the North has."

Richardson and the six other Administration officials, all members of the White House Committee on Education, conferred with leaders of seven state education advisory committees set up by the White House to help ease problems arising from the desegregation of the South's public schools.

HEW June 17 released the results of a nationwide survey apparently proving that public school integration in the South had increased dramatically in the last two years.

Other figures in the survey indicated that school integration in many of the North's large cities had shown a significant decline over the same two-year period.

According to HEW, of the total black students in the U.S., the percentage attending majority white schools increased from 23% in the fall of 1968 to 33% in the fall of 1970. The increase was attributed by HEW almost wholly to the increase in integration in the South.

In the 11 Southern states, HEW's data showed, the percentage of Negroes in schools with a white majority rose from 18% in 1968 to 39% in 1970. In the North and West, integration remained steady at 27%. Increased integration in some areas of the North and West was offset by declines in big cities.

New York, Detroit, Philadelphia, St. Louis, Boston, San Francisco and Minneapolis all showed a drop in the percentage of black students in schools with a white majority.

Los Angeles, Newark, N.J., San Diego and Denver were among the large cities in the North and West showing an increase in school integration.

Following is the table compiled by the Department of Health, Education and Welfare on the rate of integration in the nation's 100 largest school districts:

District	Total Negroes		Negroes in White Schools (In Percentages)	
	1968	1970	1968	1970
New York	31.5	34.5	19.7	16.3
Los Angeles	22.6	24.1	4.7	5.9
Chicago	52.9	54.8	3.2	3.0
Detroit	59.2	63.8	9.0	5.8
Philadelphia	58.8	60.5	9.6	7.4
Houston	33.3	35.6	5.3	8.4
Dade Co. (Miami)	24.3	25.4	12.4	21.7
Baltimore City	65.1	67.1	7.7	9.4
Dallas	30.8	33.8	2.1	2.7
Cleveland	55.9	57.6	4.8	4.2
Memphis	53.6	51.5	2.6	6.5
Washington	93.5	94.6	0.9	1.2
Milwaukee	23.9	26.0	12.4	12.2
San Diego	11.6	12.4	25.1	32.1
Duval Co., Fla. (Jacksonville)	28.2	29.4	12.6	25.6
St. Louis, Mo.	63.5	65.6	7.1	2.5
Orleans Parish, La. (New Orleans)	67.1	69.5	8.8	7.8
Indianapolis	33.7	35.8	22.4	20.5
Atlanta	61.7	68.7	5.4	6.6
Denver	14.1	14.7	20.0	44.6
Boston	27.1	29.8	23.3	18.0
Nashville-Davidson Co., Tenn.	24.1	24.6	16.8	25.0
San Francisco	27.5	28.5	15.5	14.2
Cincinnati	42.9	45.0	21.9	16.9
Seattle	11.0	12.8	44.8	40.6
Charlotte-Mecklenburg Co.	29.2	30.8	27.7	90.7
Newark	72.5	72.2	2.1	2.9
Tulsa	12.2	13.7	15.6	27.5
San Antonio	14.7	15.3	10.6	9.3
Portland, Ore.	8.1	9.2	57.4	62.1
Pittsburgh	39.2	40.3	21.3	23.3
Kansas City, Mo.	46.8	50.2	14.0	9.3
Buffalo	36.6	38.5	27.0	26.8
Mobile Co., Ala.	41.7	44.5	10.9	18.2
Oakland, Calif.	55.2	56.9	5.5	6.5
Minneapolis	7.5	8.9	70.8	57.6
Birmingham, Ala.	51.4	54.6	7.2	15.8
Toledo, Ohio	26.7	26.6	22.6	24.1
Dayton, Ohio	38.3	40.7	10.9	13.0
Akron, Ohio	25.8	27.3	37.7	36.5
Norfolk, Va.	41.9	44.9	11.5	32.9
Louisville	46.1	48.3	13.5	11.7
St. Paul	5.8	6.4	87.6	64.6
Richmond	68.3	64.2	6.4	11.7
Gary, Ind.	61.6	64.7	3.1	3.5
Rochester, N.Y.	28.9	33.1	45.6	40.9

A House subcommittee was told in New York City May 21 that voluntary school integration in the North was failing.

New York state officials and educators told members of the General Education Subcommittee of the House Education and Labor Committee that neighborhood housing patterns stood in the way of increased school integration. The six visiting representatives and witnesses also exchanged views on the value of voluntary versus mandatory school integration.

In addition to Badillo, the panel members at the hearings were Victor V. Veysey (R, Calif.), Roman C. Pucinski (D, Ill.), Mario Biaggi (D, N.Y.), Shirley Chisholm (D, N.Y.) and Louise Day Hicks (D, Mass.).

Dr. Harvey B. Scribner, chancellor of New York City's schools, said that "because this nation is composed of black housing areas and white housing areas, and because this pattern is not likely to change overnight, school integration plans will frequently have to transcend school district bondaries."

HEW reiterated Jan. 12, 1972 that integration efforts in the South had led for the first time to a smaller proportion of black students attending totally segregated schools in the South than in the North or West.

An HEW survey revealed that 9.2% of the black pupils, or 290,390, in the 11 southern states attended all-black schools, while the corresponding figure in the 32 northern and western states was 11.2%, or 325,874, and in the border states, 24.2%, or 162,578. In 1968, 68% of the South's black students had attended totally segregated schools.

Black male professionals as a percent of all professionals, by occupation, selected years, 1890–1970

Occupation	1890	1900	1910	1920	1930	1940	1950	1960	1970
Accountants	10.1	—	6.7	—	—	—	1.4	2.8	6.4
Actors	—	5.8	2.0	3.6	5.4	3.3	2.3	—	3.1
Architects	.2	.2	.2	.1	.1	.2	.3	.3	.8
Artists	.3	.5	.5	.4	.4	.5	1.5	1.4	1.3
Authors	.3	.2	.05	(1)	.08	(1)	—	(1)	.2
Chemists	—	—	.3	.5	.6	1.4	1.4	1.9	2.3
Clergy	48.1	50.3	47.0	50.1	45.1	35.8	28.6	16.9	8.7
College professors	(2)	(2)	.5	1.5	2.1	2.9	3.9	4.3	6.5
Dentists	.5	.7	1.2	2.8	3.2	3.1	2.6	2.4	1.4
Designers	—	—	.2	.3	.2	.3	1.3	3.3	1.0
Editors	.5	.7	.5	1.7	.6	1.8	.9	1.9	1.1
Engineers	—	—	.6	.5	.6	.5	2.5	5.3	9.2
Lawyers	1.7	2.3	2.1	2.5	2.2	2.1	2.2	2.4	2.3
Musicians	5.1	8.9	8.8	9.7	14.2	10.4	8.8	7.0	3.3
Nurses	—	—	.7	.4	.3	.3	.7	—	.8
Physicians	3.2	5.1	8.1	9.4	7.5	7.3	6.9	5.1	5.4
Photographers	—	—	1.0	1.3	.8	—	1.5	—	1.3
Librarians	—	—	—	.06	.06	—	.5	—	1.0
Social workers	—	—	.5	—	.4	1.9	4.0	6.8	1.0
Teachers, elementary	(2)	(2)	(2)	(2)	(2)	(2)	(2)	16.3	10.6
Teachers, secondary	—	—	—	—	—	—	—	18.0	19.4
Teachers not elsewhere classified	(2)28.7	(2)25.3	(2)18.9	(2)16.2	(2)16.1	(2)28.5	(2)29.1	3.2	—
Pharmacists	—	—	—	—	—	1.6	1.8	1.8	—

¹ Category includes editors and authors.
² Category includes college professors and other teachers of various levels.

NOTE: Dashes indicate no data available.

From *Monthly Labor Review* May 1977

The percentage of blacks attending integrated schools in the South rose to 44%, compared with 38.1% in 1970 and 18.4% in 1968.

Resegregation charged—Six civil rights organizations May 23, 1972 released a report charging that desegregation of urban schools in the South was "far from complete," and that resegregation was increasing with the complicity of all levels of government.

In a study of 43 Southern cities, the report found that at least a dozen were "operating under shockingly inadequate and outdated court orders and desegregation plans." Of 2,727 schools, over 1,000 were totally or nearly completely segregated, partly because of changing racial residence patterns fostered by "the Federal Housing Administration, local planning commissions and housing authorities, urban renewal, school boards, highways departments, realtors, and even transit companies."

The report found a trend toward disproportionate suspension of black students in integrated schools.

The study was sponsored by the Alabama Council on Human Relations, the American Friends Service Committee, the Delta Ministry of the National Council of Churches, the NAACP Legal Defense Fund, the Southern Regional Council and the Washington Research Project.

30,000 black school jobs lost. A National Education Association (NEA) survey found that over 30,000 teaching jobs for blacks had been eliminated in 17 Southern and border states through desegregation and discrimination since 1954, it was reported May 19, 1972.

The proportion of teachers who were black declined in the region in 1954–70 from 21% to 19%, although the proportion of black students increased slightly. The percentage of existing or projected black teaching jobs displaced was lowest in Alabama, which the report attributed to court orders and continued segregation, and highest in Kentucky, Missouri and Delaware.

According to Samuel B. Ethridge, NEA teacher rights director, "as early as 1968 one state department of education identified 25 counties which employed one or more black teachers in 1954, and employed none in 1968."

Few blacks among executives. The Race Relations Information Center, a group based in Nashville, Tenn., released Sept. 30, 1970 the results of a survey that showed there were only three black executives among the 3,182 senior officers of the largest 50 U.S. corporate firms.

The three black executives identified as corporate directors were Robert C. Weaver of the Metropolitan Life Insurance Co.; Clifton R. Wharton Jr. of the Equitable Life Assurance Society and Thomas A. Wood of the Chase Manhattan Bank.

Commission reports enforcement breakdown. The U.S. Commission on Civil Rights reported Oct. 12, 1970 that there had been a "major breakdown" in the enforcement of the nation's legal mandates forbidding racial discrimination.

The commission's findings were announced by the Rev. Theodore M. Hesburgh, the panel's chairman and president of the University of Notre Dame. Hesburgh said the findings, based on a six-month study of the executive departments and agencies charged with enforcing the nation's civil rights laws, showed that "the credibility of the government's total civil rights effort has been seriously undermined."

The 1,115-page report was entitled "The Federal Civil Rights Enforcement Effort." Hesburgh called it one of the most important documents "the commission has issued in its 13-year history."

At the news conference, Hesburgh emphasized that the breakdown in enforcement of the civil rights laws "did not originate in the current Administration, nor was there any substantial period in the past when civil rights enforcement was at a uniformly high level of effectiveness."

Black female professionals as percent of all professionals, by occupation, selected years, 1890-1970

Occupation	1890	1900	1910	1920	1930	1940	1950	1960	1970
Accountants	—	1.6	2.1	1.6	2.5	—	.5	.9	3.1
Actors	1.6	0	1.8	—	—	.3	.7	—	.6
Architects	.7	.6	.01	.3	.3	—	—	.4	.04
Artists	.2	.2	.4	—	.01	.2	.3	.5	.2
Authors	—	—	.03	(¹)	—	(¹)	—	(¹)	.06
Chemists	—	—	.01	.02	.02	—	.2	—	.3
Clergy	.6	1.1	.2	.6	.8	—	.8	—	.2
College professors	(²)	(²)	.09	1.4	1.7	1.5	1.5	1.3	3.1
Dentists	.02	.04	.01	.1	.05	.2	.06	—	.05
Designers	—	—	—	.1	.2	.1	.4	.3	.4
Editors	.06	.07	.07	1.2	.1	1.2	.2	1.3	.6
Engineers	—	—	—	—	—	—	.2	.1	.3
Lawyers	—	.06	.006	.01	.04	.06	.1	—	.2
Musicians	6.7	7.6	8.0	5.9	4.8	3.1	3.2	2.4	.5
Nurses	—	—	7.4	8.8	9.4	10.7	13.1	21.2	6.7
Physicians	1.3	1.0	1.5	.6	.9	.2	.8	.8	.7
Photographers	—	—	.14	.3	.1	—	.2	—	.2
Librarians	—	—	—	.1	.3	.6	1.5	—	2.8
Social workers	—	—	1.1	—	1.4	2.7	5.2	5.8	10.7
Teachers, elementary	(²)289.1	(²)286.7	(²)276.8	(²)280.0	(²)277.3	(²)280.1	(²)270.7	50.2	52.8
Teachers, secondary	—	—	—	—	—	—	.3	12.1	16.5
Teachers not elsewhere classified	—	—	—	—	—	—	—	3.9	—
Pharmacists	—	—	—	—	—	—	—	—	—

NOTE: Dashes indicate no data available.

¹ Category includes editors and authors.
² Category includes college professors and other teachers of various levels.

From *Monthly Labor Review* May 1977

Hesburgh said the commission had noted that in the past decade and a half an impressive number of laws had been passed seeking to eliminate racial discrimination.

"Each civil rights law that has been passed, each executive order that has been issued, and each court decision favorable to the cause of civil rights has been viewed as another step along the road to full equality for all Americans," Hesburgh said.

"But perhaps," he added, "what has been lost sight of is that these legal mandates in and of themselves cannot bring about a truly open society, that they must be implemented—and it is at this point that we have found a major breakdown."

Hesburgh said the report found that some of the laws had worked, notably in the areas of voting rights, public accommodations and school integration, but that these were found to be exceptions. The rights panel said it found government-wide failure in enforcement in such areas as employment, housing and use of federal grants.

The commission also said that the absence of pressures from the White House had contributed to the general breakdown in enforcement of the laws.

The annual NAACP report June 29, 1972 said that 1971 had seen more school desegregation than any year since the 1954 Supreme Court *Brown vs. Topeka* ruling, "in spite of frustrating maneuvers by the Nixon Administration." But the employment situation of urban blacks in 1971 was worse "than at any time since the great depression" the report said, with one third of black youths unemployed.

Black complaints & demands. President Richard Nixon met March 25, 1971 with black members of the House of Representatives, all Democrats, and appointed a White House staff panel to study a list of recommendations made by the group, known as the Congressional Black Caucus.

The group's recommendations, presented in a 32-page booklet, expressed the "majority" black viewpoint that rep-

resentatives of the Nixon Administration, "by word and deed, have at crucial points retreated from the national commitment to make Americans of all races and cultures equal in the eyes of their government."

"Our people," the congressmen said, "are no longer asking for equality as a rhetorical promise" but were demanding "equality of results."

At the annual convention of the National Association for the Advancement of Colored People, held in Minneapolis July 5–9, Dr. Andrew F. Brimmer, the sole black on the Federal Reserve System's board of governors, said July 6 that the job outlook for black Americans was so bleak that some had "given up" and no longer even entered the nation's labor force.

Herbert Hill, NAACP labor director, charged July 8 that the Administration's "benign neglect" policy "has now become criminal negligence." Hill accused the government of having failed to enforce laws forbidding discrimination by federal contractors. He said the government failure had contributed to the high unemployment rate among blacks.

Vernon E. Jordan Jr., scheduled to become executive director of the National Urban League, accused Nixon and his Administration July 28 of compiling a "record of ambiguity" toward black Americans. He said the Administration had let the nation's civil rights law "languish in dusty books."

Jordan's remarks were made at the closing session of the league's 61st annual conference in Detroit.

Administration claims rights gains. A White House staff report on civil rights achievements was released Feb. 15, 1972 by Communications Director Herbert Klein.

The reports included the following claims in "civil rights and related social programs":

■ Federal civilian minority employment had risen to 19.5% by May 1971, including seven black ambassadors and nearly 100 blacks in "super-grade" jobs, as opposed to 63 in 1969.

■ Blacks in completely segregated schools declined from 40% in 1968 to 12% in 1971–1972, while the Internal

Revenue Service eliminated tax-deductable status for segregated private schools.

Toward the middle of the year, the U.S. Civil Service Commission reported July 1 that the number of blacks, Spanish-Americans and other minority group members had increased in all grade levels of federal service above the lowest in the year ending November 1971. Overall federal minority employment excluding the Postal Service rose by 2.1% in the period, although the proportion of minorities in federal service dropped from 19.6% to 19.5% in the year, taking into account extensive postal job cutbacks.

The gains in high-paying jobs resulted from a one-third minority share of the 31,485 increase in U.S. white collar jobs.

U.S. criticized—Federal programs to assure equal job rights at government agencies and among contractors were criticized as ineffective in June 1972 by the outgoing head of the Office of Federal Contract Compliance (OFCC) and by the Public Interest Research Group, a Ralph Nader research organization.

George Holland, director of the OFCC since February, submitted his resignation June 1, effective July 1, charging that a recent reorganization of the agency had diminished its effectiveness in enforcing equal job opportunities in firms doing business with the federal government.

In his letter of resignation Holland charged that the reorganization, which decentralized the agency and merged its field offices with other Labor Department units, "diminishes program impact, diffuses program authority and denies program uniformity."

The Public Interest Research Group report, issued June 24, charged the Civil Service Commission with inadequate and unsympathetic supervision of job rights complaint procedures in government agencies, and with failing to require agencies to provide training and promotion programs to compensate for past discrimination against blacks and women.

The report charged that half of all complaints closed in the 1970 fiscal year and reviewed by the commission had taken over six months to process, despite regulations requiring action within two

months. Of those cases reviewed by the commission, a finding of discrimination was made in only 7.4% of the cases in fiscal 1970 and 4.8% in the first half of fiscal 1971. In 1970, supervisors were disciplined in only 1.8% of the cases, and only through reprimands or training classes. The Civil Service Board of Appeals and Review had rejected complaints in over 98% of the cases it reviewed.

Commission chairman Robert Hampton said June 24 "the data the conclusions are based on is quite dated."

Numerical Goals or Racial Quotas

Early affirmative action programs, requiring federal contractors to try to hire specific numbers or percentages of minority workers, were attacked by critics as illegal racial quotas.

Philadelphia Plan. A federal district judge in Philadelphia March 14, 1970 upheld the constitutionality of the Labor Department's "Philadelphia Plan" to increase minority employment in the construction industry. Judge Charles R. Weiner rejected a suit filed Jan. 6 by the Contractors Association of Eastern Pennsylvania requesting an injunction against the plan and a declaration that it was unconstitutional.

Weiner said in his 22-page decision that the pilot job program did not in any way violate the Civil Rights Act of 1964 which forbade racial quotas in employment procedures. Weiner said "it is fundamental that civil rights without economic rights are mere shadows." He said it did not violate the civil rights act because it "does not require the contractor to hire a definite percentage of a minority group."

(The Philadelphia plan required all contractors working on federally-funded projects to make good-faith efforts to hire specified percentages of blacks in those projects costing $500,000 or more.)

The contractors' association had contended in their suit that the plan denied them equal protection of the laws because it was being applied only in Philadelphia. But Secretary of Labor George P. Shultz later announced that similar plans were being adopted for 18 other large cities, unless those cities devised pilot plans of their own.

The Philadelphia Plan, however, was reported to have fallen short of its expected minority hiring goals, according to initial progress reports disclosed May 2. Citizen organizations in Philadelphia, where the plan was first set into motion, had reported to the department's Office of Federal Contract Compliance that contractors were abusing and disregarding the plan by not taking on additional minority group employes.

The preliminary reports were still being received by Benjamin Stanley, head of the Compliance office. Stanley said that an official count of minorities on construction job payrolls had not been completed, but that initial reports had shown that "there is no question, compliance is lagging."

gotiations, black community leaders announced they had agreed upon a program designed to train Negroes for skilled construction jobs. The accord came after black community groups had begun a drive in September 1969 to force open construction union rolls to Negroes by shutting down several state construction projects.

The agreement called for 4,000 Negroes to be trained as skilled construction workers and admitted to the Chicago unions. Earlier negotiations had broken down after construction officials had refused to accept the black demands for 9,000 on-the-job training positions. The unions offered instead to train 1,000 Negroes and to seek apprenticeship positions for 3,000 others.

Under the agreement, 1,000 Negroes who could qualify as apprentices or journeymen would be put to work immediately.

A second 1,000 would start on-the-job training as soon as possible, and another 1,000 would be slated to begin journeyman training leading to full status as skilled workers.

The other 1,000 would be given a specialized pre-apprentice training program for rudimentary construction skills.

Ohio plan. The Supreme Court Jan. 12, 1970 refused to review an Ohio state court ruling upholding an equal employment plan similar to the Nixon Administration's "Philadelphia plan" setting goals for the number of nonwhite employes on a federal construction project. The court rejected an appeal from an Ohio contractor who had been denied a contract for a federally-subsidized college building even though he had been low bidder. The contractor had refused to give assurances, required by the federal government, that he would attempt to employ a specified number of Negro workers.

Plumber apprentice plan. The Department of Labor said Jan. 27, 1970 that the United Association of Plumbers and Pipefitters had agreed to assist 500 Negro apprentices in finding jobs in areas where there was a manpower shortage. Labor Secretary George P. Shultz described the accord as an important breakthrough in federal efforts to find new jobs for Negroes and other minorities.

The agreement was in the form of a contract signed by the union, the National Constructors Association and the Labor Department. Under its terms, the 500 apprentices would be able to bypass the union's apprenticeship requirements so long as they had passed the apprenticeship age and had some experience to take jobs as soon as they were available. They would take the jobs as apprentices with guarantees that they would become

Chicago plan. Agreement was reached on a minority employment-training plan in Chicago Jan. 12, 1970. After long ne-

journeymen when fully qualified. Journeyman status represented higher wages and more union fringe benefits.

Pittsburgh plan. The Black Construction Coalition, an umbrella organization of civil rights groups, announced Jan. 30, 1970 that an agreement had been reached to employ 1,250 Negroes as workers with journeyman status in Allegheny County, Pa., during the next four years. The accord was reached by the coalition, representatives of 15 contractor associations and the Pittsburgh Trades and Construction Council, who represented Pittsburgh's craft unions.

The agreement came after more than six months of controversy marked by periodic work shutdowns because of mass picketing and demonstrations.

Spokesmen for the coalition said negotiations with individual craft unions had to be carried out before the plan could be implemented. While the terms of the agreement were not disclosed, it was reported that the settlement called for establishment of a panel to oversee a training program for minority members in the construction industry, details of workers' duties and arbitration procedures.

W. J. Usery Jr., assistant secretary of labor, who sat in on the negotiations, said the Labor Department supported the agreement. He said legal action would be instituted against any union that failed to enroll the new workers.

Formal federal approval, however, was not achieved until Oct. 24.

The government's decision to accept the plan marked the end of its freeze on $100,000 for federally assisted projects in the Pittsburgh area. The government had frozen the funds to force unions to comply with minority hiring guidelines.

The agreement called for 1,250 blacks to be employed as workers with journeyman status in the Pittsburgh area during the next four years.

New York job plan set. Labor and management leaders in the construction industry in New York City March 21, 1970 announced a job plan called the New York Plan for recruiting and training minority group members as skilled construction workers. The program was devised after the Labor Department said it would extend its job plan, the Philadelphia Plan, to 18 other cities unless they designed their own arrangements for increasing minority group employment in the construction trades.

Peter J. Brennan, president of the Building and Construction Trades Council of Greater New York, said the plan would go into effect as soon as the funds become available. He said New York Gov. Nelson Rockefeller had committed an unspecified amount of money for financing the New York Plan.

Under the terms of the arrangement, trainees were to be selected by a community screening committees for on-the-job training at participating projects. The Workers Defense League, an organization which had aided other groups in selecting and preparing blacks and other minority group members for construction trades apprenticeship programs, said March 21 that it would assist the community committees in screening potential candidates for the New York Plan. In addition to on-the-job assignments, the apprentices would be given craft training, guidance and counseling until additional on-the-job assignments could be secured.

Brennan said the plan "will combine periods of instruction, counseling and remedial education at a central training facility with periods of on-the-job training. The result will be a comprehensive work-learn program with a continuity of training, a completion of training and a reasonable assurance of entry into the industry as a qualified craftsman."

Gov. Rockefeller, Mayor John Lindsay and industry and union representatives signed the job plan accord Dec. 10.

City quits plan—New York City announced Jan. 12, 1973 that it was withdrawing from participation in the plan because it was "very disappointed in the results." According to the city, only 537 trainees had been placed by June 1972.

The city asked the U.S. Labor Department to impose minority job goals and timetables, as mandated by federal law in the absence of a local voluntary plan, on all federally aided construction in New

York. The city said it would also seek city and state legislation requiring affirmative action plans from all city- or state-aided contractors.

Thomas J. Broidrick, a construction company executive and head of the New York Plan, said the city's charges were unfair, since the city had not supplied its $100,000 share of the costs until June 1972, and the federal government had decided not to fund a central training facility.

Broidrick said 620 trainees were currently in the plan, of whom 480 were actually in jobs and 34 were journeymen. He said the record, along with other city training programs, was "the best in the country in numerical terms," which the city's announcement had not disputed.

Plan upheld after court conflict—U.S. District Court Judge Morris E. Lasker July 25, 1974 overruled the Labor Department's objections and approved a revised version of the plan. But in a decision reported Aug. 10, a state supreme court justice ruled that the city had gone beyond its authority in imposing the mandatory standards. The Labor Department said Nov. 13 that it would not appeal Lasker's decision, and the immediate struggle against the plan thus was ended.

The disputed plan had been formulated to replace the old "New York Plan" from which the city had withdrawn in 1973, citing unsatisfactory results.

The approved program required that contractors working on federally-aided municipal projects hire one minority on-the-job trainee for every four experienced workers on each project. In addition, long-term goals would require that the number of minority workers be increased so that their representation in the industry equaled their proportion of the city's population by July 1, 1978.

The Labor Department had withheld federal construction funds from the city on the ground that the city had implemented the new plan without federal approval. The city's suit to have the funds released led to Lasker's decision. The conflicting state court decision came in another suit filed by the industry and unions.

According to the Lasker ruling, the city had the authority to impose anti-discrimi-

nation rules more stringent than those approved in advance by the federal government. The ruling would also empower the city to require that contractors bidding on government-financed projects meet the same hiring standards on other operations, including private projects, during the life of the government contract.

Job pledges—The director of New York City's Office of Contract Compliance had announced March 21, 1970 that seven elevator companies had pledged to "employ immediately a significant number" of Negroes and Puerto Ricans after the city had withheld millions of dollars in payments to the companies because of alleged job discrimination. The seven companies were Otis, Armor, Westinghouse, Staley, Serge, Haughton and Burlington.

Director James D. Norton said $6.5 million in payments to the seven firms would be delayed for several more weeks while his office checked the firms' compliance with their pledge.

Norton said the firms had promised to hire at least 50 minority group members immediately, to redouble "their efforts to hire minority workers," and to re-examine those requirements now in existence as they related to employment.

Apprentices ordered upgraded—New York City Steamfitters Union Local 638 was ordered by a U.S. judge Jan. 3, 1972 to upgrade 169 black and Puerto Rican apprentices to journeyman status.

The ruling involved the largest number of reclassifications ordered in a suit brought by the federal government. The court reserved the right to rule on individual cases if the union tried to downgrade any of the 169 workers on grounds of incompetence.

Washington efforts. The Department of Transportation April 13, 1970 ordered a freeze on new roadway and airport construction contracts in the Washington, D.C. metropolitan area as part of a drive to bring more high salaried jobs to black and other minority group workers.

The director of the department's civil rights division, Richard F. Lally, reported that the suspension of funds had been ordered after three days of hearings during which contractors had been warned that if they did not implement their own job plan, the Labor Department "would be ready to impose" a mandatory job plan on the contractors. The freeze prohibited any contracts to be financed by Transportation Department funds until a regional employment and job-training program was adopted.

The freeze order also applied to projects scheduled for Virginia and Maryland, as well as Washington, D.C.

In another area action, Washington D.C.'s Public Service Commission April 15 ordered the Potomac Electric Power Co., which provided electricity to the D.C. area, to hire more black workers and other minority group members on a preferential basis. Under the order, the utilities concern must specifically request "all minority group persons contacting the company . . . to file an application for employment regardless of whether vacancies exist."

The order also provided that the firm maintain a file of applications from the minority applicants and "before consulting other sources for applicants . . . give every consideration to the hiring of applicants from this file."

Labor Secretary George P. Shultz June 1 imposed a department-devised program known as the "Washington Plan" that would require all contractors with federal jobs of $500,000 or more in Washington, D.C. to make "good faith" attempts to increase minority hiring on all their projects. Under the plan, (as reported by the Washington Post) which was to go into effect immediately, 3,500 minority group workers had to be hired in 11 skilled construction trades on such federal jobs as construction of the metropolitan subway system, highway building and federally subsidized housing projects.

The plan was an expansion of the Labor Department's controversial Philadelphia Plan which was inaugurated in 1969.

The plan was ordered into effect after Washington area contractors and labor unions had failed to come up with a voluntary hiring practice agreement by May 25, a deadline set by Shultz after bargaining sessions between the participants had failed.

The Washington Area Construction Industry Task Force, a coalition of 25 black organizations, June 4 denounced the Washington Plan as "devoid of promise" and "wholly unacceptable." The group sent a letter to Shultz demanding that 70%-80% of jobs in all crafts go to minority group workers. The federal plan called for unions to have from 25% to 43% black membership, depending on the trade, by May 31, 1974 for the Washington, D.C. metropolitan area.

The task force accused the Labor Department of diluting the plan by incorporating into it the construction sites in Virginia and Maryland. The task force's chairman, R. H. Booker, said "it serves little purpose" to offer a black construction worker a job in Virginia or some "other remote construction site when in his own city (Washington, D.C.) the overwhelming majority of jobs will continue to go to whites."

Government threatens action. James D. Hodgson, who had succeeded George Shultz as secretary of labor, warned July 9, 1970 that unless the construction industry opened up more jobs for black workers during the summer the government might begin to enforce federal hiring quotas in 73 cities. The labor secretary said "there has been too much of a lag in this work and the big push is on."

Hodgson said the 73 cities would be given an opportunity to develop voluntary plans to increase black employment in the construction trades, but unless it was done soon the Labor Department would impose quotas as it had already done in Philadelphia and Washington, D.C.

Hodgson said he was not satisfied with progress that had been made under existing voluntary agreements, but added that he was pleased that some larger cities (Boston, Los Angeles and St. Louis) had developed effective antibias job plans.

Job accord in New Orleans. New Orleans city officials joined local representatives of the construction industry, craft unions, and a coalition of area chapters of the National Association for the Advancement of Colored People (NAACP) and the Urban League to announce July 26, 1970 their agreement to a proposal to increase minority hiring and open the unions' rank-and-file membership to Negroes.

The "New Orleans Plan" was designed to place more members of minority groups, mainly blacks, in the construction industry labor pool in the New Orleans area. One official said, however, that the plan was put together to prevent the federal government from implementing more stringent racial hiring guidelines in the New Orleans area.

A similar plan had been designed for Atlanta by local groups in July but it was rejected by the NAACP and Urban League, whose negotiators quit a meeting with local construction industry representatives, calling the plan "weak and pallid."

A spokesman for the New Orleans NAACP-Urban League coalition said the Atlanta plan had been rejected because it did not mention a minority group quota for union membership. The plan agreed to by NAACP-Urban League officials in New Orleans contained a provision calling for a 20% minority group membership in all New Orleans construction trades and crafts unions.

Illinois fund ban lifted. Secretary of Transportation John A. Volpe announced June 6, 1970 that a 23-month government freeze of federal construction funds for two counties in East St. Louis, Ill. that had been imposed because of discrimination charges against blacks had been lifted. It was reported the ban had fallen short of its desired objectives to increase minority group employment in the East St. Louis area.

The freeze for St. Clair and Madison Counties was imposed July 1, 1968 after civil rights groups had lodged complaints with various federal agencies that the construction companies were discriminating against black workers. The freeze of federal funds was then ordered by the Bureau of Public Roads.

The freeze was in effect at the same time that the Labor Department ordered a pilot job training program to increase minority group hiring in the building trades in the city.

Volpe said he was lifting the freeze after receiving assurances from Illinois Gov. Richard B. Ogilvie that efforts would be made to increase black employment in the area. Volpe said he was also prompted to lift the ban after a federal court handed down consent decrees requiring three East St. Louis union locals to operate nondiscriminatively.

Ogilvie's assurances included a pledge that he would see to it that a new employment arrangement was implemented in the city. The Ogilvie plan called for the establishment of a six-member local opportunity committee to oversee recruitment, training and placement of blacks in jobs in the construction projects then under way in East St. Louis. Six training programs would be established with 300 persons enrolled in 1970 and 600 in 1971.

Job gains at GM. James M. Roche, chairman of the board of the General Motors Corp. (GM), reported Feb. 6, 1970 that the company had made significant gains in its minority group hiring, although the number of salaried blacks at GM remained relatively low. He said that at the end of 1969 97,150 of its U.S. employes, or 15.3%, were Negroes, Orientals, Indians or Spanish Americans. Roche said that in 1965 the figure was 66,469 or 11.5%.

Roche said that "since 1965, 60% of the employes we have added, both hourly and salaried, have been minority Americans." Roche said that in the last year the number of GM's salaried employes who were minority group members had increased 30%, to 5,086 from 3,894. General Motors had about 143,000 salaried employes, meaning that minority group members made up about 3.5% of the salaried worker total.

Film-makers set job plan. Seventy-two movie studios and television companies said March 31, 1970 that they had agreed to implement immediately an equal employment plan for their industries that included hiring, training and upgrading of minorities and setting racial quotas. The agreement was worked out with the aid of lawyers from the Justice Department who entered the negotiations after the movie and television industry had been criticized during hearings in 1969 for practices of racial discrimination in hiring.

Among the major companies signing the agreement were Columbia Pictures Industries, the Columbia Broadcasting System, Warner Brothers, Metro-Goldwyn Mayer, Bing Crosby Productions, Paramount Pictures Corp., Lucille Ball Productions, Walt Disney Productions and 20th Century Fox Film Corp.

The agreement would ban all job discrimination within the movie-making industry and the affiliated unions that served it. The jobs were nonacting employment, such as hair stylists, make-up artists, set designers, film editors and electrical technicians. The firms also agreed to prohibit discriminatory job testing and to set up a minority pool in some jobs in which two of every five new employes would be members of a minority group. The firms also agreed to establish a job-training program with participation consisting of two-fifths Negroes and two-fifths Mexican-Americans, with all of them guaranteed jobs within the industry.

Shipyard job plan. A spokesman for the Maritime Administration announced April 9, 1970 that the Newport News, Va. shipyard, largest in the U.S., had agreed to end racial discrimination among its 20,000 workers by implementing a pilot job plan. Maritime Administrator Andrew E. Gibson, the chief negotiator for the government during talks between the yard's officials and black workers, called the plan "a milestone" and "one of the most forward looking of any major industry."

The agreement removed the yard, the Newport News Shipbuilding and Dry Dock Co., from the government's blacklist, which had prohibited the company from signing contracts with federal agencies. (The yard had been placed on the black list March 12 when the Maritime Administration ordered the company to

"produce an affirmative action plan" to meet the equal job opportunities provision of the 1964 Civil Rights Act.)

Under the plan, the yard would open up more skilled jobs for black workers. The plan also set a numerical target for the number of blacks to be employed in the yard's executive offices. About 5,600, or 28% of the yard's workers were black.

Trucking suit. The Justice Department announced Sept. 1, 1970 that a U.S. judge in Cleveland had entered a consent decree requiring the nation's third largest trucking concern to implement an equal employment program. The order brought to a close the department's first suit seeking to enjoin job discrimination throughout a company's nationwide operation.

The court order entered by Judge Thomas D. Lambros against Roadway Express Inc., of Akron, Ohio, enjoined the firm from engaging in any act or practice that had the purpose of denying Negroes equal employment opportunities in hiring, upgrading and promotions. The decree also ordered Roadway, which had freight terminals in 28 states, to offer job opportunities on a first available vacancy basis to nearly 105 individuals, with seniority and other benefits for 45 of them.

The department had filed the suit against Roadway in May 1968, charging that Negroes had been discriminated against in job placement and opportunities.

Steel industry & racial job quotas. The chairman of the United States Steel Corp. accused the Justice Department Dec. 14, 1970 of threatening a law suit to force the company to hire more black office and clerical personnel at its plant in Fairfield, Ala.

According to E. H. Gott, the chairman, when the corporation refused to accept the government's racial job quota, the Justice Department filed suit against U.S. Steel, charging it with discrimination.

(The Justice Department had filed a suit in federal district court in Birmingham Dec. 11, charging the steel firm with discriminating against blacks at its Fairfield plant. The suit also charged the United Steelworkers of America, the AFL-CIO and 12 Alabama steelworker locals with violating the 1964 Civil Rights Act and being parties to the alleged discriminating practices.)

Gott said Justice Department officials demanded Dec. 10 that U.S. Steel, the nation's largest steel company, allocate 50% of all office and clerical jobs at its Fairfield division to blacks within five years. Another Justice Department demand, Gott said, was that blacks constitute 40% of all personnel promoted to management levels through 1975 at the Fairfield steelworks.

Gott said the hiring figures "were the price U.S. Steel was asked to pay to forestall immediate filing of a pattern and practice suit against Fairfield Works by the Justice Department." He termed the government's proposals "grossly outrageous demands." U.S. Steel rejected the figures the same day they were received.

The Justice Department confirmed Dec. 14 that it had used the figures cited by Gott in negotiations with the company. The spokesmen said, however, that it was erroneous to characterize the proposed hiring figures as demands. He added that "resolution of these issues would not have stopped the filing of the suit."

When the suit was filed Dec. 11 in Birmingham, U.S. Steel issued a statement denying "any pattern or practice of discrimination at its Fairfield operations. The company included in the statement a listing of the programs it had initiated to help black workers.

Gott said the government's proposed racial job quotas were "in direct opposition to the premise of Title VII of the Civil Rights Act, which provides there be no discrimination in employment and upgrading because of race, color, creed, national origin or sex." He said the quotas' provisions exceeded the ratio of blacks to whites in Jefferson County, where the Fairfield plant was located.

Bethlehem Steel charged with job bias— The Bethlehem Steel Corp., second largest steel producer in America, was accused by a federal labor panel Jan. 5, 1971 of discriminating against Negroes through its seniority system. A report compiled by the panel was forwarded to Secretary of Labor James D. Hodgson.

In a statement accompanying the report, Bethlehem denied the charge but agreed to set new hiring, promotion and training quotas for Negro employes. A company spokesman said Jan. 5 that the firm was studying the federal report.

The three-member federal panel delivered a unanimous decision against Bethlehem but disagreed on what corrective measures should be taken. Two of the panelists accepted the company's new job quotas, but the third termed the quota proposal "seriously deficient" and asked for adoption of a plan presented by the federal government.

The plan, which was drawn up by the Office of Federal Contract Compliance, was rejected by the majority as unworkable and inappropriate in the steel industry.

Court rules vs. Bethlehem—The 2nd U.S. Circuit Court of Appeals June 21, 1971 ordered the United Steelworkers of America and Bethlehem Steel Co. to permit black workers to transfer from "hotter and dirtier" jobs at Bethlehem's plant in Lackawanna. N.Y. to higher paying and cleaner jobs with no loss in seniority or pay.

The decision was believed to be the first time a federal court had outlawed transfer and seniority provisions that violated Title VII of the Civil Rights Act of 1964. Such violations were interpreted as penalizing black employes who sought to shift their jobs within a plant.

In a unanimous ruling, the court held that "in hiring, jobs were made available to whites rather than to blacks in a number of ways. There were no fixed or reasonably objective standards and procedures for hiring." The court also said that over 80% of the black workers at the Lackawanna plant were placed in departments "which contained the hotter and dirtier jobs in the plant." Blacks, the court held, were excluded from "higher-paying and cleaner jobs."

The case was brought to the appeals court by the federal government. The government had succeeded in getting a lower court to rule that the company and union did discriminate, but could not obtain a lower court order that "would have made the exercise [of transfer rights] more attractive."

Bethlehem changes ordered—The Labor Department Jan. 16, 1973 ordered into effect a series of changes in the seniority practices at Bethlehem Steel's Sparrows Point, Md. plant, to wipe out the continuing effects of past discrimination in job placement of blacks.

The order, which a department spokesman called "the most far-reaching" affirmative action program so far imposed, was issued under the Executive Order enforcing job rights in federal contracts, but Labor Secretary James D. Hodgson rejected a request by the Office of Contract Compliance that sanctions be imposed, "in light," he said, "of the company's spirit of cooperation." The order was the first to concern seniority rights.

A federally appointed panel had reported at the beginning of 1971 that as of November 1967, 81% of the 7,864 black workers at the plant had been employed in all-black or predominantly black departments with lower pay and less sought-after jobs, including refuse disposal and coke oven maintenance, while most of the 12,602 white employes worked as timekeepers and sheet metal workers. Changes in hiring practices since March 31, 1968 eliminated discrimination against new workers, the government ruled, but limited transfer rights perpetuated the effects of previous policy.

The order provided that all employes hired before March 31, 1968 who had never transferred out of a black department be given written transfer offers, provided they could perform the new job "with minimal training." Bethlehem was ordered to see that "reasonable requirements" be set for jobs, and training be provided.

Employes asking for transfer to a predominantly white department would be hired for the first "available permanent vacancy" on the basis of total years of "plant service" in any department. Blacks transferring to a white department would retain their accrued seniority and their pay, if higher than the new job would otherwise provide.

Bethlehem, along with the United Steelworkers of America, had agreed to comply with a federal court order imposing a similar program at a Lackawanna, N.Y. plant in 1971.

Steel industry signs job pact—Nine major steel companies, the United Steelworkers of America and the U.S. government April 15, 1974 signed agreements providing back pay and expanded job opportunities for minorities and women. The accord, similar to earlier broad settlements in the trucking and communications industries, was contained in consent decrees filed in U.S. district court in Birmingham, Ala., resolving a Justice Department discrimination suit filed at the same time.

The companies were: Allegheny-Ludlum Industries, Inc., Armco Steel Corp., Bethlehem Steel Corp., Jones & Laughlin Steel Corp., National Steel Corp., Republic Steel Corp., U.S. Steel Corp., Wheeling-Pittsburgh Steel Corp. and Youngstown Sheet & Tube Co. According to the Justice Department, the companies produced about 73% of the nation's raw steel and employed 347,679 workers, of whom 52,545 were black, 7,646 Spanish-surnamed and 10,175 women.

Under the agreement, back pay totaling $30.9 million would be distributed to about 34,000 minority male employes hired for production and maintenance jobs before 1968 and to 5,600 women currently in such jobs. Individual amounts would range from $250 to more than $3,000.

The accord also set timetables under which half of the openings in trade and craft positions would be filled by minorities and women, and additional first-year goals calling for women in 20% of production and maintenance vacancies, minorities in 15% of technical and clerical openings, and selection of minorities and women for 25% of vacancies in supervisory positions and for management training.

Employes would also be allowed to transfer to departments or seniority categories offering better advancement opportunities previously reserved for white males, without suffering pay cuts even if the new job had a lower wage scale.

The National Association for the Advancement of Colored people, which had opposed the settlement as inadequate and an obstruction to other litigation under the Civil Rights Act, filed suit in the Birmingham court April 23 to have the consent decrees set aside.

Black workers win back pay—A federal appeals court Oct. 11, 1975 overturned a district court judge's ruling that 2,700 black workers at the U.S. Steel Corp.'s Fairfield (Ala.) Works should not have back pay sought on grounds of racial discrimination by the company and the United Steelworkers of America union.

Judge Sam C. Pointer Jr. had awarded back pay to 61 employes but denied it to workers on the production and maintenance force because he lacked the resources to determine individual awards.

In reversing the decision, the Fifth Circuit Court of Appeals in New Orleans stated that the fact that so many persons had been discriminated against neither lessened the liability of the company nor made the individual workers any less entitled to back pay.

Unions vow to fight quotas. The nation's building and construction unions Feb. 10, 1971 rejected accusations that they practiced racial discrimination as "reckless rhetorical and political pandering," and vowed to resist proposed federal job quotas for nonwhite workers.

A statement issued by the Building and Construction Trades Department of the AFL-CIO said the group rejected "quotas under any name."

The government's proposed quota rules were published in the Federal Register Jan. 29, attracting little public attention at the time. They were promulgated by Labor Secretary James D. Hodgson. According to the apprenticeship rules, which could be altered or withdrawn within 30 days after they first appeared in the register, unions with federally registered trainee programs would be required to adopt "affirmative

action plans" to bring more nonwhites into the programs.

In rejecting the proposed job quotas the unions maintained that "the goal of equal employment opportunity in apprenticeship has generally been achieved under existing regulations."

Although the proposed rules would give the craft unions some flexibility in drawing up programs to carry out "affirmative action," basically they required the unions to place a specified quota of nonwhites in the apprenticeship programs.

The federal quotas were reportedly designed to do on a national scale what various job programs had accomplished in local areas—bringing more blacks into the building and construction trades.

Court upholds Philadelphia Plan. The Nixon Administration's Philadelphia Plan, its pilot affirmative action device for employment of minorities, overcame another legal challenge April 23, 1971 when the U.S. Court of Appeals for the 3rd Circuit upheld its legality.

In the most recent case, the court was asked by the Contractors Association of Eastern Pennsylvania to declare the plan illegal because it denied the group equal protection of the laws. The contracting group, in the suit it filed in January 1970, also charged that the plan violated the 1964 Civil Rights Act because it required racial "quotas."

The court upheld a lower court's ruling that the plan did not violate the 1964 rights act because the contractors were not required to hire a "definite percentage" of a minority group.

The Supreme Court upheld the ruling without comment Oct. 12.

U.S. to impose quotas. The Labor Department announced May 3, 1971 that it would soon impose mandatory racial hiring quotas on federally-sponsored construction projects under way in San Francisco, St. Louis and Atlanta.

Discussions to set up a similar job plan for federal construction in Chicago were also being held by Labor Department aides, Chicago officials, civil rights leaders and union and industry representatives.

The established plans for St. Louis, San Francisco and Atlanta varied slightly in their formats. Overall, however, the quotas required contractors bidding on federal or federally-sponsored projects to agree to hire a fixed goal of minority group members by a certain date.

The mandatory plan for San Francisco was put into effect June 3.

San Francisco's minority job program was the third such plan set for the construction industry.

Like the Philadelphia and Washington plans, the San Francisco program would affect only federal construction projects costing over $500,000.

The Atlanta job plan was put into effect June 18. Arthur A. Fletcher, an assistant secretary of labor, said that he expected that "compliance would come even easier" in Atlanta than it had in other cities. He said his investigation of labor practices in metropolitan Atlanta had indicated that leaders of the higher paid craft unions would turn to the heavily black laborers unions where men had worked as skilled laborers for many years and invite them into their unions.

Mandatory plan for Chicago—The Labor Department said June 4, 1971 that it was withdrawing its support of Chicago's voluntary equal hiring plan for federal construction projects and would impose mandatory racial quotas on federally-assisted projects throughout the city.

Chicago's voluntary plan collapsed after 18 months. Known as the Chicago Plan for Equal Opportunity, the program called for training and hiring 4,000 minority group members. By June 4, however, only 885 Negroes and Spanish-Americans had been taken on for apprentice training and only a few had obtained membership in Chicago's construction unions.

The federal move coincided with the disappearance of Alderman Fred D. Hubbard, program director, and the discovery that $94,500 of its funds were missing.

U.S. job quotas set for Seattle. The Labor Department ordered federal mi-

nority-group hiring quotas for U.S.-assisted construction work in Seattle June 17, 1971. It rejected a city plan as ineffective. Secretary of Labor James D. Hodgson said the quotas went into effect at once.

The Seattle plan required all contractors to submit minority-hiring goals and job training quotas with their project bids. The goals would be required to fit within federal guidelines that sought to have each contractors' work force show a 9.7 to 13% increase in minority-group employes by 1973.

Hodgson said the Seattle plan would affect all construction crafts except four—iron workers, sheet metal workers, plumbers and pipefitters and electricians—that were covered by a minority-hiring plan ordered by federal courts.

Equality for Women

The 1970s was a period of unprecedented activity in the long struggle to win equality for women. Legislative and legal action in this cause was often allied with the movement for racial equality, and the same charges were soon heard that affirmative action to secure job rights for women ultimately produced illegal quotas.

Federal guides vs. bias. The Labor Department June 9, 1970 issued guidelines prohibiting sex discrimination in employment by government contractors and subcontractors. Elizabeth Duncan Koontz, director of the department's Women's Bureau, announced the guidelines, which applied to companies with government contracts of $50,000 or more or those that employed more than 50 people.

At the same time the White House released a 33-page report by the President's Task Force on Women's Rights and Responsibilities. The guidelines were one of the recommendations in the report, which was completed nearly six months before its release.

The guidelines, to take effect immediately, prohibited sex discrimination in employment opportunities, wages, hours or other job conditions. Advertisements for employes could not express a sex preference, unless sex was "a bona fide occupational qualification." Distinctions between married and unmarried employes were to be applied equally to men and women, and an employer could not discriminate against a woman with young children "unless the same exclusionary policy exists for men." Women could not be penalized for taking time off to bear children.

The guidelines prohibited seniority based solely on sex and banned "discriminatorily restricting one sex to certain job classifications and departments." In addition, an employer could not discriminate against a woman on the basis of state laws requiring the protection of female employes.

The regulations were to be enforced by the Labor Department's Office of Federal Contract Compliance. Contracts could be withheld from employers who failed to comply.

Goals & timetables planned—To implement the federal ban against sex discrimination by employers with government contracts, the Nixon Administration said July 31 it would require contractors to set goals and timetable to increase employment of women. Labor Secretary James D. Hodgson said in a statement: "The federal government is convinced that the under-utilization in employment throughout the nation constitutes a waste of national resources and talent." He noted that the goals and timetables concept was the method used to curb racial discrimination by government contractors.

The task force report was prepared by a 13-member panel headed by Virginia R. Allan, executive vice president of Cahalan Drug Stores Inc. (Wyandotte, Mich.). The report declared, "the United States, as it approaches its 200th anniversary, lags behind other enlightened and indeed some newly emerging countries in the role ascribed to women."

In addition to the new guidelines, the task force recommended establishment of a permanent office of women's rights and responsibilities; a 1970 White House conference on women's rights; and new legislation providing better enforcement of federal bans against sex discrimination, liberalizing Social Security and income tax laws applying to women employes and their husbands and providing child-care assistance for working mothers.

Other recommendations in the report called for enactment of a Constitutional amendment to assure men and women equal protection under laws governing marriage, guardianship, dependents, property and business ownership, dower rights and domicile. The panel also asked for a special women's unit in the U.S. Office of Education to end bias in higher education.

Hodgson Dec. 2 ordered all federal contractors and subcontractors to take "affirmative action" that would bring an end to "under-utilization of women" in all areas of employment. The order, to take effect in 120 days, required federal contractors to consider the supply of women in the local work force, their skill levels, and the training necessary if skills were lacking, in determining whether under-utilization existed.

First government suit. Attorney General John Mitchell said Dec. 7, 1970 that the government's first suit seeking equal employment rights for women had been concluded successfully with the filing of a consent decree in U.S. district court in Toledo, Ohio.

The Justice Department had charged Libbey-Owens-Ford Co., Inc. and the AFL-CIO United Glass and Ceramic Workers of North America and its Toledo local with discrimination against women in hiring and advancement opportunities at the company's Toledo area plants.

Under the decree, the company agreed to correct certain specific discriminatory practices charged in the suit and undertook what was described as a "continuing obligation not to discriminate on the basis of sex with regard to its future recruitment, hiring and assignment of new employes."

The suit, filed July 20, had accused Libby-Owens-Ford of a long-time policy of hiring women in only one of its five Toledo plants, of assigning them to lower-paying jobs with the least opportunity for advancement and of firing women employes first when layoffs occured. The suit said the company and union had contracts "which establish seniority systems and procedures for promotion, demotion, layoff, recall, and transfer which . . . deprive female employes of an equal opportunity to compete with their male contemporaries for the more desirable, better-paying jobs."

A spokesman for Libbey-Owens-Ford said July 21 that the company was making every effort to comply with the 1964 Civil Rights Act but was hampered by Ohio laws requiring the protection of female employes. The company employed 200 women and 5,200 men in its Toledo plants.

The case had been referred to the Justice Department by the Equal Employment Opportunity Commission (EEOC) in March. A commission spokesman said July 20 that the number of complaints about job bias against women had risen sharply in recent months, "mostly as a result of women's liberation and the publicity they have gotten." The spokesman estimated that as many as 25% of complaints currently received by the commission charged sex discrimination. He said the EEOC received 17,000 complaints in the fiscal year ending June 30, 1969, alleging sex and racial bias and other forms of job discrimination. The Justice Department said it had participated in other sex discrimination cases as a "friend of the court."

Suit for women & blacks—In the first federal suit charging job discrimination against both blacks and women, the Justice Department asked a federal court in East St. Louis, Ill. to enjoin discrimination by the Obear-Nester Glass Company of that city, the Wall Street Journal reported Sept. 9, 1971.

Clothing pay bias—The Labor Department Nov. 2, 1971 reported it had won a suit against City Stores, Inc., a national retail chain charged with paying salesmen and male tailors more than saleswomen and female tailors. The U.S. District Court in Montgomery, Ala. ordered the firm to pay the women back wages plus interest, rejecting claims that selling and altering men's clothing was more difficult than selling and altering women's clothing.

Bias against mothers barred. The Supreme Court ruled Jan. 25, 1971 that companies could not deny jobs to women with pre-school children unless the same criterion applied to men. In its first sex discrimination ruling on equal hiring provisions of the 1964 Civil Rights Act, the court said the law forbids "one hiring policy for women and another for men."

The case was an appeal by Mrs. Ida Phillips, who had been denied a job by the Martin Marietta Corp. at its Orlando, Fla. plant. Lower courts had dismissed her appeal on the ground that she had not been denied employment only because of sex but because of her sex plus the fact that she was the parent of young children. The case had gained prominence when feminists cited G. Harrold Carswell's support of the "sex plus" argument in opposing Carswell's nomination to the Supreme Court.

The Supreme Court returned the case for further evidence, contending that "the existence of such conflicting family obligations, if demonstrably more relevant to job performance for a woman than for a man, could arguably be a basis for distinction." Justice Thurgood Marshall concurred in the outcome of the case but said sex could only be a job qualification in unusual cases, such as employment of actors and fashion models.

Mrs. Phillips' appeal had been argued by the NAACP Legal Defense Fund Inc. joined by the Justice Department and the Equal Employment Opportunity Commission.

State job laws voided. The U.S. Court of Appeals for the 9th Circuit ruled June 1, 1971 in San Francisco that California laws permitting sex discrimination in employment violated provisions of the 1964 Civil Rights Act. The court said the federal act invalidated sections of the state labor code, which limited female working hours and forbade employment of women on jobs requiring the lifting of heavy weights.

The ruling upheld a lower court ruling in a case brought by Mrs. Leah Rosenfeld, who had been refused a job by the Southern Pacific Co. The appellate court endorsed Federal Equal Employment Opportunity Commission guidelines that persons should be considered for jobs "on the basis of individual capacity and not on the basis of any characteristics generally attributed to a group."

Similar provisions of an Ohio employment law had been declared invalid in March by a federal district court judge in Dayton. In this case, the Ohio law— challenged in suits against two divisions of the General Motors Corp., two union locals and the Ohio Department of Industrial Relations—forbade the employment of women on jobs requiring "frequent or repeated lifting of weights over 25 pounds" and limited a woman's working days and hours per day.

The plaintiffs in the suit said the law denied them opportunities available to males, such as overtime work and better paying jobs. U.S. District Court Judge Carl A. Weinman based his ruling on the 1964 Civil Rights Act.

General Electric Co. filed suit March 26 in federal court in Cincinnati asking for a clarification of conflicts in state and federal employment laws regarding women. A state appeals court in Columbus had ruled March 9 that the Ohio law regulating women employes was valid and that if it was discriminatory, "it is a discrimination in favor of female employes." Other sections of the Ohio law required suitable seats and lunchtime breaks to be provided for female employes.

Judge Edwin J. Martin, of Allegheny County (Pa.) Common Pleas Court, ruled March 24 that Pittsburgh's two daily newspapers must run employment advertisements under a single category rather than classifying jobs according to male help wanted and female help wanted.

Martin noted two federal court precedents in his ruling, but he said it was the first time a state court had been required to rule on the issue. A spokesman for the Pittsburgh chapter of National Organization for Women (NOW), which had filed the original complaint, said it was a "landmark case." She noted that some cities had local ordinances requiring that help wanted ads not be segregated.

News magazines settle with women. The management of Newsweek magazine Aug. 26, 1970 signed a pledge to accelerate the recruitment and promotion of women. The document had been worked out in negotiations with representatives of 46 women employes, who had filed a sex discrimination complaint in March with the U.S. Equal Employment Opportunity Commission.

Time, Inc., publisher of four magazines, reached an agreement Feb. 6, 1971 with over 140 women employes under which all jobs in the company would be open to qualified candidates regardless of sex or marital status. The agreement provided for committees to resolve future complaints of sex discrimination.

In complaints to the New York attorney general's office, the women charged that they were limited to jobs as researchers at Time, Life, Fortune and Sports Illustrated. New York Attorney General Louis J. Lefkowitz worked out the agreement, and the State Division of Human Rights was to review periodically salaries of men and women in the same job category at the magazines. In addition, the editors agreed to masthead changes that would "reflect more adequately the significant contributions being made by women."

Federal bias banned. The Civil Service Commission ruled May 12, 1971 that "men only" and "women only" designations must be eliminated for almost all federal jobs. Sex specifications would be permitted only if the job required that the employes sleep in common quarters or in certain institutional jobs, such as matron in a women's prison.

According to the ruling, women could no longer be excluded automatically from jobs requiring physical strength or from law enforcement jobs requiring the carrying of weapons. A spokesman for the commission said a number of complaints had been received from women turned down for federal police jobs.

(Four women were among 81 graduates of the Treasury Department's training school for sky marshals April 8. The four were the first women to be trained for the special security force created in September 1970 to guard against airliner hijackings.)

Women in top U.S. jobs studied. The Democratic National Committee, in a study published May 27, 1971, said the percentage of women in policy-level positions in the federal government had increased by only .2% in the last three years. The study said there were currently 3,854 policy-level jobs, those in the top two Civil Service grades and the major appointive jobs, and that women held 63 (1.6%) of these positions. In 1968, the study said, women held 1.4% of the top federal positions.

In a Washington news conference, Mary Lou Burg, vice chairman of the Democratic National Committee, said the data indicated that "the Nixon Administration is not keeping up with the dynamic movement toward equal employment opportunity for women."

Mrs. Burg said she was unimpressed by the Administration's contention that 200 women had been appointed to key positions. She said the majority of these appointments were to advisory committees "and there is some question of the impact they have on policy."

Miss Burg said that of the 200 women appointees cited by the Nixon Administration, "62 are on a single committee—the Advisory Committee on the Arts of the John F. Kennedy Center for the Performing Arts." She noted that advisory committee appintments were "part-time, unpaid" positions.

The study showed there were 36 federal agencies, with a total of 1,209 policy-making positions, that employed no women. Among these agencies were the Office of Management and Budget, the Small Business Administration, the Commission on Civil Rights, the Commerce Department, the Office of Science and Technology and the Smithsonian Institution.

U.S. agencies charged with bias. Charges of sex discrimination in hiring were filed against the Federal Bureau of Investigation (FBI) Aug. 4, 1971. In another case, a charge of State Department bias against a woman foreign service officer was settled in favor of the complainant Aug. 25.

The suit against the FBI, Attorney General John Mitchell and FBI Director J. Edgar Hoover was filed in federal court in Washington by Cynthia Edgar, 24, an attorney on the staff of Rep. Bella Abzug (D, N.Y.). The suit was joined by Sandra Rothenberg Nemser, 28, also a lawyer.

Miss Edgar said at a press conference that FBI agents had told her in April that women need not apply because they "do not command enough respect" and "could not handle combat situations." Her lawyer, Philip Hirschkop, commented that a woman "can tap a phone as well as the next person." The suit was backed by the American Civil Liberties Union.

In the State Department case, Alison Palmer, 39, charged that she had been denied three consecutive posts in 1965 and 1966 as political officer to Tanzania, Uganda and Ethiopia because of her sex. In arguing against her appointment in Ethiopia in 1966, U.S. Ambassador Edward M. Korry had written the State Department that a woman would not receive enough respect to carry out her duties. The statement reportedly coincided with a department policy to exclude women from certain foreign posts "for compelling reasons of foreign policy."

The case was settled in favor of Miss Palmer Aug. 25 by Deputy Undersecretary William B. Macomber Jr., who also admitted "a pattern of discrimination" against women in the foreign service. Acting on the Aug. 19 recommendations of Civil Service hearing examiner Andrew B. Beath, Macomber said women would no longer be excluded for the "compelling reasons" cited in

Miss Palmer's case. He said she would be offered "a desirable African assignment" and her record would be amended to note that her career had been adversely affected by discrimination.

Macomber also said he would move on Beath's general recommendations for a comprehensive policy regarding women employes and an increase in the authority of the department's Equal Employment Opportunity office. Macomber said he had appointed two women foreign service officers to deal with women's problems in the department—Mary Olmsted, to be deputy director of personnel, and Gladys Rogers, to be Macomber's special assistant for women's affairs.

Pay gap narrowing. Department of Labor statistics, reported by the Washington Post May 15, 1971, showed that the gap between women's and men's wages in the U.S. began to narrow in 1968 and 1969. The median annual wage for women, as compared to men, had reached a low of 57.8% in 1967, representing a decline since the mid-1950s when women earned 64% as much as men.

The Labor Department said that in 1969, the latest year in which a breakdown was available, women earned a median wage of $4,977, 60.5% of the male median wage of $8,227. In 1968 women earned 58.2% of the male median wage. The department said some of the difference in wages earned by men and women was due to the lower average educational level attained by women and because of a larger concentration of women in lower-paying, lower-skilled jobs.

Citing data on specific job categories, the department said women who were full professors at universities had a median salary of $11,649 compared with the male median of $12,768 in 1965–66, the latest data available. In 1968, median salaries for women scientists were $1,700–$4,500 lower than for all scientists in their respective fields.

The Post quoted a study by the Women's Division of the Wage and Labor Standards Administration concluding that federal legislation prohibiting sex discrimination "has not been enough to date to close the gap between the earnings of women and men. . . . In addition to enforcement of these laws, it is also imperative for employers to review their recruitment, on-the-job training, and promotion policies to give well-qualified women the opportunity to move into more of the better paying jobs than they now hold."

Women mark suffrage day. Women in cities across the country celebrated the 51st anniversary of their right to vote Aug. 26, 1971 with rallies, fund raising events and protests. Although the demonstrations were generally quieter and smaller than those a year ago during the "Women's Strike for Equality," more specific political goals and plans were voiced, as exemplified by the newly formed National Women's Political Caucus.

In Washington, Labor Secretary James D. Hodgson proposed that employers with federal government contracts be required to set quotas for the hiring of women.

Sen. Fred Harris (D, Okla.), in Tampa, Fla., said women made up 53% of the population and should have 53% of the Democratic Convention seats. In support of one of the major Woman's Political Caucus goals, Harris said he would challenge any state delegation that did not have equal representation of women.

University bias cases. Owen P. Kiely, director of contract compliance for the Health, Education & Welfare Department (HEW), announced Jan. 19, 1971 that the government had negotiated an "historic" plan to end sex discrimination in employment at the University of Michigan. Kiely said the university had agreed to equalize salaries and job opportunities and to increase participation of women on employment committees. Kiely said HEW was investigating sex bias complaints against 29 other colleges and universities.

The department Dec. 4 suspended three federal contracts with Columbia University totalling $688,000, and threatened suspension of another contract worth

Women in Government

The President's Memorandum for the Heads of
Executive Departments and Agencies.   *April 21, 1971*

... The Nation's many highly qualified women represent an important reservoir of ability and talent that we must draw on to a greater degree. In this Administration we have firmly espoused the rights of women, and we must now clearly demonstrate our recognition of the equality of women by making greater use of their skills in high level positions.

Our efforts to date in appointing women have offered some encouragement. I have appointed a number of women to top posts and have named more than 200 to Presidential Advisory Boards and Commissions. However, I am convinced that we can and must do better.

To this end, I am now directing that you take the following actions:

—Develop and put into action a plan for attracting more qualified women to top appointive positions (GS–16 and up through Presidential appointees) in your Department or Agency by the end of this calendar year. This plan should be submitted to me by May 15.

—Develop and put into action by May 15 a plan for significantly increasing the number of women, career and appointive, in mid-level positions (GS–13 to 15). This plan should directly involve your top personnel official.

—Ensure that substantial numbers of the vacancies on your Advisory Boards and Committees are filled with well-qualified women.

—Designate an overall coordinator who will be held responsible for the success of this project. Please provide this name to me by May 15.

· · ·

I intend to follow personally the results of this project; I look forward to your giving it the fullest degree of cooperation. ...

RICHARD NIXON

nearly $2 million because the university had failed to submit an affirmative action plan to eliminate discrimination against women and minority group members. Columbia was alleged to have practiced discrimination in hiring for both faculty and service staffs.

The action was taken under a 1967 executive order prohibiting discrimination by federal contractors, which HEW had been delegated to enforce for universities. Columbia had been under investigation by HEW's Civil Rights Office since 1969, and had failed to provide employment data despite repeated requests. All of its contracts could be terminated, HEW warned in a Nov. 4 letter to university president William J. Mc-Gill.

The contracts suspended included two from the Agency for International Development and one from the National Institute on Child Health and Human Development. Federal grants and loans to Columbia and its students were not affected.

The University of Oregon had already pledged that it would try to name women and minority group members to half its faculty vacancies in 1972–73. The commitment came while the university was under Civil Rights Office investigation.

School Integration Pressed

The federal government continued heavy pressure on the South and throughout the country as the 1970s opened to bring about racial balance in public schools. Affirmative action plans to achieve such balance by shifting children among a community's schools—often by busing them to schools more distant than their neighborhood schools—met vehement resistance.

High Court sets deadline. In a brief, unsigned order Jan. 14, 1970, the Supreme Court overturned a Dec. 1, 1969 U.S. Fifth Circuit Court of Appeals ruling that set September 1970 as a pupil desegregation deadline for public schools in Alabama, Florida, Georgia, Louisiana, Mississippi and Texas. The court set a Feb. 1, 1970 desegregation deadline, rejecting a Justice Department request that the September deadline be approved.

Acting on appeals backed by the NAACP Legal Defense and Educational Fund Inc. involving 14 school districts in five of the states, the court said: "Insofar as the Court of Appeals authorized deferral of student desegregation beyond Feb. 1, 1970, that court misconstrued our holding in Alexander v. Holmes County Board of Education" –the court's Oct. 29, 1969 decision ordering desegregation "at once." The court had issued orders Dec. 13, 1969 instructing the districts to be prepared to meet a Feb. 1 deadline if the appeals court decision were overturned.

Although there were no dissents to the order, Chief Justice Warren E. Burger and Justice Potter Stewart signed a "memorandum" stating that they did not join the action because they felt the court should have considered arguments pertaining to the decision of the appeals court, which, they said, "is far more familiar than we with the various situations of the several school districts." Justices John M. Harlan and Bryon R. White stated that they concurred with the ruling but suggested that the court set eight weeks as the maximum allowable time between a court integration order and actual desegregation of a school district. Justices Hugo L. Black, William J. Brennan Jr., William O. Douglas and Thurgood Marshall termed the eight-week period a "retreat" from the court's Oct. 29 position.

Southern resistance pledged. Four Southern governors vowed Jan. 10–23 to defy the government's plan to implement student busing arrangements in their home states to achieve desegregated school systems. Govs. Lester G. Maddox of Georgia, John J. McKeithen of Louisiana, Albert P. Brewer of Alabama and Claude R. Kirk Jr. of Florida offered different strategies for dealing with the busing issue, but all four promised their constituents that they would not accept any busing plans designed by the federal government or the courts.

Maddox moved to block busing in Georgia Jan. 10 by calling for the state legislature to abolish the state's compulsory school attendance law. The governor said the legislature should make the attendance law "inapplicable where children are denied their inherent constitutional and divine right to attend the school of their choice."

Maddox joined white citizens' organizations in demanding that the government accept "freedom of choice" school plans as a suitable alternative to total school desegregation. The U.S. Court of Appeals for the Fifth Circuit Jan. 21 denied Georgia's petition for a temporary injunction to reinstate the freedom of choice plans and instead adopted the Supreme Court's Jan. 14 order calling for total school desegregation by Feb. 1.

In a news conference following his appearance before the legislature, Maddox called on Georgia's students to stay away from their schools and for teachers to refuse to teach until Georgia's freedom of choice plans were restored by the courts.

Kirk appeared before the Supreme Court Jan. 19 and said that Florida was "financially and physically unable" to desegregate its schools immediately as the court had ordered. He said he was ordering Florida school districts not to change their school calendars during mid-year.

Two attorneys representing school districts in Louisiana also appeared before the court Jan. 19 requesting an emergency rehearing on the Feb. 1 deadline. The two attorneys said the Louisiana districts were trying to abide by the court's decision but were meeting difficulties.

Louisiana Gov. McKeithen vowed Jan. 19 that he would never allow his own children to be bused to achieve racial balance in the state's schools. In a speech before the Louisiana School Board Association, McKeithen said "I will not allow it," when asked about his plans for sending his children to schools in outlying districts.

Alabama Gov. Brewer said Jan. 21 that the federal courts do not have the constitutional authority to order busing simply to achieve racial balance in Ala-

bama schools. Brewer declared that the state would not comply with the government's plans for busing. He urged the other Southern governors to join him in forming a united front to face the issue. Brewer promised he would use all the executive powers of his office to block any attempts at busing Alabama schoolchildren.

Florida Gov. Kirk told a federal district court judge Jan. 22 that he intended to issue an executive order to block further desegregation of Florida public schools.

Kirk told Judge C. Clyde Atkins, sitting in Miami: "I do not want to issue the order, but in the dilemma of the moment, I see no other alternative." Kirk said he would order Florida's school boards to defy the Supreme Court's Jan. 14 ruling even if it meant "going to jail."

20 districts ignore deadline—Southern school officials in 20 districts in Alabama, Georgia and Mississippi Feb. 1 refused to implement the federal integration plans. Some administrators closed their schools temporarily, while others supported boycotts by white parents and students. In two Alabama districts the court orders were ignored.

Only a few of the 40 school districts under the court order implemented desegregation plans, including three in Louisiana, two in Mississippi and one district in Florida. Fifteen of the districts under order had been granted delays by federal district court judges.

Many of the officials in the 20 districts that chose to disobey the court's order arbitrarily closed their schools to await further rulings on their appeals for delays. In Alabama and in Mississippi, some school administrators had sought to implement desegregation plans, but boycotts by white students and parents effectively resegregated the district schools.

In Mobile, Ala., school officials refused to implement a federal plan that would have transferred 6,000 of the city's 73,000 school children to new schools to achieve racial balance.

In Bessemer, Ala., school officials said they would not comply with the integration orders.

In Georgia, the Burke County school system opened its schools under a "freedom of choice" arrangement that the court had invalidated.

Panama City, Fla. was one of the few districts to comply fully with the court orders. About 1,000 of its 17,500 students were transferred to new schools to achieve racially balanced schools. In Louisiana, the parishes of Bossier, Claiborne and Jackson complied with the court's orders. The orders were also accepted in Leland and Western Line, Miss.

4 governors discuss action—The governors of four Southern states met in Mobile, Ala. Feb. 8 in an attempt to devise a uniform strategy to circumvent federal plans to desegregate the South's public schools. But they failed to produce a plan of action. Govs. Albert P. Brewer of Alabama, Lester G. Maddox of Georgia, John J. McKeithen of Louisiana and John Bell Williams of Mississippi issued a statement at the close of the meeting, however, specifically rejecting violence as a recourse to the court-ordered desegregation arrangements.

Williams called for the meeting after the governors had independently pledged Jan. 10–23 to battle federal court orders calling for the busing of students to achieve immediate school desegregation.

An aide to the Mississippi governor said invitations had been extended to Govs. Claude R. Kirk Jr. of Florida and Robert E. McNair of South Carolina, but he said they were unable to attend. (McNair had counseled South Carolina's school administrators to comply with the court orders.)

Brewer said later that the four governors had agreed to combat the court orders by encouraging legislation from Southern congressmen.

South Carolina to obey courts. South Carolina Gov. Robert E. McNair, disavowing the plans of other Deep South governors, had announced Jan. 27 that his state would comply with court orders to desegregate its public school system.

McNair, in a statewide telecast, said: "We've run out of courts, and we've run out of time, and we must adjust to new circumstances." The governor said he would oppose any attempt to close down South Carolina schools. He emphasized that he would move to block any attempt

to repeal the state's compulsory attendance law.

"We don't want to bring up another generation of illiterates," he said. McNair said the people of South Carolina "were going to have to maintain, support and strengthen our public school system."

Nearly 12,000 students transferred schools with "grace and style" Feb. 18 in Greenville, S.C. after the U.S. Court of Appeals for the Fourth Circuit Jan. 21 struck down the district's "freedom-of-choice" plans for student enrollment and ordered the schools to desegregate immediately. About 5,000 white and 7,000 Negro students were transferred to give each school in the Greenville district a composition of 80% white and 20% black.

The Nixon Administration June 6 approved a school desegregation plan for Columbia, S.C. that left four all-black elementary schools unchanged and eight others nearly 95% black. The plan, drawn up by Columbia school administrators after two of the President's chief civil rights officers told them that there could be no more delay, was accepted by Stanley Pottinger, director of the Department of Health, Education and Welfare's (HEW) Office of Civil Rights.

Under the provisions of the plan, the faculty ratio in all of Columbia's schools would be approximately 65% white and 35% black, and 750 of the district's 1,900 teachers would be assigned across racial lines. All school principals currently in office, including the black principals, would retain their positions at the schools that they were then heading.

Fifteen of the 19 junior and senior high schools in the district would be reshuffled to have an enrollment that would be 35% to 40% black, including a formerly all-black high school. The other four would have an enrollment that would be more than 70% black. Fifteen of the city's 43 elementary schools would remain more than 80% black and 11 would remain more than 80% white.

The total enrollment in the Columbia public school system was estimated at 39,000 students, 53% white and 47% black. Nearly 13,000 students would be assigned to new schools in the fall term to accommodate the desegregation plan. Of those 13,000, most of them would be students in grades 7 to 12.

There would be no busing of students except in cases where it was needed to relieve overcrowding.

Debate in Senate. Sens. John C. Stennis (D, Miss.) and Strom Thurmond (R, S.C.) led a parade of a dozen Southern senators who took the Senate floor for over three hours Feb. 5, 1970 demanding that the new federal school desegregation guidelines be applied to Northern school districts or be abandoned altogether.

Stennis's action opened his campaign to amend a House-passed education bill to bar compulsory busing of schoolchildren to achieve racially integrated schools in the South, and to restore "freedom of choice" school arrangements where they had been struck down by federal courts.

The amendment that Stennis and the other Southern senators sought to attach to the bill was almost an exact copy of a law passed by the New York State Legislature in 1969 prohibiting the assignment of students "on account of race, creed, color, or national origin or for the purpose of achieving equality in attendance or increase attendance or reduced attendance at any school of persons of one or more particular races, creeds, colors or national origins."

Thurmond maintained that approval of an antibusing measure "would prevent our schools from becoming the laboratories of fanatical social reformers and race-obsessed judges."

Sen. Sam J. Ervin Jr. (D, N.C.) noted during the debate that the amendment sought by the Southern senators had been approved and signed into law by "that great liberal in the field of civil rights, Gov. Nelson Rockefeller."

Sen. Abraham A. Ribicoff (D, Conn.) Feb. 9 was the first Northern liberal to announce his intention to vote for a Stennis amendment to require uniform enforcement of school desegregation guidelines. He called on other Northern senators to drop their "monumental hypocrisy" and admit that Northern school systems were just as racially segregated as those in the South.

Ribicoff said: "if Sen. Stennis wants to make honest men of us Northern liberals, I think we should help him." "Northern communities have been just as systematic and consistent as Southern communities in denying to the black man and his children the opportunity that exists for white people."

Ribicoff's speech was immediately hailed by both Senate conservatives and liberals. Sen. George D. Aiken (R, Vt.), a liberal, praised Ribicoff for "your courage and if I may use the term, nobility, in standing up before the Senate and telling the truth."

Another Senate liberal, Claiborne Pell (D, R.I.), agreed that many Northerners "go home and talk liberalism to each other, but we don't practice it."

Ribicoff emphasized that he would not support the amendment also sponsored by Stennis that would prohibit busing to achieve racial balance. Ribicoff warned that such an amendment would "bring to a halt federal efforts to enforce school desegregation."

Administration position—The Nixon Administration, in a series of releases, presented its views on Stennis' proposals.

The first statement outlining the Nixon Administration's position was released Feb. 6 in a letter from Commissioner of Education James E. Allen Jr. to Sen. Clairborne Pell (D, R.I.), the floor manager of the education bill. Allen said the Administration was opposed to any Southern-sponsored legislation that would preserve racially segregated schools in the South.

Allen said that he was "convinced that segregation by races in our nation for any reason is unsound educationally, regardless of geography." He added, however, that there were "serious questions as to the legal effect and implications" of the Southern-backed proposal to press school desegregation in the North.

White House Press Secretary Ronald L. Ziegler indicated Feb. 12 that President Nixon believed the North and the South should be subject to federal school desegregation orders. Ziegler indicated that the President was not opposed to Stennis' efforts to extend to school districts in the North the same desegregation guidelines being enforced in the South.

Ziegler told newsmen that to "the extent the uniform application amendment offered by Sen. Stennis would advance equal application of the law, the Administration would be in full support of this concept."

Ziegler re-emphasized that Nixon had "consistently opposed and still opposes compulsory busing of school children to achieve racial balance."

President Nixon said Feb. 17 that although he understood the confusion and disruption caused by massive school desegregation, the courts had ordered an immediate end to school segregation. He said the law must be obeyed. In a formal statement, Nixon promised federal assistance to school districts "in complying with the courts' requirements."

The President made the statement during his announcement of a cabinet-level committee to aid schools as they implemented court-ordered desegregation arrangements.

Bill modified—The education bill, after compromises made in Senate House conference committee, was passed by the Senate April 1 and the House April 7 and was signed by President Nixon April 13.

The House-Senate conferees, however, had nullified the Stennis amendment. They retained the proposal's requirement that guidelines for ending federal aid to school districts for failure to eliminate segregation must be applied "uniformly" in all regions of the U.S. But the conferees added a provision to require separate federal policies for de jure and de facto segregation, a policy expounded by President Nixon in an earlier statement on school desegregation. The conferees added a proviso that nothing in the amendment should dilute enforcement of the 1964 Civil Rights Act requirement ending federal funds to areas practicing segregation.

Southern Senators, joined by Sen. Abraham A. Ribicoff (D, Conn.), protested the new provisions March 24, but a Ribicoff motion April 1 to return the bill to conference to restore the original Stennis amendment was rejected by a 43–32 vote. The new version was backed by Senate Republican leader Hugh Scott (Pa.) and defended April 1 by Sen. Jacob

K. Javits (R, N.Y.), who viewed the dispute as one of attempting to set an unattainable goal, elimination of de facto segregation, so as to slow up an attainable goal, elimination of de jure segregation.

Later, an anti-busing proposal was enacted in a $4.4 billion education appropriation bill passed by the House July 16 and the Senate July 28. The bill was vetoed by President Nixon as inflationary Aug. 11, but the veto was overriden by votes of the House Aug. 13 and Senate Aug. 18.

As enacted, the bill retained a House amendment barring use of the funds to force school closings or busing or transfer of pupils without parental consent to promote school desegregation. In the Senate debate July 28, Sen. Charles McC. Mathias (R, Md.) read a letter from Elliot L. Richardson, secretary of health, education and welfare, stating that the provision would not interfere with the Administration's desegregation program in the South.

Another House amendment—to bar use of funds to implement any plan denying students choice of public schools because of race or color—was dropped from the bill during the House-Senate conference.

State school & busing legislation. Tennessee Gov. Buford Ellington Feb. 19, 1970 signed into law a measure providing that there should be no racial discrimination in the state's pupil assignment plans. Two other bills, which would have in effect banned busing in the state, were voted down by the Tennessee Legislature.

Two other governors Feb. 23 signed measures that would prevent court-ordered desegregation arrangements from using the transferring of students and teachers to achieve racial balance in their states' schools.

Georgia Gov. Lester G. Maddox said the bill he signed would supersede any court orders requiring transfers in Georgia's schools.

Maddox said the bill, which was passed by the Georgia legislature Feb. 21, did not contain any provisions for enforcement of the new law. But he said he hoped that parents, students, teachers or officials would file civil suits against school administrators who did not abide by the law.

Maddox said the law was based on a New York statute that he said had been upheld in court. Several other leading Southern officials had also said they would seek adoption of a New York law signed May 2, 1969.

The bill signed by Gov. John J. McKeithen of Louisiana provided that there would be no racial discrimination in the state's school systems but prohibited the transfer of students to achieve a racial balance, unless elected school administrators approved such a plan.

McKeithen said the new law would do little to alleviate the pressures of mass integration in Louisiana, but would make the rest of the nation aware of his state's problem in the area of school desegregation.

(School administrators in Houston County, Ga. Feb. 25 ignored Maddox's call for defiance of court-ordered desegregation. They told a U.S. district judge that public schools in the district were reopening under integration arrangements. Gov. Maddox warned Feb. 23 that any school official who implemented new student assignments would be violating state laws.

(U.S. District Judge George L. Hart Jr. April 23 dismissed a suit by the State of Georgia asking the court to require the federal government to apply its school desegregation guidelines on a national uniform basis.

(Georgia had taken its case to the district court in Washington, D.C. after various judges across the nation had refused to intervene and grant Georgia's request, which at one time or another, had been joined by several other Deep South states. These states had sought relief in the courts after the Senate had rejected two amendments that would have forced the federal government to apply uniform desegregation guidelines or abandon them altogether.)

Kirk yields school control. Florida Gov. Claude R. Kirk Jr. capitulated to the federal district court in Bradenton April 12, 1970 and pledged to end week-long acts of defiance against a Supreme Court-approved school desegregation

plan for the Manatee County public schools. Kirk, who had suspended the Manatee district school officials on the day before the plan was to be implemented April 5, had been repeatedly warned by the federal court that he faced contempt citations and fines of $10,000 a day until he relinquished control of the county's public schools.

Kirk made the announcement that he was reinstating the district's officials in a taped TV broadcast. He said he would officially put the school board members and the local school superintendent back in control and direct them to put the desegregation plan into operation April 14. The desegregation plan ordered by U.S. District Judge Ben Krentzman began operation April 14 with 2,600 students bused cross-county to new schools.

Kirk said he had agreed to relinquish his control over the Manatee schools because "the solutions to our problems must lie in the duly constituted courts." The "problem" Kirk referred to involved the implementation of the school desegregation plan, which Kirk termed "illegal" because it required the forced cross-county busing of students to achieve a racial balance in the Manatee schools.

The drama unfolded April 3 when the Supreme Court rejected a request by Manatee County officials for a delay in implementing the desegregation arrangement. Soon after the court's decision was announced, Manatee's school board announced it would implement the plan immediately.

Kirk flew to Bradenton April 5 and ordered the district's 17,000 public school pupils to ignore the court order and continue to attend the neighborhood schools in which they were presently enrolled. He suspended the school board and the local superintendent, he said, by the power of "executive order" and said he was assuming personal control of the district's school system.

Judge Krentzman April 7 ordered Kirk to relinquish control of the Manatee schools and return control immediately to the local officials. He also ordered that the controversial busing plan be put into operation by April 9. He said that any orders issued by Kirk to the contrary were to be disregarded.

Kirk, however, ignored Krentzman's order to have the busing arrangement set in motion and returned to Bradenton April 8 to insure that the integration plan was not implemented. Two of the governor's aides took physical possession of the school board offices while Kirk himself warned that any Manatee school official who agreed to implement the plan would be suspended.

U.S. Attorney John Briggs announced April 9 that the federal government would assume control of the Manatee county public schools despite a phalanx of heavily armed Florida state troopers and a reported warning that federal marshals would be fired upon if they moved against the school offices. Kirk moved into the offices late April 9 and said he would resist any effort of the federal marshals to take control of the schools.

Kirk vacated the Manatee County school board offices April 10.

Alabama integration ordered. Three federal judges, who for a six-year period had handled a statewide desegregation suit involving 100 Alabama school systems, ordered the rural county of Sumter to desegregate its schools completely June 13, 1970. The judges said they were forced to approve what they considered a harsh desegregation plan after the Justice Department had rejected a plan submitted by the Sumter County school board that coupled zoning patterns and freedom of choice to achieve integration.

The judges, Richard T. Rives, Frank M. Johnson and H. H. Grooms, said the insistence of the Justice Department on strict compliance with "clear mandates" of recent desegregation decisions of the Supreme Court and other U.S. district courts had left them no choice but to hand down an order that they said could cause a "white flight" from the public schools.

Sumter County's school system included about 1,000 whites and 4,000 blacks. Under the order handed down by the judges, blacks would outnumber whites—in some cases by 10-1—in the county's seven public schools.

School Policy & Action

Advisory panel formed. President Nixon established a Cabinet-level task force Feb. 16, 1970 to give aid and counsel to school districts under court orders to desegregate their schools immediately. The President said the group, which he termed "an informal Cabinet-level working group," would work with school administrators to execute the desegregation orders and still preserve the public education system.

Chairman of the group was Vice President Spiro Agnew. Vice chairman: George P. Shultz, secretary of labor. Other members were Attorney General John N. Mitchell, Postmaster General Winton M. Blount, Secretary of Health, Education and Welfare Robert H. Finch, Donald Rumsfeld, director of the Office of Economic Opportunity, and Presidential counselors Bryce Harlow and Daniel P. Moynihan.

Nixon states policy. President Nixon pledged March 24, 1970 that the Nixon Administration would not abandon or undermine the school desegregation gains since the Supreme Court's 1954 ruling outlawing "separate but equal" facilities. The President said it was his "personal belief" that the 1954 decision "was right in both constitutional and human terms."

The President's commitment was included in an 8,000-word document on the problems of elementary and secondary school desegregation. White House officials said it was the most comprehensive statement by any president on the issue of school integration.

In his report, Nixon vowed to apply all of the government's available resources towards elimination of officially imposed, or de jure, segregation in the South's public schools. He said, however, that until the courts provided further guidance he could not require elimination of de facto segregation, in the North or South, resulting from residential housing patterns.

Nixon said the Supreme Court had ruled on de jure segregation when it handed down the landmark decision in

Brown vs. Board of Education in 1954. The President pledged to carry out the court's mandate by relying on the "good faith" efforts of local Southern officials to comply with the court's orders.

The President said, however, that the courts had not spoken out on what, if anything, to do to overcome de facto segregation. He said that while segregation as a by-product of housing patterns was undesirable in practice, it remained fully constitutional in theory. Nixon said he was offering a set of possible remedies at an administrative level.

Nixon's suggestions encompassed two positions that he had often stated before. He repeated his opposition to student busing simply as a means of achieving racially balanced schools without improving the quality of education, and he said that he was in favor of the neighborhood-school concept.

His main proposal was to offer funds for technical assistance to public school districts in the North and South that wanted to eliminate de facto segregation on their own initiative or to mitigate the effects of segregation by providing compensatory educational guidance to minority group children in segregated schools. The President proposed $500 million for the 1971 fiscal year, beginning July 1, and an additional $1 billion in fiscal 1972.

The President said it would be the purpose of his Administration "to carry out the law fully and fairly." Nixon said he had instructed Attorney General John N. Mitchell, Secretary of Health, Education and Welfare Robert H. Finch and other "appropriate officials of the government" to be guided by the basic principles and policies laid down in his statement.

The President offered these principles:

Deliberate racial segregation of pupils by official action is unlawful, wherever it exists. In the words of the Supreme Court, it must be eliminated "root and branch"—and it must be eliminated at once.

Segregation of teachers must be eliminated. To this end, each school system in this nation, North and South, East and West, must move immediately, as the Supreme Court has ruled, toward a goal under which "in each school the ratio of white to Negro faculty members is substantially the same as it is throughout the system."

With respect to school facilities, school administrators throughout the nation, North and South, East and West, must move immediately, also in conformance with the Court's ruling, to assure that schools within individual school districts do not discriminate with respect to the quality of facilities or the quality of education delivered to the children within the district.

In devising local compliance plans primary weight should be given to the considered judgment of local school boards—provided they act in good faith and within constitutional limits.

The neighborhood school will be deemed the most appropriate base for such a system.

Transportation of pupils beyond normal geographic school zones for the purpose of achieving racial balance will not be required.

Federal advice and assistance will be made available on request, but Federal officials should not go beyond the requirements of law in attempting to impose their own judgment on the local school district.

School boards will be encouraged to be flexible and creative in formulating plans that are educationally sound and that result in effective desegregation.

Racial imbalance in a school system may be partly de jure in origin, and partly de facto. In such a case, it is appropriate to insist on remedy for the de jure portion, which is unlawful, without insisting on a remedy for the lawful de facto portion.

De facto racial separation, resulting genuinely from housing patterns, exists in the South as well as the North; in neither area should this condition by itself be cause for Federal enforcement actions. De jure segregation brought about by deliberate school-board gerrymandering exists in the North, as the South; in both areas this must be remedied. In all respects, the law should be applied equally, North and South, East and West.

The President also outlined what he called his "policies for progress:"

In those communities facing desegregation orders, the leaders of the communities will be encouraged to lead—not in defiance, but in smoothing the way of compliance. One clear lesson of experience is that local leadership is a fundamental factor in determining success or failure. Where leadership has been present, where it has been mobilized, where it has been effective, many districts have found that they could, after all, desegregate their schools successfully. Where local leadership has failed, the community has failed—and the schools and the children have borne the brunt of that failure.

We shall launch a concerted, sustained and honest effort to assemble and evaluate the lessons of experience: To determine what methods of school desegregation have worked, in what situations, and why—and also what has not worked. The Cabinet-level working group I recently appointed will have as one of its principal functions amassing just this sort of information and helping make it available to the communities in need of assistance.

We shall attempt to develop a far greater body of reliable data than now exists on the effects of various integration patterns on the learning process. Our effort must always be to preserve the educational benefit for the children.

We shall explore ways of sharing more broadly the burdens of social transition that have been laid disproportionately on the schools—ways, that is, of shifting to other public institutions a greater share of the task of undoing the effects of racial isolation.

We shall seek to develop and test a varied set of approaches to the problems associated with de facto segregation, North as well as South.

We shall intensify our efforts to insure that the gifted child—the potential leader—is not stifled intellectually merely because he is black or brown or lives in a slum.

While raising the quality of education in all schools, we shall concentrate especially on racially impacted schools, and particularly on equalizing those schools that are furthest behind.

The President said the federal government was limited in its enforcement of school desegregation orders. "If we are to be realists," Nixon said, "we must recognize that in a free society there are limits to the amount of government coercion that can reasonably be used; that in achieving desegregation we must proceed with the least possible disruption of the education of the nation's children..."

Comment on Nixon's policy—Secretary of Health, Education and Welfare (HEW) Robert H. Finch indicated April 7 that President Nixon's March 24 policy statement would not change his department's enforcement of desegregation. He said there would be no "backward motion."

Finch told newsmen that he and his HEW aides foresaw no change in the department's practice of busing as one means of enforcing either court-ordered or HEW-ordered school desegregation in the South.

Finch said that since nearly 90% of the South's public schools used student busing "it's not as though we're calling for a whole new lot of buses."

One of Finch's key aides, Jerry H. Rader, HEW's equal educational opportunity director, said that where busing already was used to maintain segregation, there would be little problem in rearranging it to accommodate school desegregation.

The Commission on Civil Rights, an independent federal agency, criticized Nixon's statement April 11 as inadequate, overcautious and possibly signaling a major retreat on the issue of school integration.

In a formal, unanimous statement from the group's Washington, D.C. headquarters, the commission said what was needed above all was "the continuing example of courageous moral leadership from the President of the United States." The group's report suggested that the President had failed to provide such leadership.

The commission had no enforcement powers but had frequently played an outspoken role in advocating equal civil and educational rights for all black Americans.

The language used in the commission's 27-page analysis and rebuttal of President Nixon's statement was moderate but critical.

The panel acknowledged that the President had pledged to carry out the U.S. Supreme Court's mandate of an immediate end to legally sanctioned dual school systems. But, the commission said, "much more, however, is necessary." The commission reported that it feared "that the President's statement well may have the net effect, though unintentional, of signaling a major departure from the policy of moving toward integrated schools and that open society of which he spoke so well in his statement."

The six members also disputed Nixon's distinction between de facto and de jure segregation. They took issue with the President's statement that "de facto racial separation, resulting genuinely from housing patterns exists in the South as well as the North." The commission reported, however, that extensive de jure segregation existed in the North. Indeed, the panel reported, so much segregation, even in the North, was traceable to official acts that there was "probably little legal substance to the concept of de facto school segregation."

Coleman calls school integration vital. James S. Coleman, principal author of a 1966 study of comparative educational opportunities for black and white children, said March 7, 1970 that integration was the most effective instrument available for upgrading the education of poor black children.

(The Coleman Report of 1966, commissioned by the Congress when it passed the Civil Rights Act of 1964, was the first study of its kind to report that integration was the only known educational device to have significant impact on the disadvantaged black child. By 1975, however, Coleman had concluded that integration was less helpful than his early studies had indicated it would be.)

Coleman, a Johns Hopkins University sociologist, said if the nation yielded to growing pressures to curb integration "we strongly risk creating all over the country the same kind of apartheid that had existed in the South since Reconstruction."

Coleman said that "school integration was vital not merely for some vague generalized social purposes, but because it was the most consistent mechanism for improving the quality of education of disadvantaged children." He indicated that the nation's educational administrators seemed transfixed with busing as the only means of integration—when, in his opinion, there were a variety of mechanisms to make integration work. Coleman said too often it appeared that federal and state officials "attempt only to satisfy the forms of law rather than to make integration succeed."

Coleman said he was pleased that President Nixon paraphrased part of the Coleman Report when he delivered his education message. "Quality," Nixon said, "is what education is all about; desegregation is vital to that quality." But Coleman said the statement did not go far enough because the President "didn't follow the statement with anything at all about how to make integration work."

Coleman maintained that so long as middle-class students remain in the majority in a given school, they set the achievement standard. By attending such a school, disadvantaged youths make more consistent educational gains than from any other educational mechanism. He stressed that the achievement level of the middle-class children would not suffer.

Coleman said the issue was not whether integration worked but rather how to make the benefits of integration possible. He put some of the responsibility for the current crisis over school desegregation on the federal government, which Coleman said, had used a punitive rather than helpful approach in implementing desegregation guidelines.

Segregation harms whites?—Dr. Kenneth B. Clark, a leading psychologist and director of a social research organization, testified at a Senate hearing April 20 that segregated schooling was more damaging to white schoolchildren than to minority pupils. Clark, director of the Metropolitan Applied Research Center, Inc., of New York and Washington,

was the first witness to appear before the hearings convened by the Senate's Select Committee on Equal Educational Opportunity.

The hearings, directed by committee chairman Walter F. Mondale (D, Minn.), were reported to be in response to President Nixon's March 24 policy statement on the progress of school desegregation and the admission that the Nixon Administration would not require elimination of de facto segregation until the courts provided additional guidance.

Clark told newsmen after his testimony that President Nixon had totally defaulted on leadership in achieving progress in the area of school desegregation. Clark said the President "acted as if the issue could be dealt with politically. He missed the basic point that the issue is moral and ethical and educational. His statement [March 24] has taken away some of the momentum the federal courts and some segments of society had built up."

Clark told the senators that "segregated schools are destroying the human development of sensitive white children more surely than that of black children."

'Unreasonable' busing scored. Attorney General John N. Mitchell said April 16 that every citizen had "the right to reject unreasonable requirements of busing and to send their children to neighborhood schools." Mitchell said this right was "just as important as the right of all of our citizens to be assigned [to the schools] without regard to their race." Mitchell's antibusing remarks drew cheers and applause from many of the 1,200 Republicans who were attending the party's 1970 leadership conference in Washington, D.C.

The attorney general told the GOP leaders that despite the balancing of constitutional rights and antibusing rights, the Nixon Administration "has brought about more school desegregation than any previous administration." He said he hoped that by the beginning of the next school year in September "this burning issue of school desegregation will be behind us and be laid to rest."

Allen to press integration. James E. Allen Jr., U.S. commissioner of education, announced April 27, 1970 that he intended to continue his work to end school segregation whether it was de facto or de jure. Allen's statement apparently put him at odds with President Nixon's policy statement March 24 that his Administration could do nothing about de facto segregation resulting from neighborhood residential patterns.

Allen said in his statement, "in the position of national leadership which I occupy I shall continue to emphasize the educational value of integration and the educational deprivation of segregation regardless of cause." He called on educators to intensify their efforts to achieve school desegregation and to take the lead by educating others about "the harmful educational effects of segregation on all our people."

U.S. pledges integration drive. Three of the Nixon Administration's chief civil rights officers pledged in separate statements June 25–29 that the government intended to force recalcitrant Southern school districts to comply with school desegregation orders when their schools reopened for the fall term.

One of the officials, Jerris Leonard, chief of the Justice Department's Civil Rights Division, warned that unless state and local officials worked out acceptable desegregation arrangements for their districts, the government would begin filing desegregation suits against their districts.

The first disclosure that a concerted effort was under way to force compliance was made June 25 by Elliot L. Richardson, the new secretary of health, education and welfare (HEW). Richardson, who was appointed June 6 by President Nixon to replace the departing Robert H. Finch, warned that the federal government was prepared to terminate federal funds to those school districts that continued to ignore desegregation orders. Richardson, speaking in Washington, D.C. at his first news conference as head of HEW, said the funds cutoffs would come where necessary. "In any case where appropriate," Richardson said, "I would take that action." (In his final 12 months in office Finch had terminated federal aid to only one Southern school district.)

Richardson also said the government would prosecute any discrimination

against black students or faculty members in otherwise desegregated schools. He said that the "ending of officially sanctioned racial discrimination should and must go beyond the assignment of students by race. This means desegregation not only at the point of entry but integrating education within the building as well."

Leonard's statement warning Southern school administrators that they faced possible court action was made June 26 during a week of meetings with Southern public school officials in Augusta, Ga. Leonard told the officials that no further delay would be tolerated in about 50 school districts that had avoided court scrutiny while maintaining token integration arrangements under freedom-of-choice school plans.

Leonard was joined in Jackson, Miss. June 29 by J. Stanley Pottinger, head of HEW's Office of Civil Rights, to conclude negotiations with Southern school officials over desegregation orders. The two federal officials asserted that most Southerners were convinced that the Nixon Administration intended to force compliance with the law when schools reopened for the fall term. Pottinger said his office would "conduct on-site reviews" of those school districts that were reneging on desegregation orders. He said those districts that failed to comply with desegregation orders would be referred "immediately to the Justice Department for action."

U.S. school suits filed. The Nixon Administration, which vowed June 26 that it would no longer tolerate delays or excuses from recalcitrant Southern school districts, took action to carry out its threat July 9 as the Justice Department haled into federal court 46 Deep South school districts for failing to produce acceptable desegregation arrangements.

Attorney General John N. Mitchell announced that the department had sued the state of Mississippi and a number of individual school systems in South Carolina, Arkansas and Florida. The suits involved 19 districts in Mississippi, 10 in South Carolina, nine in Arkansas and eight in Florida.

The government, filing the suits simultaneously in seven federal courts, asked for immediate orders to bring the districts into compliance with the law before the start of the 1970–71 school year. The suits asked for court orders to require the officials named as defendants in each case to work with the Department of Health, Education and Welfare to develop acceptable school desegregation plans.

Mitchell said that the suits were designed to "clean up the remnants—those few districts which could not or would not come into compliance."

In the statewide Mississippi case the department contended that the state's Constitution required dual, racially segregated school systems and that state agencies and officials had permitted, endorsed and encouraged the segregation. In the other cases the government charged that individual school districts "operate dual school systems based on race with the knowledge and consent of the state and its agencies and officials."

The department sued six more Florida school districts July 10 and thus raised to 14 the number of districts in the state facing possible court litigation for refusing to implement voluntary desegregation plans. The department said the suit covering all six districts brought into court all of the remaining Florida school systems that had not desegregated or had not approved desegregation plans for the 1970-71 school year. The suit was filed in U.S. District Court in Jacksonville against the Baker, Bradford, Flagler, Pasco, St. John's and Seminole school districts. The six systems had 79 public schools attended by 35,655 whites and 9,993 blacks.

Integration reaction polls. A survey conducted exclusively in the South indicated that the percentage of white Southern parents who would object to sending their children to public schools where Negroes were enrolled had dropped from 61% in 1963 to 16% in 1970, according to a Gallup Poll released May 2, 1970. The report said the findings represented one of the most dramatic shifts in the history of opinion sampling.

The American Institute of Public Opinion, which conducted the poll, said the figures represented answers to a question involving schools with only a few black pupils. Of the white parents

questioned, 43% said they would object to their children attending schools where more than half the enrollment were Negroes. In 1963, 78% of the whites questioned had said they would object to their children attending predominantly Negro schools.

The poll also conducted a sampling of Northern white parents' opinions on the same issue. Of those questioned, 6% said they objected to having their children attend classes with a few Negro students. (In 1963, 10% had objected.)

The Gallup organization had reported April 4 that by nearly an 8-1 margin, people questioned about the busing of schoolchildren said they would oppose the busing of black and white students to achieve racial balance in schools. The final statistics: Those who favored busing totaled 11%, 86% were opposed to it; and 3% said they had no opinion.

More than 70% of whites surveyed by the National Opinion Research Center (NORC) supported racial integration of schools and public accomodations, Scientific American magazine reported in its December issue.

Sentiment for integration had been increasing since NORC's first survey in 1942, although residential integration and intermarriage were still opposed by about half the 1970 sample, and only 16% opposed the statement that "Negroes shouldn't push themselves where they're not wanted," compared with 25% opposition in 1963.

Slight differences were reported between regions and ethnic groups. About half the Southerners sampled favored school integration, compared with 75% nationally. Catholics of German or Irish descent registered somewhat higher support for integration than Northern Protestants, who were in turn slightly more integrationist than Catholics of Southern and Eastern European ancestry.

Thurmond attacks school policy. Sen. Strom Thurmond (R, S.C.), who in 1968 had promised Southern voters they would find Republican school desegregation efforts easier to tolerate than Democratic ones, lashed out bitterly at the Nixon Administration's school policies July 17. He said that "such unreasonable policies" could lead to President Nixon's defeat in 1972.

"I can only conclude," Thurmond said in a speech to an almost empty Senate floor, "that a group of liberal advisers around the President are misleading him, and that their advice will bring disruption to the nation." The South Carolina senator said that Nixon's liberal advisers had advanced a "Northeast policy."

Thurmond, considered instrumental in preventing Southern Republicans from bolting to George C. Wallace in 1968, said that some of the Administration's more recent desegregation policies were the sort he had come to expect from Democratic Administrations of old.

He assailed a July 16 report that the Justice Department was planning to send 100 lawyers and staffers to the South in August and September to monitor the effects of the Administration's school desegregation efforts. Thurmond said: "I condemn these actions. I strongly condemn them. They are wrong as social policy and they are wrong as law."

Thurmond also attacked the Internal Revenue Service's July 10 decision to revoke the tax-exempt status of private academies that continued to practice racial discrimination in their admissions policies.

Nixon defends policy—President Nixon replied to Sen. Thurmond's charges July 20 during an impromptu news conference at the White House. Nixon did not deny the reports that the Justice Department was planning to send lawyers to the South to monitor school desegregation, but he said that the Administration had no intention of sending "vigilante squads" to the South "to coerce the Southern school districts to integrate."

The President also said that he was not surprised by Sen. Thurmond's reaction to the reports. He said: "I am not surprised at the reaction, but I believe that as thoughtful people in the South consider not only what we have done in the past but what we do in the future, they will recognize that we finally have in this country what the South has wanted and what the South deserves, a one-nation policy—not a Southern strategy and not a Northern strategy, but a one-nation strategy.

"As far as the South is concerned, the statement that Senator Thurmond made partially objected to an action we have not taken and have no intention of taking,

and that is of sending vigilante squads, in effect, from the Justice Department, lawyers, in to coerce the Southern school districts to integrate. We have not done that; we are not going to do that.

"Our approach is one of recognizing this terribly difficult problem of cooperating with the educational leaders and other leaders in the South in bringing them into compliance with the law of the land as it has been interpreted by the Supreme Court. Our policy, in other words, is cooperation rather than coercion.

"Now I would say finally that I know that some people in the South would prefer a policy that was perhaps not as evenhanded as this, but I believe this is the right policy insofar as carrying out the Constitutional mandates are concerned. I think it also is the fair policy. I think in the long run, too, it is in the interest of the South, because when we look at this difficult school problem there cannot be instant integration, but segregation must be ended. That is the law of the land and it is necessary for us to go forward and to end it with a transition period which will be as least difficult as possible."

Plan for monitoring South—White House counselor Robert H. Finch, the former HEW secretary responsible for many of the Administration's desegregation policies, said July 19 that Thurmond's attack was based on "erroneous" information. Finch was apparently referring to Thurmond's denunciation of the plan to send aides to oversee desegregation in recalcitrant Southern districts.

Newspaper reports of the Justice Department plans had been confirmed July 16 by Jerris Leonard, chief of the department's Civil Rights Division. But Attorney Gen. John N. Mitchell said July 17 that the published reports "purporting to give actual details of the program are premature." Mitchell said the details "are not necessarily wrong, just premature."

According to Leonard, the 100-man federal task force was to establish five regional command posts throughout the South in an effort to reduce the potential for disturbances as hundreds of Southern districts implemented desegregation arrangements for the first time.

The five field command posts were reported to be set for Jackson, Miss.; Montgomery, Ala.; and in undetermined cities in North or South Carolina, Georgia or Florida and Texas. Each post would be headed by a senior lawyer from Justice's civil rights division and staffed by HEW officials. About 50 lawyers would operate in the field reporting to the regional command posts.

Leonard also confirmed reports that all of the in-field lawyers would be accompanied by a deputy U.S. marshal to provide enforcement if it proved necessary. He also said that the normal field bureaus of the Federal Bureau of Investigation (FBI) would be relied on for immediate investigations sought by any one of the task force command posts.

Schools in South integrate. More than 200 school districts across the South that had resisted integration since it was ordered by the Supreme Court in 1954 reopened Aug. 31, 1970 with newly desegregated classrooms. Nearly 300,000 Negro schoolchildren from Virginia to Louisiana began classes with whites as threatened school boycotts organized by parents protesting desegregation plans failed to materialize.

Despite the compliance in the 200 districts, 175 others continued to be regarded by Nixon Administration officials as holdouts. Most of the 175 recalcitrant districts were involved in litigation on the controversial issue of student busing and other desegregation problems. Some of the others were involved in meetings with government officers in an attempt to dismantle the dual school systems.

School administrators in the 11 Southern states reported that the transition in the 200 districts was orderly and generally peaceful.

Southern educators said that despite the successful integration in most of the schools in the 200 districts, the government still faced two significant problems: the busing issue and the rise of segregated private academies.

The most pressing problem was reported to be opposition to busing. White parents in Augusta, Ga. picketed a newly desegregated school the week of Aug. 24, insisting that their protest had nothing to do with desegregation of the school. They said that they were protesting the busing

plans set for their children. The federal courts had handed down busing orders in cities and large towns where all-black schools were located in all-black neighborhoods to increase the incidence of desegregation.

The courts handed down the orders despite requests by officials in the Nixon Administration that busing be kept at a minimum. Parents had joined school administrators in some districts in filing suits and appeals to seek delays in opening their schools until the busing issue was resolved.

The Charlotte-Mecklenburg County, N.C., school board, which had been conducting a series of legal battles to delay implementation of a desegregation plan that called for extensive busing, was denied a petition for a delay Aug. 25 by U.S. Chief Justice Warren E. Burger. At the same time Burger refused to grant similar delays sought by Winston-Salem, N.C.; Forsyth County, N.C.; Broward County, Fla. and Dade County, Fla. All four districts had asked the chief justice to set aside the busing orders until the Supreme Court decided the busing issue.

Burger's refusal to grant the motions for stays of the orders meant that the busing plans ordered by lower courts for the districts would go into effect before the next regular Supreme Court session.

Burger rejected without comment Aug. 29 a similar appeal submitted by the Richmond, Va. school board. Officials on the Richmond board contended that the the busing plan, which would involve 13,000 students, would cause mass disruptions in the schools.

Southern officials and administrators also expressed concern over the proliferation of private segregated academies. Despite the Internal Revenue Service's July 10 directive to revoke the tax-exempt status of private schools practicing racial discrimination in admission, the number of such schools seemed to be growing.

A three-judge federal court panel Aug. 26 turned down a request by the Nixon Administration to have a suit pending against federal tax exceptions for the private all-white academies in the South dismissed. The panel in Washington, D.C. also turned down a request by the civil rights groups bringing the suit that all such academies have their tax-exempt status revoked immediately.

The government's lawyers told the court that the IRS would no longer grant tax exempt status to private schools practicing a policy of racial discrimination in admissions policies, but that for the present the government had taken the word of the schools in determining whether they were willing to desegregate.

A new round of desegregation in the Deep South began Sept. 9, marked by stiffening white resistance to federal integration orders and confusion over new student assignments. More disruptions accompanied the reopening of schools Sept. 9 than had occurred when most of the South's schools desegregated peacefully Aug. 31.

In Mobile, Ala. school officials placed the responsibility of enforcing a court-ordered desegregation plan on federal authorities. Members of the school board blamed the federal government for the confusion that accompanied the reopening of schools Sept. 9.

While the board met to discuss the enforcement of the order, white parents defied a federal court order and tried to enroll their children in neighborhood schools from which they had been removed and reassigned. Other white parents kept their children home.

The NAACP Legal Defense Fund, Inc. charged in federal court in Mobile Sept. 10 that the school board had discriminated in the deployment of 225 school buses. The defense fund argued that some of the buses should be used in the inner city where many youths had to travel farther to school than a year ago under the terms of the desegregation order. The board replied that it had neither the time nor funds to buy more buses to handle inner city busing.

The Justice Department accused the school board Sept. 14 of ignoring repeated violations of the desegregation order and sought a court order to stop it. Federal Judge Daniel H. Thomas signed the order banning the board from circumventing the school orders "by providing or . . . allowing the use of space, facilities and equipment . . . for the instruction of students" in schools other than those with desegregated student bodies.

There was little resistance Sept. 9 as the Charlotte-Mecklenburg, N. C.

school system, one of the largest in the South, began to reopen its schools under a court-ordered desegregation plan. Although students in only four grades reported back to school, most of them were quietly brought in by a busing plan that had stirred up much community opposition in Charlotte.

A black civil rights lawyer charged the week of Sept. 7 that the Nixon Administration and school officials in Jefferson County, Ala. were allowing 10,000 white students to attend classes in schools where they had not been assigned in violation of a U.S. court's desegregation order. The attorney, U.W. Clemon, filed a motion for contempt against the school administrators of Jefferson County, which included Birmingham. Clemon, an attorney for the NAACP Legal Defense Fund, Inc., said "the Nixon Administration had encouraged the whites to resist and defy the court orders, especially in districts where they know that local federal judges won't hold them in contempt."

Antibusing resolution adopted. A pair of conservative Deep South governors outmaneuvered the more moderate members of the Southern Governors Conference Sept. 21, 1970 and persuaded the group to vote adoption of a strongly worded antibusing resolution at their meeting in Biloxi, Miss.

Govs. John Bell Williams of Mississippi and John J. McKeithen of Louisiana, who pushed the resolution through over parliamentary objections from other governors, hailed its passage. The middle-of-the-road position taken at the 1969 conference was that some forms of busing were acceptable.

The resolution drafted by Williams and McKeithen opposed busing children from one neighborhood to another to achieve "racial balance," the phrase already enacted by an amendment in the Civil Rights Act of 1964. The measure passed with the support of 10 other governors.

The conference also adopted a measure asking Congress to enact a uniform national policy for enforcing school desegregation guidelines.

Busing & antibusing action. Gov. Ronald Reagan of California Sept. 12, 1970 signed into law a bill barring busing of students "for any purpose or for any reason without the written permission of the parent or guardian."

(An antibusing amendment to the California constitution was approved by California voters by vote of 4,905,247 to 2,877,596 Nov. 7, 1972. It banned involuntary pupil transfers for integration.)

Pasadena, Calif. residents narrowly voted down Oct. 14 three referendums to recall three members of the local school board who had supported a school integration plan that called for extensive cross-town busing.

The plan was implemented when the Pasadena schools reopened for the fall term. Under its terms, 30,000 students were to be bused at a cost of $1 million to Pasadena and three neighboring communities which were involved in the busing arrangement.

Final but unofficial returns showed that Albert C. Lowe, the board president, was retained by a vote of 23,522 to 21,610. Mrs. LuVerne Lamotte retained her seat by a vote of 23,009 to 22,410 and Dr. Joseph Engholm kept his seat by a vote of 23,281 to 22,258.

The recall campaign was started during the spring after the three board members voted not to appeal to a higher court the March 4 decision of the U.S. federal district judge who approved the integration plan.

New York State's 17-month-old antibusing law was voided as unconstitutional Oct. 1, 1970. A three judge federal court in Buffalo held that it violated the 14th Amendment. The statute had made it illegal for appointed school boards to reshuffle pupil assignment plans to achieve racial balance without the consent of their parents.

The law had been copied by school administrators in the Deep South seeking to forestall desegregation in their district's classrooms.

The judges held in their 24-page decision that the law violated the U.S. Constitution because it "constitutes an explicit and invidious racial classification and denies equal protection of the law." They granted a permanent injunction against all future enforcement of the law.

The order was signed by Circuit Judge Paul R. Hays, Chief Judge John O. Henderson of the Western District of New York and District Judge Harold P. Burke.

The law, which was enacted in May 1969, applied to appointed school boards, but not to elected school boards. The litigation challenging the law was brought by a group of black and white Buffalo parents.

The judges said that an examination of the objectives and effect of the law "supports the proposition that the statute serves to continue segregation in the school and thus significantly encourages and involves the state in racial discrimination."

Affirmative Action in Schools North & South

North Carolina: *Charlotte busing upheld* — The legality of busing for the purpose of racial integration in schools was upheld by the U.S. Supreme Court in 1971 in a group of decisions involving Charlotte, N.C. and other Southern communities.

The Nixon Administration had joined the case April 8, 1970. It suggested that a federal district court judge who had ordered a busing plan to be implemented had committed "an abuse of discretion." The action was in the form of a brief filed by the Justice Department in the U.S. Court of Appeals for the Fourth Circuit in Richmond, Va.

The National Education Association (NEA) entered the case the same day with a brief representing the Negro schoolchildren of Charlotte. The NEA argued that the busing order, handed down by Judge James B. McMillan, was the proper means of achieving desegregation and would not place a burden on the Charlotte-Mecklenburg County school district.

According to the terms of McMillan's order, a maximum of 13,300 pupils would be added to the 24,000 then being bused. The order also would require the pairing of schools so that no school in the district would be more than one- third black. He had ordered the plan to be put into operation by April 1, but March 25 he amended it to take effect Sept. 1. The Fourth Circuit and the Supreme Court upheld the change.

The Fourth Circuit Court opened its hearings on the appeal April 9 in Richmond and heard a government attorney say that it was time that the Supreme

Court ruled on the legality of all-black schools. The attorney, David L. Norman, deputy assistant attorney general for civil rights, told the court that Nixon Administration policy permitted the existence of predominantly Negro schools in urban centers and said the Supreme Court should decide whether judicial policy would be the same.

Norman concentrated his case on the question of whether Judge McMillan's order for busing was too "extreme." Norman said that the Justice Department and the Department of Health, Education and Welfare (HEW) "have drawn hundreds of desegregation plans at the instruction of the courts and we do not have one that resembles" the arrangement ordered by McMillan.

One of the attorneys representing the NEA and the Negro schoolchildren of Charlotte was Stephen J. Pollak, a former deputy attorney general for civil rights in the Johnson Administration. Pollak argued that the existence of segregated neighborhoods could not be used in the Charlotte case as a basis for maintaining all-black schools since, he said, the school segregation was not de facto, or segregation resulting from housing patterns.

The appeals court May 27 ruled, 4–2, that it was not always necessary for every school within a district to be integrated in order to fulfill the Supreme Court's demand that de jure school segregation be eliminated at once.

The decision set aside the order for implementation of the desegregation plan that would have made it necessary for the district to bus 13,300 more students than the 24,000 already participating in the busing arrangement. The ruling left standing the original order for integration of the district's junior and senior high schools but ordered that a new plan for the district's elementary schools be drawn up.

The majority decision, written by Judge John D. Butzner Jr., said busing of students was a "permissible tool" for achieving integration but no "panacea" for solving all problems that arise out of school desegregation.

"Not every school in a unitary school system need be integrated," the court said.

The majority view said if a school board had made "every reasonable effort to integrate the pupils under its control," an "intractable remnant of segregation" should not void an otherwise sound plan for the establishment of a unitary school system.

In effect, the court upheld sections of McMillan's Feb. 5 decision but ordered one part re-examined for a "rule of reasonableness."

In another development in Charlotte, the only Negro on the district school board was defeated in a runoff election May 31 that completed a sweep of the board's seats by antibusing candidates. Two other anti-busing candidates were elected to the board May 3.

McMillan Aug. 3 upheld his earlier ruling and ordered the school administrators to begin using a student busing plan when the schools reopened for the fall term Aug. 31. The busing plan, which McMillan had approved Feb. 5, was designed to increase the incidence of desegregation in the county's public schools.

McMillan gave Charlotte officials the option of adopting portions of a plan drawn by its liberal minority. That plan would require busing of more students but generally over shorter distances than the ones incorporated in McMillan's ruling.

In sustaining his Feb. 5 decision, McMillan said that constitutional rights take precedence over reasonableness. He wrote in his decision: "Reasonable remedies should always be sought. Practical rather than burdensome methods are properly required. . . . However, if a constitutional right has been denied, this court believes that it is the constitutional right that should prevail against the cry of unreasonableness. If, as this court and the circuit court have held, the rights of children are being denied, the cost and inconvenience of restoring those rights is no reason under the Constitution for continuing to deny them."

The Supreme Court Oct. 12–14 heard arguments on the Charlotte and Mobile, Ala. school desegregation cases as well as on busing and racial balance in Deep South schools in general.

During the three days of hearings, lawyers for Negro schoolchildren, the U.S. solicitor general representing the federal government and attorneys for Southern school officials called on the Court to adopt different proposals to solve the busing problem.

Attorneys for the N.A.A.C.P. Legal Defense and Educational Fund, Inc., representing the Negro children, argued Oct. 12 that each black child had a constitutional right to be enrolled in a school that was not recognizably "black." The lawyers said that based on this premise, any school plan that did not eliminate every all-black school should be adjudged inadequate. The Fund attorneys told the court that it would be undermining its own 1954 decision in Brown vs. Board of Education if it now permitted some Southern school districts to maintain some recognizably "black" schools.

Solicitor General Erwin N. Griswold, arguing for the Justice Department, rebutted the Fund's arguments Oct. 12 and 14. He said Oct. 12 that the Fund's petition amounted to a demand for racial balance in the schools and "I cannot find that in the Constitution." He told the court that if a school board had done everything feasible to eliminate all traces of state-imposed segregation, then it had satisfied the Constitution even if some all-black schools remained. In response to a question by Justice Thurgood Marshall, who argued the Brown vs. Board of Education case before the court in 1954, Griswold said it was "surely an objective" of a school board to see that each Negro child received a desegregated education, but that the court could not require it because "it's not in the 14th Amendment."

In his second appearance before the bench, Griswold warned Oct. 14 that white students might flee the South's public schoolrooms if school desegregation were pressed too vigorously. He insisted that the plan advocated by the Fund—abolition of all recognizably black schools—would in the long run produce less integration. Griswold said that "if you require too much, you aggravate the problems of withdrawals. There suddenly comes a place where the whites' fleeing is accelerated or becomes complete."

At the same time Griswold rejected arguments by lawyers for the Mobile and Charlotte districts that the Constitution prohibited assigning children to schools on the basis of race in order to break up segregated schools. He also accepted the idea that limited busing of children to schools outside their imme-

diate neighborhood might be necessary to achieve integration.

Lawyers for the school districts told the court Oct. 13 that the 1954 Brown vs. Board of Education decision was being violated by court-ordered integration plans that assigned children to schools by race. A group of the Southern lawyers argued that the 1954 ruling required "color-blind" assignment of students and that the busing of schoolchildren to increase the incidence of integration was unconstitutional.

Lawyers for the Southern appellants repeatedly used the 1954 Brown decision to bolster their arguments against the integration plans ordered for the Mobile and Charlotte districts. An attorney for a group of white and black parents whose children were bused away from their local schools when the Charlotte schools were reopened Sept. 9 asserted that "we plead the same constitutional rights here that the plaintiffs pleaded in Brown."

In a series of unanimous decisions April 20, 1971, the Supreme Court told the Charlotte-Mecklenburg County school system and all other Southern school districts that busing children to dismantle dual school systems was constitutional.

The rulings brought to a close final legal efforts by Southern school boards to stave off busing students to achieve racially-balanced schools.

Chief Justice Warren E. Burger wrote the opinions for the entire court in the four cases on which it ruled.

In addition to upholding a far-reaching school desegregation plan for the Charlotte-Mecklenburg district, the court struck down as unconstitutional an anti-busing statute enacted by the North Carolina legislature, ordered Mobile, Ala. school officials to use "all available techniques" to correct segregation in their schools and overturned a Georgia Supreme Court ruling that had said certain desegregation efforts in Athens were unconstitutional.

"Desegregation plans cannot be limited to the walk-in school," Burger wrote for the court. The justices held that busing schoolchildren was proper unless "the time or distance is so great as to risk either the health of the children or significantly impinge on the educational process." The court added that at times busing was an indispensable method of eliminating "the last vestiges" of racial segregation.

The court made it clear, however, that the rulings in the Charlotte and its companion cases did not apply to de facto segregation, caused by neighborhood housing patterns and found most often in the North.

In upholding the constitutionality of busing, the court brushed aside the arguments of the Nixon Administration and the Justice Department which had backed Southern school officials seeking relief from the court. The department lawyers had contended that Southern school districts should be permitted to assign students to schools in their own neighborhoods even if it slowed down the pace of desegregation.

Lawyers for the Southern districts argued that in the North, communities were allowed to have neighborhood schools and that it would be discriminatory if the South were not allowed the same "privilege."

(Several hours after the decision was announced, White House Press Secretary Ronald L. Ziegler, speaking for President Nixon, said "the Supreme Court has acted and their decision is now the law of the land. It is up to the people to obey that law." He declined to answer questions of whether the President was pleased or dissatisfied with the ruling.)

The court imposed some limits on its decisions. It stopped short of ordering the elimination of all-black schools or of requiring racial balance in the schools. In addition, the court said that young children may be improper subjects for busing if it was over long distances.

The major portion of what Burger described as "guidelines" for the "assistance of school authorities and courts" came in a 28-page decision involving the Charlotte school district. The court upheld the action of U.S. Judge James B. McMillan who approved a school desegregation plan that required massive crosstown busing of schoolchildren to increase the incidence of integration.

In the other North Carolina case, the justices ruled that the legislature violated the Constitution when it enacted an anti-busing law and that the statute, "apparently neutral" and "color-blind" in form, "would render illusionary" the concept of a unitary school system.

Burger wrote that bus transportation had been an "integral part of all public educational systems" and that it was unlikely that an effective remedy could be devised "without continued reliance upon it."

In the Mobile case, the justices overturned a desegregation plan that city officials had devised and ordered further desegregation.

The court held in an Athens, Ga. action that, contrary to the ruling of the Georgia Supreme Court, Athens and its surrounding county (Clarke) were within the law to take race into account in devising their own voluntary desegregation plans. White parents had challenged the efforts on the grounds that they violated the 14th Amendment.

Chief Justice Burger said Aug. 31 that he feared federal judges were "misreading" the Supreme Court's April 20 ruling on busing to achieve racial desegregation by interpreting it to require racial balance in every school. Burger delivered a clarification of the landmark busing decision, which he had written for the court, in refusing to stay the enforcement of a court-ordered busing plan for the Winston-Salem, Forsyth County, N.C. school system.

Burger rejected the plea for a stay because of the lateness of the appeal and the lack of sufficient information to overturn the plan ordered by Judge Eugene A. Gordon. Schools there had opened Aug. 30 under a plan involving busing of 34,000 of the district's 50,000 students.

In his 10-page opinion, unusual in a denial of a stay, Burger said the unanimous April ruling did not require "a fixed racial balance or quota" in order to constitutionally desegregate schools. He said a school district's racial balance should be used as "a starting point" to determine "whether in fact any violation existed."

But he quoted language from the Charlotte ruling saying that judges need not require "that every school in every community must always reflect the racial composition of the school system as a whole."

California: *Court acts re Pasadena*—A federal district court judge in Los Angeles Jan. 20, 1970 ordered the Pasadena school district to submit a plan to desegregate its public schools by Feb. 16. The plan, covering all the schools in the suburban Los Angeles district, was to go into effect September.

The Pasadena case was the first of the government's suits against Northern school districts to be acted upon. The ruling ordered that the plan submitted by the Pasadena district must produce no school with a majority of nonwhite students. Federal Judge Manuel L. Real also ordered that the plan must cover new teaching assignments, hiring and promotional practices and the construction of new school buildings.

(The suit was filed in August 1968 by the parents of three schoolgirls. The Justice Department joined the suit in November 1968.)

The plan submitted by the Pasadena school administration was approved by Real March 4. He rejected a petition by the attorneys general of Alabama, Mississippi and Louisiana to enter the case as a "friend of the court."

The Southern officials had sought to enter the Pasadena case because in their view the time allowed Pasadena educators to design a desegregation arrangement was excessive. The Southerners contended that the California district should be ordered to "integrate now," which, according to the attorneys general, was the order handed down to their states.

The plan approved by Judge Real called for busing students up to 10 miles within zones set up inside the district.

The Department of Health, Education & Welfare informed Pasadena school officials April 11, 1974 that the district had failed to comply with the court-ordered desegregation plan, forcing the department to cut off the city's share of federal integration-aid funds, provided under the Emergency School Aid Act of 1971.

In a decision upholding Pasadena's desegregation record, however, the U.S. Supreme Court ruled, 6–2, June 28, 1976 that the public schools could not be required by the courts to readjust attendance zones in line with population trends after initial compliance with desegregation orders.

The decision was written by Justice William Rehnquist. The ruling, he wrote, applied even to cases where the system lacked full compliance with other parts of a court-ordered desegregation plan, such as in the hiring of teachers.

If a "racially neutral" system of pupil assignment had been reached with the initial compliance, Rehnquist said, the court had "fully performed its function of providing the remedy for previous racially discriminatory attendance patterns."

Justices Thurgood Marshall and William Brennan Jr. dissented.

The case was Pasadena City Bd. of Education v. Spangler (75–164).

Los Angeles order reversed—Superior Court Judge Alfred E. Gitelson in Los Angeles Feb. 11, 1970 ordered officials of the city's school system, the U.S.' second largest, to present a formula by June 1 for the integration of the district's 555 schools and to implement it by September 1971. Gitelson issued the order in a suit instituted by the American Civil Liberties Union (ACLU) on behalf of Mexican-American and Negro schoolchildren.

According to Judge Gitelson, the Los Angeles district set boundaries "preventing or prohibiting or impeding minorities from attending white or substantially white schools."

Los Angeles school superintendent Robert F. Kelly said the order required the busing of 240,000 of the district's 674,000 students. He warned that the costs of reshaping the district "would mean the virtual destruction of the school district."

Judge Gitelson said in his ruling that the district was guilty of "expending millions in tax funds for the protection, maintainance and perpetuating of its segregated schools . . . " The judge also accused the district of building new facilities "knowing that the schools, would be, upon opening, segregated or racially imbalanced."

The 2nd District Court of Appeals of California March 10, 1975 overturned Gitelson's ruling. The panel held that the school board had not "intentionally discriminated against minority students by practicing a deliberate policy of racial segregation." The panel, returning the case to a lower court, said that "segregation was ignored rather than intentionally fostered."

The city board of education March 3, 1977 adopted a new busing plan that included a number of options and delayed mandatory busing for a year. Rides would be limited to no more than 20 minutes for those students who were bused, under the plan. The plan was designed to provide all pupils with at least two years of "an integrated educational experience." Segregated schools were defined as those with a student body more that 75% minority or white.

Superior Court Judge Paul J. Egly rejected the plan July 6 as "ineffective," similar to plans that had been ruled unconstitutional in other cities. Egly said the Los Angeles plan "does not desegregate any school in the district."

The court ruling ordered the school board to submit within 90 days a revised proposal that would "realistically commence the desegregation of this district by no later than February 1978." (A voluntary desegregation program had been adopted for use until then.)

The school board April 14 assigned 116 schools to "educational leagues" as part of the district's desegregation plan.

The assignment marked the end of the plan's voluntary phase and beginning of mandatory desegregation.

Predominantly Anglo and predominantly minority schools within the leagues were required to pair or cluster before the September term, when the league system would be initiated. If schools did not agree to pair or cluster, the board would mandate the groupings.

The plan encompassed only grades four through eight. Voluntary integration activities were encouraged in the other grades.

Students in racially isolated schools left outside the leagues, generally because of distances involved or poor access, would be given preference in assignment to magnet schools. These schools were designed with special educational programs to attract interracial enrollment from throughout the school district.

Special educational programs also were planned for the racially isolated schools and their class sizes would be reduced.

San Francisco plan—Federal District Judge Stanley A.Weigel in San Francisco April 28, 1971 held the city board of education responsible for widespread school segregation and ordered it to produce a plan that would fully integrate San

Francisco's elementary schools by the next school year. The board adopted such a plan June 4 and it went into effect Sept. 8.

Weigel ordered integration of the 48,000 elementary pupils in light of the Supreme Court's April 20 decision upholding busing as a means of ending school segregation.

Weigel said he found that only 29% of the 48,000 pupils in the city's 102 elementary schools were black, but that 80% of the blacks were concentrated in 27 schools.

Weigel said the district had advanced segregation by zoning new schools and attendance boundaries in a manner that perpetuated the racial imbalance.

A school board study of the city's first year of integration found a slight rise in reading levels, an improvement in racial attitudes among children and reduced parent opposition to busing, it was reported Nov. 16, 1972.

Inglewood plan abandoned—Superior Court Judge Max F. Deutz May 10, 1975 permitted school officials of the city of Inglewood to abandon a five-year old plan to desegregate the city's schools. "As a practical matter, we are now busing black children from predominantly black schools to other predominantly black schools," said Deutz, who noted in his decision that the district's 17 schools had gone from 62% white in 1970 to 19.5% in 1975. School authorities said that families with school-aged children had moved out of the district or sent their children to private schools.

Michigan: Uncertainty in Detroit—Detroit underwent at least six years of struggle for an accepted school desegregation plan. The city's school board April 7, 1970 had agreed to a busing plan for about 3,000 of the city's high school pupils and a decentralization plan aimed at dispersing the white minority students among the district's secondary schools.

The 3,000 students to be bused would be entering their first year of high school. They would be switched from their neighborhood schools to schools in other areas of Detroit. The board said the goal of the busing arrangement, which would involve both Negro and white students, was to alter the racial makeup of 11 Detroit high schools having about 34,000 children.

In addition to the busing arrangement, the board had approved a state-ordered decentralization plan which split the Detroit district into seven districts, each of which would have its own school board. Under this plan, black students would be sent into practically all-white schools on the district's outer perimeter, while more white students would be assigned to schools in the inner city area. There were no formal provisions for busing, but some school board members estimated that some students would have to ride city buses five miles to get to their new schools.

Legislation adopted by the State Legislature was designed to reverse or modify the controversial plan. Both houses approved a bill to block the boundary changes which were part of the decentralization formula, and to eliminate the jobs of board members who voted for the zoning changes. The bill, however, would not take effect until the spring of 1971, too late to prevent the integration which was ordered for the 1970 fall school term.

The U.S. Court of Appeals for the 6th Circuit ruled that the state could not block a local desegregation plan. Detroit's new school board then gave the federal court a choice of plans.

U.S. District Court Judge Stephen Roth, asked to choose a desegregation plan from among several proposed, picked one Dec. 3 that called for the establishment of "magnet" high schools throughout the city, specializing in vocational, science, arts or business programs, with students picking the school and the program they wanted. The arrangement was unlike other school desegregation plans which most frequently used compulsory busing to achieve increased integration.

In his ruling, Judge Roth said that "integration for integration's sake alone is self-defeating; it does not advance the cause of integration, except in the short haul, nor does it necessarily improve the quality of education."

As the legal dispute continued, however, Roth said Sept. 27 that he would delay ordering specific plans pending further hearings. He ruled that the school system had been deliberately segregated.

Roth's decision came in a 13-month civil suit still being contested. The suit was filed by the National Association for the Advancement of Colored People (NAACP) as a class action suit on behalf of all the city's schoolchildren and their parents.

According to Roth, the Detroit system promoted segregation by constructing small primary schools, redrawing attendance zones to circumvent integration and using busing to move some black students to other black schools rather than white ones. He said "state and local government actions have played a substantial role in promoting segregation" of the schools.

But he added that "there is enough blame for everyone to share." "Government actions and inactions at all levels—federal, state and local—have combined with those of private organizations such as loaning institutions, real estate associations and brokerage firms" to cause a pattern of housing segregation, Roth said. He said segregated housing fostered segregated schools.

Roth also put some of the blame on blacks, who to some degree he said, "like other ethnic groups in the past, have tended to separate from the larger group and associate together."

A week later Roth directed the Michigan Board of Education Oct. 4 to propose within four months a school integration plan that would encompass Detroit's inner city schools and schools in outlying suburban areas.

In his instructions, Roth said the plan should result in the creation of a metropolitan school district integrating inner city and suburban schools. He said that only some type of metropolitan plan appeared to have "a chance to succeed."

Roth insisted that he had not decided on any integration plan, but his comments on an inner city-suburban district stirred fears in the suburbs that the plans would require cross-district busing of schoolchildren.

In a related development, Michigan's top Democratic party leadership went on record Oct. 2 endorsing busing "as an imperfect and temporary mechanism to help erase the imbalances in our educational system." Among those who signed the busing statement were Sen. Philip A. Hart, State Attorney General

Frank Kelley, Secretary of State Richard Austin, Democratic State Chairman James M. McNeely and Jerome Cavanagh, former mayor of Detroit.

But Gov. William G. Milliken warned Nov. 3 that Michigan would appeal a busing order. In a statewide broadcast, Milliken said "children—white or black —don't learn by riding buses." He added that "busing to achieve racial balance treats only a symptom of segregation," which Milliken said was fostered by housing and working patterns.

Milliken said "even the suggestion of cross-district busing to achieve racial integration has stirred a storm of emotions and uncertainty that threatens to tear the very fabric of our whole public educational system."

The state Board of Education submitted six different plans to Roth Feb. 3, 1972, without expressing preference, ranging from a merger of 36 metropolitan school districts into six regions with equal black-white ratios, to a simple increase of funds and community control for black schools in Detroit.

Rejecting all three plans, Roth said school district lines were arbitrary, and could not be used to deny constitutional rights. He called it his "duty" under the 1954 *Brown* decision to "look beyond the limits of the Detroit school district for a solution." The judge ruled March 28 that "relief of segregation in the public schools of the city of Detroit cannot be accomplished within the corporate geographical limits of the city."

Roth June 14 issued an order that required a massive busing operation to integrate Detroit city and suburban schools. It was the most extensive desegregation order issued by a federal court.

Under the plan, which was based largely on a proposal of the National Association for the Advancement of Colored People, 310,000 of 780,000 pupils in Detroit and 53 suburban school districts would be bussed across Detroit city lines. City high school districts would be paired or clustered with suburban districts, and teachers would be reassigned so that each school had at least 10% black faculty and staff.

Roth wrote that under his order, "the greatest change would be in the direction of the buses," and set a general maximum of 40 minutes for a one-way ride. But he added that "transportation

of kindergarten children for upwards of 45 minutes one way, does not appear unreasonable, harmful or unsafe in any way."

Roth set up a nine-member panel to fill in the details and establish a schedule within 45 days, with full implementation set for the fall 1973 term. Problems of adjusting administration, personnel contracts and financing with the plan were expected to be complicated by a Detroit fiscal crisis. The Detroit School Board had adopted an emergency budget plan June 6 reducing the 1972-73 school year from 180 to 117 days, in a plea for more state aid.

The Detroit schools had 290,000 students, about 65% black, while 29 of the 53 suburban districts were all white and the rest overwhelmingly white.

Roth issued orders to the state of Michigan July 10 to buy 295 buses to begin implementing the first stage of his plan, though state officials argued that they had no constitutional or legislative authority to purchase the buses.

After two stays July 21 and Aug. 24, Roth's decision was upheld Dec. 8 by a three-judge panel of the 6th U.S. Circuit Court of Appeals. The panel held that the city-suburb school integration plan was necessary to assure equal rights for black schoolchildren in Detroit.

Nearly a year later the full 6th U.S. Circuit Court June 12, 1973 likewise upheld the principle of merging city and suburban school districts to achieve racial balance.

The issue of metropolitan area busing had remained open after the U.S. Supreme Court refused May 21 to uphold a similar plan for Richmond, Va. Because of a tie vote in the Supreme Court, no precedent was set.

Writing for the 6–3 majority in the Detroit case, Chief Judge Harry Phillips said the constitutional right to equality before the law could not be "hemmed in by the boundaries of a school district."

The court set aside the original busing plan on the ground that the suburban districts had not been given proper opportunity to object in court. Also set aside was an order that Detroit immediately buy 295 school buses to implement the plan. While returning the case to the federal district court, the appeals court suggested that the best solution might come from the state legislature. But if the legislature failed to correct segregation, the court said, "a federal court has both the power and the duty to effect a feasible desegregation plan."

In a dissenting opinion, Judge Paul C. Weick urged a new trial to consider a Detroit-only plan. A merger, he said, would deny individual children "their right not to be substantially burdened solely on account of their race."

In 1974 the Supreme Court July 25 rejected the plan for integrating Detroit and suburban schools. The high court, in a close 5–4 decision, all but banned desegregation through the busing of children across school district lines.

Chief Justice Warren E. Burger, author of the court's majority opinion, was joined by Justices Harry A. Blackmun, Lewis F. Powell Jr. and William H. Rehnquist, all appointees of President Nixon, and Potter Stewart, named to the court by President Eisenhower.

In his opinion, Burger noted reasoning by lower courts that Detroit's schools, which were 70% black, would not be truly desegregated unless their racial composition reflected the racial composition of the whole metropolitan area. However, Burger challenged what he called the lower court's "analytical starting point"—that school boundary lines might be casually ignored and treated as mere administrative conveniences.

Such notions were contrary to the history of public education in the U.S., Burger wrote. "No single tradition in public education is more deeply rooted than local control over the operation of schools; local autonomy has long been thought essential both to the maintenance of community concern and support for public schools and to quality of the educational process. . . ."

Moreover, Burger continued, consolidation of 54 historically independent school districts into one super district would give rise to an array of new problems concerning the financing and operation of the new district. In the absence of a complete restructuring of the laws of Michigan relating to school districts, the proposed interdistrict remedy would cause the federal district court to become "first, a de facto 'legislative authority' to resolve these complex questions, and then the 'school superintendent' for the entire area," Burger said.

"Disparate treatment of white and Negro students occurred within the De-

troit school system and not elsewhere, and on the record the remedy must be limited to that system. The constitutional right of the Negro respondents residing in Detroit is to attend a unitary school system in that district. Unless petitioners drew the district lines in a discriminatory fashion, or arranged for white students residing in the Detroit district to attend schools in Oakland and Macomb counties, they were under no constitutional duty to make provisions for Negro students to do so. . . . We conclude that the relief ordered by the district court and affirmed by the court of appeals was based upon an erroneous standard and was unsupported by record evidence that acts of the outlying districts affected the discrimination found to exist in the schools of Detroit."

In a dissent, Justice Thurgood Marshall charged that the court's answer to this problem was to "provide no remedy at all. . . , thereby guaranteeing that Negro children in Detroit will receive the same separate and inherently unequal education in the future as they have been unconstitutionally afforded in the past."

Failing to perceive any basis for the state's erection of school boundary lines as "absolute barriers" to the implementation of effective desegregation remedies, Marshall castigated the court majority for seeming to have "forgotten the district court's explicit finding that a Detroit-only decree . . . 'would not accomplish desegregation.' "

The state, not simply the Detroit board of education, bore the responsibility for curing the condition of segregation in the Detroit schools, he asserted. Marshall pointed out that the state, under the 14th Amendment, bore responsibility for the actions of its local agencies. Given that Michigan operated a "single, statewide system of education, Detroit's segregation could not be viewed "as the problem of an independent and separate entity," Marshall said.

Two proposals calling for the forced busing of a minimum of 50,000 children to integrate the Detroit public school system were rejected by U.S. District Court Judge Robert E. DeMascio Aug. 16, 1975. DeMascio ordered the Detroit Board of Education to devise a less sweeping plan that emphasized quality education and employed a variety of integrationist techniques involving a lessened amount of busing.

DeMascio's decision was reached after nine weeks of hearings that ended June 25. During the hearings, the board had put forward a desegregation plan that entailed busing at least 50,000 children. Although the plan was intended to eliminate "white identifiable schools" by reassigning pupils so that no more than half the students in any school would be white, it left a number of all-black schools.

An alternate proposal, advanced by the National Association for the Advancement of Colored People, involved the busing of a minimum of 80,000 students in such a way as to bring every Detroit school to within 15% of the racial make-up of the system as a whole.

The guidelines finally established by De-Mascio incorporated a part of the Board of Education's plan, including comprehensive programs for in-service training, bilingual multi-ethnic studies, a non-discriminatory testing program and improved school-community relations. Without setting a specific timetable, De-Mascio ordered the board to draw up a plan under which no school would be any less than 30% black.

DeMascio Nov. 4 ordered Detroit to begin in January 1976 a new integration plan that would involve busing more than 20,000 students.

The plan was devised by DeMascio with the aid of Prof. John E. Finger of Rhode Island College and was aimed at increasing to just over 50% the proportion of black students in those Detroit schools that were still heavily white.

DeMascio said the purpose of his plan was to keep white students (who made up only 23% of Detroit's 247,500 public school students) from moving to avoid an integration order.

The DeMascio-Finger plan would affect about 28,300 students; 21,200 would be bused and 7,100 others reassigned.

The integration plan went into effect Jan. 26, 1976 with no disturbances.

The limited nature of the desegration plan—busing less than 10% of the students, and affecting only 107 of the system's 240 schools—was cited by some to explain the peacefulness which attended its implementation. However, the plan also drew criticism on the ground of its limited scope; the NAACP had appealed it unsuccessfully as inadequate.

Pontiac integration & arson—Federal District Judge Damon J. Keith in Detroit Feb. 17, 1970 ordered the city of Pontiac, Mich. to completely integrate its schools at the student, faculty and administrative levels by the fall of 1970. In his order, Keith instructed that "such integration shall be accomplished by the revising of boundary lines for attendance purposes, as well as by busing so as to achieve maximum racial integration."

The board submitted a plan March 21 but served notice that it was appealing. The board argued that if Keith accepted its formula it would be so costly to the school district that it would impair the quality of education for all of Pontiac's 24,000 students.

Under the plan submitted by the school board, each pupil in grades one through six would attend his neighborhood school for two years and transfer to other area schools for the other four grades. This would mean that every child in the Pontiac system would be bused for four of his first six school years.

Keith's order was sustained by the U.S. 6th Circuit Court of Appeals May 28, 1971, and the Supreme Court Oct. 26 declined to hear the appeal that followed.

By refusing to hear the case, the court avoided ruling on the controversial issue of busing in the North to achieve racially-balanced schools.

For the most part, school segregation in the North was fostered by neighborhood housing patterns, or de facto segregation. In the South, school segregation was generally the result of officially constituted acts or de jure segregation. The court had yet to rule on de facto segregation.

The court's action in the Pontiac case meant that lower court judges would remain free to order school busing plans in other Northern school cases.

The court did not give reasons for refusing to hear the appeal by the Pontiac school board, which maintained that school segregation in Pontiac was a result of neighborhood patterns and not of discriminatory actions by either school or public officials.

In the meantime, violence erupted in the Pontiac situation. Arsonists Aug. 30, 1971 set fire bombs that destroyed 10 buses scheduled for use in the integration plan. Detroit District Court Judge Lawrence Gubow May 21, 1973 found five former Ku Klux Klan members guilty of conspiracy to bomb the buses.

The five were found guilty of conspiring to interfere by force with the execution of a court-ordered desegregation plan and of conspiring to intimidate black children in the exercise of their right to attend public schools.

Ferndale guilty of segregating—A hearing examiner for the U.S. Department of Health, Education & Welfare (HEW) ruled Sept. 28, 1970 for the first time that a Northern school district had violated the nation's civil rights laws by illegally segregating its elementary school pupils.

The examiner recommended that $275,000 in federal aid be withheld from the Ferndale, Mich. school district.

Horace H. Robbins, the hearing examiner, said he found that local and state zoning laws contributed to school segregation in the district. He supported the government contention that Ferndale officials in 1926 opened the U.S. Grant school to segregate black students after racial disorders in Ferndale in 1925. Robbins said that "the school board's course of conduct for 44 years has been consistently one of segregating the Negro children residing in the Grant area and the township from the Ferndale city elementary schools."

HEW, which had initiated the action against the district in April 1969, contended that Ferndale intentionally segregated its elementary schools by assigning all but 31 of its 396 black schoolchildren to the Grant school.

The federal funds were withheld April 19, 1972, and the school district became the first in the North to be cut off from federal aid because of violation of desegregation laws April 19.

Tennessee: Memphis integration—The Supreme court ruled, 7–0, March 9, 1970 that the Memphis school system must end racial segregation immediately. The court said the U.S. Court of Appeals for the Sixth Circuit and the district court judge had erred in declaring that Memphis had already achieved a unitary school system and in not ordering prompt integration action.

The Memphis school system served 74,000 Negro students and 60,000 whites. It included 35 all-white schools, 50 all-black schools, 47 schools that were predominantly white and 17 that were predominantly black. The lower courts had already ordered faculty integration but had refused to move beyond a "freedom of choice" plan for pupil integration.

The Memphis Board of Education Oct. 17, 1972 approved a $252,000 budget item to begin busing some 12,000 students in 1973.

The 6th U.S. Circuit Court of Appeals, in a split decision, had ordered the plan into effect Aug. 29. In the majority opinion, Judge Anthony Celebreeze wrote that the school board had failed to prove that the 128 of 162 schools that were segregated were not "in any way the product of its past or present discriminatory conduct," which would be the only way the board could refute charges that it had "failed to eliminate its dual system," according to Celebreeze's interpretation of Supreme Court decisions.

Dissenting Judge Paul C. Weick said the court had "given scant consideration to the "constitutional rights" of "black and white children who do not want to be bused away from their neighborhood schools."

The first stage of the desegregation plan went into effect Jan. 24, 1973, and the second stage started Aug. 27.

The U.S. 6th Circuit Court of Appeals Dec. 4 upheld the desegregation plan, rejecting contentions by the National Association for the Advancement of Colored People that the plan left too many all-black schools.

Citing Supreme Court precedents, the court said there was a "necessity of tolerating some one-race schools because minority groups concentrate in urban areas."

The court also upheld a lower court's finding that the city of Memphis had acted improperly by cutting its transportation budget in an attempt to avoid implementation of the busing order.

The U.S. Supreme Court April 23, 1974 refused unanimously to reconsider the lower court order upholding the Memphis school desegregation plan that retained 25 all-black schools in the interest of saving money and limiting busing. Justice

Marshall did not participate in the ruling, which was made without comment.

Nashville busing ordered—A federal district judge in Nashville, Tenn. June 28, 1971 approved a crosstown busing plan submitted by the Nixon Administration to desegregate the Nashville-Davidson County public school system.

Judge L. Clure Morton adopted the integration plan drawn up by the Department of Health, Education and Welfare (HEW) with some modifications.

Morton's order was upheld by the U.S. 6th Circuit Court of Appeals May 30, 1972.

U.S. District Judge Frank Gray Jr. ruled Dec. 19, 1973 that a Department of Health, Education & Welfare refusal to consider applications for transportation aid funds had "impeded" busing in Nashville and was "illegal and unconstitutional."

The HEW plan would require the daily busing of about 47,000 students, an increase of some 13,500 over the number bused during the 1970-71 school year. The Nashville-Davidson school system, the second largest in Tennessee, had an enrollment of about 95,000 students. Under the plan, the system's all-black schools would be completely eliminated, although 36 of the system's 141 schools would remain mostly white.

The number of black schoolchildren required to ride buses would almost double while the number of whites to be bused would increase by only one-third.

Chattanooga integration ordered—The U.S. 6th Circuit Court of Appeals April 30, 1973 ordered the implementation of a lower court plan for the integration of the public schools in Chattanooga, Tenn.

The plan established a ratio of not less than 30% but not more than 70% of any race in all but five of the city's elementary schools and in junior high schools.

The Supreme Court June 10, 1976 refused to review the decision.

Jonathon Mapp, whose suit had resulted in the original ordering of the plan in 1971, contended before the court that the plan placed a disproportionate burden on black students by ordering the closing of some black schools but not white schools. The Chattanooga Board of Education said the plan went too far in requiring pairing and clustering of schools and large expenditures for the purchase of buses to transport students.

Knoxville plan upheld—The U.S. 6th Circuit Court of Appeals July 18, 1973 upheld a desegregation plan for the Knoxville, Tenn. schools calling for pairing of schools, adjustment of school zones and the closing of two schools—one all black and the other all white. The plan did not provide for busing.

The ruling affirmed a 1971 order by District Court Judge Robert L. Taylor, who had said busing of a large number of pupils "to obtain a certain percentage of black students in each school" was not required.

The plan put 59% of the city's black students in nine schools that were 64% or more black.

The ruling was upheld by the Supreme Court Jan. 21, 1974. Justices Lewis F. Powell Jr. and Byron White dissented.

Georgia: Atlanta desegregation plan—A school desegregation plan ultimately accepted for Atlanta left most of the city's schools virtually all black.

U.S. District Court Judge Frank A. Hooper had ruled March 20, 1970 that 56 of the city's public schools that were either all-black or all-white did "not exist because of discrimination" but rather evolved from the city's residential patterns and could not be further desegregated by any other plan acceptable to the court. He said there was no legal precedent that would require him to order massive student busing.

Hooper's ruling was part of an order requiring that students in Atlanta be assigned to schools on the basis of geographic zoning. His order eliminated an earlier order under which two high schools and two elementary schools were paired for integration purposes. Judge Hooper said under his plan, desegregation in Atlanta's public schools would be increased from 57.5% to 64.5%.

Since the filing of a National Association for the Advancement of Colored People (NAACP) suit in 1958 that led to the ruling, Atlanta's schools had become over 75% black.

The 5th U.S. Circuit Court of Appeals in New Orleans Oct. 21, 1971 overruled two federal district court judges who had said there was no point in ordering busing or any further desegregation of Atlanta's public schools. The district court judges, Sidney O. Smith and Albert J. Henderson Jr., had dismissed a busing plan for

Atlanta as neither "reasonable, feasible nor workable."

A three-judge panel of the appeals court Oct. 17, 1972 overruled two more district court decisions. The appeals judges ordered the school board to devise a plan that would "at a minimum" use "pairing or grouping of contiguous segregated schools," paying "special attention" to 20 schools "which have never been desegregated" and remained "all or virtually all white." Superintendent of Schools Ed Cook said the number of such schools had declined to 17.

The U.S. district court in Atlanta had rejected an NAACP plan in June which the appeals court had ordered it to consider, which would have bused 33,000 of Atlanta's 95,000 pupils.

A compromise school integration plan was ordered into effect by the U.S. district court in Atlanta April 4, 1973. The plan had been devised by the school board and the local NAACP chapter but then rejected by the NAACP national office and the NAACP Legal Defense and Educational Fund, an independent group whose attorneys had participated as counsel for the black plaintiffs in the long-standing desegregation suit.

The plan, which left more than 60% of Atlanta schools black, was accepted by the appeals court Oct. 24, 1975. "Based on live, present reality," the court said, Atlanta's school system "is free of racial discrimination and . . . wears no proscribed badge of the past."

The 1973 plan had called for the desegregation of the school system's administration and staff and the redistribution of teaching assignments in exchange for limited voluntary busing. As a result of the plan, the system's superintendent was black, two-thirds of all administrators were black and 60% of the teachers were black. (The system's student population of 80,000 was 90% black.)

"The aim of the 14th Amendment guarantee of equal protection . . . is to assure that state-supported educational opportunity is afforded without regard to race; it is not to achieve racial integration in the public schools," the court said.

"Conditions in most school districts have frequently caused courts to treat these aims as identical. In Atlanta, where white students now comprise a small minority and black citizens can control

school policy, administration and staffing, they no longer are," the court said.

The decision was praised by Warren Fortson, legal counsel to the Atlanta school board, who said the appellate court had recognized that "the mere fact people are segregated doesn't necessarily mean that they are discriminated against."

However, a spokeswoman for the Atlanta branch of the American Civil Liberties Union said the decision showed that "desegregation could not be accomplished within a city system" and that the only solution was the merger of all public school systems in the Atlanta metropolitan region.

Pennsylvania: *Harrisburg busing*—The Harrisburg, Pa. school board May 9, 1970 adopted a school desegregation arrangement that included plans for a limited amount of busing public school children despite the objections lodged by members of Harrisburg's black and white communities. The plan, approved by a 7-2 vote, called for busing about 3,700 of the city's 13,000 public school children.

The two board members who voted against the plan argued that the arrangement would overcrowd the city's two senior high schools. About 200 people attended a board meeting May 5 and nearly all voiced objections to the plan. Both whites and blacks complained that the board had failed to involve the public in developing the plan, that its cost was excessive, and that the money used to formulate it could have been used in upgrading teachers' salaries.

Philadelphia & Pittsburgh orders— Pennsylvania's Human Relations Commission ordered the Philadelphia and Pittsburgh school districts June 18, 1971 to end racial imbalance by stepping up the pace of integration in their schools.

Philadelphia was directed to integrate 20% of its schools which had failed to meet integration standards by September and all such recalcitrant schools by 1974. The Pittsburgh district was handed a similar order.

The Pennsylvania Human Relations Commission was a 16-year-old state agency empowered by state law to act to end discrimination in education, employment, housing and public accommodations.

***State antibusing bill vetoed*—**The Pennsylvania legislature March 9, 1976 approved a bill which would bar state agencies from ordering busing to achieve desegregation. Busing ordered by federal courts would not be affected by the bill.

Gov. Milton J. Shapp, who had previously vetoed two similar bills, vetoed the bill March 19, saying it could have created "disorder and unrest."

Nearly 60% of the students in Philadelphia were black, while 40% of Pittsburgh's student population was black. According to commission figures, about 25% of Pittsburgh's black students were in schools with a white majority. In Philadelphia, 7.4% of the black pupils were attending majority white schools.

The order required that by September 1974 no school have an enrollment with more than 79% of the students members of one race. That order was to be carried out even if widespread busing was necessary to achieve the integration.

Colorado: *Denver integration*—A federal District Court Judge May 23, 1970 ordered the Denver public school system to desegregate 15 of its minority-group schools by 1972 and enact sweeping changes at two others. Judge William E. Doyle, ruling in a segregation suit filed against the Denver Board of Education by eight Denver families, said desegregation was essential to improving the quality of education at the 17 schools.

Each of the schools had an enrollment of at least 70% black or Spanish-American, with the exception of one, which was 60% black. The drawing up of desegregation plans was left to the school district and the plaintiffs' lawyers, but Doyle set down several guidelines. He ordered the 14 elementary schools covered by his ruling to be desegregated by the fall of 1972. At least seven of them had to be desegregated by the fall of 1971. When integrated, each school had to have a white, non-Spanish enrollment of more than 50%. Doyle also ordered one predominantly Spanish-American junior high school fully desegregated by the fall of 1972.

Doyle also touched on the sensitive issue of student busing. (In February nearly one-third of Denver's school buses were dynamited in a parking lot. Authorities believed the blasts were linked to opponents of a plan to use busing to integrate Denver's schools.)

Doyle said mandatory busing should be avoided "to the extent possible" but that it "may well be necessary to effectuate much of the court's plan."

Doyle April 8, 1974 ordered the Denver school system to integrate in the 1974–75 school year, largely by redrawing the boundaries and pairing black, white and Mexican-American pupils to share classrooms on a half-day basis. An integration plan had been ordered drawn up by the Supreme Court in 1973.

Doyle rejected the school board's planned closing of 12 schools as a tactic "to avoid adoption of a desegregation plan." He also ordered the merger of two high schools and implementation of bilingual programs in schools with large numbers of Mexican-American students.

The order provided that elementary schools have between 40% and 70% white enrollment and that white enrollment in secondary schools be between 50% and 60%.

Virginia: *Norfolk busing order*—A busing plan was ultimately ordered for Norfolk after the U.S. 4th Circuit Court of Appeals June 22, 1970 rejected a school desegregation plan that, according to the court's 6–1 decision, "preserves the traditional racial characteristics" of Norfolk's public schools.

The court said the school board's "rigid adherence to its quota" plan in designing school districts had resulted in a pattern "which is the antithesis of a racially unitary system." The court said the ruling was made after closely examining the racial makeup of Norfolk's schools during the 1969-70 school year.

The court said 86% of Norfolk's Negro school children attended 22 schools that were more than 92% black. In contrast, the court said, 81% of the city's white students were enrolled in 25 schools that were more than 92% white. The court said the situation "clearly depicts a dual system of schools based on race."

The board's plan that was rejected by the court would have altered the racial makeup of the district so that "each school attended by white pupils will have a majority of whites." The school board, the court said, "aimed for a 70% white majority, but accepted 60% as a minimum."

A court-ordered busing plan was later approved by the appeals court, and the Supreme Court refused in an 8–0 decision

May 15, 1972 to review a further ruling that Norfolk must provide free transportation to the 24,000 children who had been assigned to schools beyond walking distance under the integration plan. The court also voided a stay issued by the appeals court that plaintiffs said would have prevented implementation of the integration plan in the coming school year.

Norfolk had argued that it had never provided free school transportation, and that the court had intervened in budget decisions and imposed its views "as to what constitutes wise economic and social policy." The appeals court ruled that it would be "a futile gesture" and a "cruel hoax" to "compel the student to attend a distant school and then fail to provide him with the means to reach that school."

Richmond school merger barred—A proposal to integrate Richmond's schools by merging the city school district with suburban districts was rejected by the federal courts after initial approval by a district court judge.

The Richmond school board had applied Aug. 16, 1971 for a court order for such a city-suburban school merger.

The board told Federal District Court Judge Robert R. Merhige Jr. that it could not reduce the large black majorities in many of Richmond's public schools without a merger with the Henrico and Chesterfield Counties' school systems. Merhige was told that even widespread crosstown busing—which he had approved April 5—would not sufficiently increase integration because too many whites had moved to the suburbs.

Richmond officials conceded that the consolidation would mean that more black students would attend predominantly white schools in Henrico and Chesterfield counties. According to Richmond officials, no school in either county would have as many as 30% blacks and the consolidated district would be two-thirds white.

The merger would also mean more long-distance busing to achieve a white majority in each school, but Richmond officials advised Merhige that little more busing would be needed than under his order.

Merhige ordered the proposed merger Jan. 10, 1972. He described it as "the only remedy promising immediate success"

to end an increasing pattern of unequal and segregated education.

Merhige's ruling focused on the public schools of Richmond, which were 70% black, and those of suburban Henrico and Chesterfield Counties, whose schools were about 90% white.

In his 325-page opinion, Merhige held that busing schoolchildren within a predominantly black school system like Richmond had not increased integration. His decision, in effect, held that the constitutional requirement that blacks and whites have an opportunity to attend an equal, unitary school district loomed as more important than the right of local governments to set educational boundaries.

Merhige wrote:

"The court concludes that the duty to take whatever steps are necessary to achieve the greatest possible degree of desegregation in formerly dual systems by the elimination of racially identifiable schools is not circumscribed by school division boundaries created and maintained by the cooperative efforts of local and central state officials.

"Just as the city's geographic borders, viewed as limits upon pupil assignment, do not correspond to any real physical obstacles, so also are they unrelated to any marked practical or administrative necessities of school operation. The boundaries of Richmond are less than eternal monuments to a city planner's vision."

The merger order, however, was overturned June 6, 1972 by the U.S. 4th Circuit Court of Appeals. It held, 5–1, that Merhige had interpreted the Fourteenth Amendment in an "excessive" manner when he ruled that governmental actions had helped lead to an increasingly black central city and a ring of white suburbs, and that the resulting school segregation was unconstitutional whatever the cause. In "exceeding his power of intervention," the court said, Merhige had slighted the "principle of federalism incorporated in the 10th Amendment," which reserved powers to the states.

Judge James Braxton Craven Jr. wrote for the majority:

"Neither the record nor the opinion of the district court even suggests that there was ever a joint interaction between any two of the units involved (or by higher state officers) for the purpose of keeping one unit relatively white by confining blacks to another. We think that the root causes of the concentration of blacks in the inner cities of America are simply not known, and that the district court could not realistically place on the counties the responsibility for the effect that inner city decay has had on the public schools of Richmond."

The court said the mere fact that the city school population was 70% black while the suburban school population was 90% white did not constitute a constitutional violation. Any county actions to enforce segregation had been "slight" compared to other "economic, political and social" factors. Furthermore, "school assignments cannot reverse the trend" of racial concentration.

Suburban Henrico and Chesterfield counties had been joined in their appeal of Merhige's ruling by the Justice Department after President Nixon set down new antibusing guidelines March 16.

The appellate ruling barring the merger was upheld by a 4–4 Supreme Court decision May 21, 1973.

Texas: 26 school districts sued—The Justice Department Aug. 7, 1970 brought into federal court the State of Texas and 26 Texas school districts that had balked at developing voluntary school desegregation arrangements.

The department said the suits named as defendants the Texas Education Agency, State Commissioner of Education J.W. Edgar and the 26 districts. The suits were filed in federal district court in Dallas, Houston, Austin and Tyler.

The suits charged that the districts had continued to operate dual school systems with both student and faculty segregation, "with the knowledge and consent of the Texas Education Agency." The complaints charged that some of the districts involved discrimination against Mexican-Americans as well as against Negro students.

The districts named in the suits had 466 schools with a student enrollment of 214,299 whites, 46,160 Negroes and 32,207 Mexican-Americans and other minority students.

Named in the Dallas suit were Ferris Independent, Garland Independent, Lubbock Independent, Richardson Independent, San Angelo Independent and Wichita Falls Independent.

Named in the Houston suit were Galena Park Independent, Katy Independent, Klein Independent and Madisonville Independent.

Named in the Austin suit were Austin Independent, Calvert Independent, Hearne Independent, La Vega Independent, Midland Independent, Temple Independent and Ector County Independent.

Named in the Tyler suit were Carthage Independent, Elysian Fields Independent, Jefferson Independent, Kilgore Independent, Lufkin Independent, Port Arthur Independent, San Augustine Independent, South Park Independent and Sulphur Springs Independent.

Mexican-Americans—U.S. District Judge Woodrow Seals ruled June 4, 1970 that the Supreme Court's 1954 decision outlawing school segregation applied to Mexican-Americans as well as Negroes.

Acting on a suit filed by Mexican-American parents against the school system of Corpus Christi, Tex., Seals asserted that Mexican-Americans were an "identifiable ethnic minority with a past pattern of discrimination" against them. Seals accused the school board of perpetuating segregation by maintaining integrated classes for Negroes and Mexican-Americans, but leaving both groups segregated from the white students.

After a busing plan had been drawn up in 1972 by the Health, Education & Welfare Department on Seals' request, the U.S. 5th Circuit Court of Appeals in New Orleans Aug. 2, 1972 reversed the court order for its implementation and rejected the use of crosstown busing until all neighborhood-oriented remedies had been tried.

The appeals court ordered the trial of a new pupil reassignment plan. The court also ordered the use of pairing and clustering of schools, and relocation of portable classrooms. But pairing of noncontiguous school districts would be barred "until the court had exhausted every other possible remedy which would not involve increased student transportation."

The court ruled that Mexican-American pupils had suffered unconstitutional discrimination in both cities, although they had never been officially segregated by state law, because school boards had failed to act against neighborhood ethnic concentrations, and had used pupil assignment and building location to reinforce segregation.

Policy Conflicts & Uncertainty

Federal Action on Schools

Critics charged the Nixon Administration with half-heartedness in its program to enforce affirmative action in schools that remained segregated.

Officials warn of aid cutoff. Two of the Nixon Administration's chief civil rights officials told a Senate subcommittee Feb. 10, 1971 that 51 Southern school districts faced a cutoff of special federal desegregation funds for violating civil rights laws.

Elliot L. Richardson, secretary of health, education and welfare (HEW), and J. Stanley Pottinger, head of HEW's Office for Civil Rights, appeared before the Senate Labor and Public Welfare Committee's education subcommittee to give a progress report on the status of the Administration's $75 million fund to ease school desegregation problems.

Richardson disclosed that HEW-sponsored checkups on school districts receiving funds revealed "in many cases, problems . . . akin to those noted" by six civil rights groups which had called the Administration's plan a "fraud upon Congress."

As a result of the HEW investigations, Richardson said, 11 Southern districts had received notices that their grants would be terminated for failure to comply with federal requirements for

biracial advisory school committes and non-discriminatory treatment of faculty and students.

Pottinger told the subcommittee that an additional 40 Southern districts might soon be notified that they too were losing their grants.

College integration demanded—About a year earlier, HEW Feb. 26, 1970 sent letters requiring that Florida and Georgia draw up plans for complete desegregation of their public institutions of higher education. The orders brought to 10 the number of states asked to present desegregation arrangements to HEW officials. (The others were Oklahoma, Louisiana, Arkansas, Mississippi, North Carolina, Virginia, Maryland and Pennsylvania.)

The letters told Florida and Georgia state officials that they had been operating racially identifiable colleges in violation of the federal antidiscrimination laws. Florida was told that data had shown that one of its schools, Florida A & M University, was almost 100% Negro while six other public universities had nearly all-white student bodies.

U.S. warns 39 school districts. The Nixon Administration notified 39 school districts in 11 Southern and Border states June 22, 1971 that they would probably be required to extend integration under guidelines the Supreme Court issued April 20 in its decision upholding the constitutionality of busing for desegregation.

In letters from the Department of Health, Education and Welfare's (HEW) Office for Civil Rights, the districts were told they would have to comply with the court's new orders or face the loss of federal aid to their schools. The civil rights office said that 80-100 districts in the Southern and Border states would get warning letters.

The first 39 letters were sent to districts in Delaware, Florida, Kentucky, Maryland, Mississippi, North Carolina, Oklahoma, South Carolina, Tennessee, Texas and Virginia.

The letters represented the first step taken by the Nixon Administration toward enforcing compliance with the court's desegregation guidelines. The 39 districts which were to get the letters had been desegregating under executive enforcement of the Civil Rights Act of 1964, which prohibited discrimination in any federally-assisted program. Most other school districts across the U.S. were integrating under federal court order.

J. Stanley Pottinger, director of the Office for Civil Rights, indicated that although the court said that a precise racial balance in every school would not be required, the existence of schools easily identified as a "white school" or a "black school" by the makeup of student enrollment, faculty or faculties was sufficient evidence of a violation of the Constitution.

Pottinger also noted in the letters that the court had called for additional busing, merging of attendance zones and other steps for desegregation, which HEW did not require as part of President Nixon's policy on integration.

Pottinger wrote that "to the extent that policy issued by this office in the past may conflict with or are different from rulings by the Supreme Court, the court holdings of course must prevail."

(Another 41 districts ultimately received similar HEW notices.)

Nixon bars busing pressure. The White House said Aug. 11, 1971 that President Nixon had warned federal aides, orally and in writing, that they risked losing their jobs if they sought to impose extensive busing as a means of desegregating schools throughout the South.

Nixon's directive was made public by White House Press Secretary Ronald L. Ziegler eight days after the President had dissociated himself from his Administration's proposal for a school desegregation plan for Austin, Tex. that would require extensive crosstown busing.

Ziegler said Nixon had warned officials in the Justice Department and the Department of Health, Education and Welfare that he wanted the busing of schoolchildren for integration purposes kept to the minimum required by law. Ziegler told newsmen that while the federal bureaucracy had not always been responsive to Presidential directives, "they are going to be responsive" to the busing order.

"And those who are not responsive," Ziegler warned, "will find themselves involved in other assignments or quite possibly in assignments other than the federal government."

According to Ziegler, the Administration did not object to busing plans drawn up by local school officials and would enforce any direct court orders requiring widespread busing.

But he said the President had instructed government personnel to carry out school desegregation without using the busing of schoolchildren as a "major technique."

U.S. panel criticizes bus policy—The U.S. Commission on Civil Rights said Aug. 12 that President Nixon's directive to keep busing for racial integration to a minimum would undermine efforts to desegregate schools.

The panel sharply criticized Nixon's policy in a statement adopted unanimously by its six members.

The commission said the "transportation of students is essential to eliminating segregation." The panel added that for purposes other than integration, "busing has been a common feature of American education."

The commission said that "what is at issue in this matter is not—to use the President's phrases--busing for the sake of busing or even busing solely for racial balance. The major issue is the kind of education available at the end of the trip."

The panel pointed out that a school desegregation plan drawn up by the Department of Health, Education and

Welfare and based on extensive cross-town busing for Austin, Tex. had been "courageously accepted" by Austin officials as the standard.

"What the nation needed was a call to duty and responsibility, for the immediate elimination of the dual school system, and for support of all those officials who are forthrightly carrying out their legal obligations," the commission said.

"Unfortunately, the President's statement almost certainly will have the opposite effect, the effect of undermining the desegregation effort."

Busing resistance in North, West. For the first time since the Supreme Court ordered an end to racial segregation in public education in 1954, resistance to court-ordered integration centered in the North and West as schools reopened for the fall Aug. 30–Sept. 8, 1971.

In the South, which for years had been the citadel of resistance to integrated schooling, newly desegregated schools reopened quietly and without major incident, even those with new busing plans.

Some federal and state officials had voiced fears over the possibility that there would be widespread and turbulent protests over the flood of new busing plans ordered for school districts across the nation. Except in a few communities, there were no extensive protests.

Southern school officials expressed satisfaction with the way in which the latest round of school integration was achieved with a minimum of friction and tension.

The stiffest resistance to busing and newly implemented integration plans was focused in the North and West.

In Pontiac, Mich., eight white students and one black youth were injured Sept. 8 in fights during protests against a busing plan. Earlier, arsonists set firebombs that gutted 10 school buses that were to have been used to carry out the integration plan.

The protests in Pontiac over busing were among the most violent in the U.S.

Parents of about 300 children assigned to a new racially-balanced elementary school in Boston refused Sept. 8 to enroll their children in the new school and instead took them to the neighborhood schools they attended the previous term. There was no violence.

In Evansville, Ind., students enrolled in the same schools they attended during the 1970–71 academic year in defiance of a federal order that the district submit a new "racial balance" plan.

Integration took place without incident in Indianapolis, Minneapolis and Kalamazoo, Mich.

There was little protest activity in the South, even in districts where children rode buses to distant schools.

There were scattered protests in Chattanooga, Tenn., Columbus, Ga., Kannapolis, N.C. and Pembroke, N. C. And in Norfolk, Va., controversy over a court-ordered plan increasing the number of pupils bused to achieve racial integration led the school board to delay for at least a week the reopening of Norfolk's schools.

Indian parents armed with hatchets and machetes staged a demonstration Sept. 2 in Pembroke to protest the busing of their children.

In Little Rock, Ark., schools reopened Aug. 30 with new busing and pairing plans which produced a consistent 2–1 white-black ratio throughout Little Rock's 24,000-pupil system. There was no public opposition in the city where federal troops once protected black schoolchildren from angry whites.

More than 110,000 children returned to integrated classrooms in Birmingham, Ala., and in adjacent Jefferson County Aug. 30 without incident.

Downstate in Mobile, more than 6,000 schoolchildren were bused out of their neighborhoods. Despite a suggestion by Gov. George C. Wallace that the city defy the court-ordered busing plan, the new busing arrangement worked smoothly and did not evoke appreciable opposition.

In Nashville, Tenn., elementary school children registered without incident Sept. 8. There was some opposition, however, to a federal court-ordered busing plan. A final effort to block the forced busing plan had failed Sept. 2 when Supreme Court Justice Potter Stewart refused to stay its implementation. Under the plan, about

47,000 of the city's 96,000 pupils were to be bused.

Opposition to busing drops. The Gallup Poll said Sept. 11, 1971 that while an overwhelming majority of Americans continued to oppose the busing of pupils to achieve more racially-balanced schools, there had been some decline in antibusing sentiments since the preceding poll, taken in March 1970.

In the new survey, involving interviews with 1,525 persons, 18 and older, 18% of those polled said they favored busing to further racial integration. Nearly 76% expressed opposition to busing.

In the March 1970 survey, 14% had said they supported busing, while 81% expressed opposition.

One of the sharpest increases in support of busing was found among college-educated persons, with the proportion nearly doubling since 1970—from 13% to 23%.

Integration pressure eased. The Nixon Administration Sept. 18, 1971 eased its publicized drive to pressure 80 school districts in Southern and Border states to integrate further to meet new guidelines laid down by the Supreme Court.

Officials in the Department of Health, Education and Welfare's Office for Civil Rights confirmed that the U.S. had dropped cases against nine of the systems that still maintained predominantly black schools.

The districts were in Wilmington, Del.; Henry County, Ga.; Charles County, Md.; Somerset, Md.; West Jasper, Miss.; Lenoir County, N.C.; Vance County, N.C.; Richland County No. 2, S.C.; and Kershaw, S.C.

Federal officials also said action would not be pressed against many of the 35 districts involved in other school cases.

Rights panel assails Administration. The U.S. Commission on Civil Rights again used stern language Nov. 16, 1971 to accuse the Nixon Administration of failing to adequately enforce the nation's civil rights laws.

It was the third time in 13 months that the panel had sharply rebuked the Administration on civil rights. The new report added a new dimension to the attack by including a performance rating in which the White House and 29 U.S. agencies were reviewed for their commitment to civil rights.

The panel used four performance levels—poor, marginal, adequate and good—for its rating system. In some instances, the commission used a variety of those marks.

The White House fared better than any of the 29 agencies rated by the commission, but it only received a "less than adequate" mark.

None of the agencies investigated received a rating of adequate. The Office of Management and Budget, which was under the auspices of the White House, scored the best of any agency with a rating just below the adequate level.

The panel report criticized President Nixon, saying that he had not clearly defined his civil rights policy despite position statements on school busing and housing.

"The net effect of the President's statement has not been to provide the clear policy direction necessary to encourage the federal bureaucracy to step up its efforts to enforce civil rights laws," the panel said.

Nixon's disavowal of school busing for purposes of racial integration was singled out by the commission. "For example, as this commission has pointed out, the President's comments opposing busing to facilitate school desegregation, by failing to offer a realistic alternative, may well be interpreted as a sign of a slowdown in the federal desegregation effort," the report charged.

The commission noted that some progress had been made by many of the U.S. agencies, mainly the establishment of an apparatus to begin enforcement.

Defiance Continues

New Jersey: *Trenton plan voided*—New Jersey's commissioner of education Nov. 14, 1970 annulled Trenton's controversial school busing plan in the wake of a boycott by white parents who had kept their children at home rather than have them bused to schools outside their neighborhoods.

The action came a month after racial disorders stemming from dissatisfaction with the busing plan forced the Trenton school board to shut down many of its schools.

In a 26-page decision canceling the plan, Commissioner Carl Marburger said that "meaningful school integration cannot be achieved by the involuntary busing of chidren in urban areas where the majority of the public school youngsters consist of children of the nation's minority groups." His decision cited "serious procedural defects" in the busing plan as cause for its cancellation.

Under the proposed plan, 55 white children were to be bused to a school with a 95% black enrollment. As part of the plan, about 100 black and Puerto Rican students were to be bused to several predominantly white schools.

The violence erupted Oct. 29 when fighting broke out between 100 black and white youths at a school in the city's predominantly Italian section. The fighting spread into the downtown district when bands of black youths surged into the area, hurling bottles at policemen and breaking store windows. State troopers joined local police and county detectives in bringing the disorders to an end.

More than 200 persons were arrested during the three days of disorders.

School district lines to stand—A three-judge federal court in Newark May 18, 1971 let stand the state's existing public school district lines despite its finding that the boundaries had led to "extreme racial imbalance in some districts."

The court said that the segregation in some New Jersey districts was directly traceable to local housing patterns that discriminated against Negroes. The panel then said that the issue of school segregation caused by neighborhood patterns had been left unresolved when the U.S. Supreme Court failed to rule on it in its latest series of school desegregation cases.

The federal court had been asked to nullify the existing lines on the grounds that school segregation resulting from housing patterns violated the 14th Amendment, which guaranteed equal protection of the law to all Americans.

The suit asking for new boundaries was filed in the name of two black Jersey City schoolchildren as a class action on behalf of all black New Jersey students. Named as defendants were State At-torney General George M. Kugler Jr., Dr. Carl L. Marburger, the state commissioner of education, and the state Board of Education.

The court's decision was signed by Judges Reynier J. Wortendyke and George H. Barlow.

Alabama: *Wallace defies court orders*—Gov. George C. Wallace, ignoring a federal judge's ruling that his instructions to have two Alabama school boards defy school desegregation plans were "legally meaningless," ordered two more school boards Aug. 18, 1971 to ignore a court-approved integration plan.

Wallace's latest action came after a week in which he called upon the Nixon Administration to join him in his crusade to stop the busing of Alabama's schoolchildren as a means of racial integration.

In his Aug. 18 order, Wallace directed the boards of education of Calhoun County and the city of Oxford to disregard orders from a federal district court to pair an all-black school in Hobson City with two predominantly white schools in Oxford.

The Oxford school board asked the federal court for a rehearing on the desegregation orders, but board members indicated that they would comply with Wallace's orders.

Calhoun County school officials indicated that they would also follow Wallace's instructions.

At a news conference in Hobson City, Wallace made it clear that he was purposely attempting to challenge the Nixon Administration and the Justice Department over busing.

"They're watching me, I know," Wallace said. "They're watching close and what they're seeing is a governor just trying to help the President and the attorney general [John Mitchell] keeping their antibusing promises."

(President Nixon had said in a policy statement Aug. 3 that "I have consistently opposed the busing of our nation's school-children to achieve a racial balance, and I am opposed to the busing of children simply for the sake of busing." Nixon had warned Aug. 11 that government officials risked losing their jobs if they sought to impose extensive busing.)

Wallace's instructions to the Oxford and Calhoun County school boards came two days after a federal district judge in

Montgomery described his previous orders to two other Alabama boards as "legally meaningless."

Wallace's earlier steps were to order the Jefferson County-Birmingham school board to transfer a white student from a court-assigned predominantly black school to a predominantly white school nearer her home and to order the Limestone County school board to reopen a predominantly black school that had been closed by federal court order.

'In both instances, Wallace issued executive orders to have the boards comply with his directives. His order to the Jefferson County-Birmingham district was issued Aug. 12. The executive order to the Limestone board went out Aug. 13.

The federal judge, Sam C. Pointer, Jr., ruled Aug. 16 that Wallace's Aug. 12 and Aug. 13 orders carried no legal weight and told the board members involved to ignore them. Pointer said the primary responsibility for responding to the orders of the court was the boards' and not the governor's. Pointer called Wallace's executive orders merely an exercise of free speech.

(Pointer's ruling was in response to motions filed Aug. 13 by U. W. Clemon, a black attorney representing the NAACP Legal Defense Fund. Clemon had asked the U.S. court in Birmingham to make Wallace a defendant in a suit seeking to guarantee compliance with a desegregation plan for the Jefferson County-Birmingham district. Pointer denied that motion, but told the school board it would not be free to disobey federal court orders regardless of what Wallace might say.)

Mobile settlement—The NAACP Legal Defense Fund and the Mobile school board agreed July 8, 1971 on a desegregation plan leaving at least 10 public schools in Mobile with nearly all-black student bodies until September 1972.

Attorneys for the defense fund said they had accepted the board's plan only to avoid another year of litigation before a federal district judge they regarded as hostile to desegregation.

The Mobile district, a combined city-county system and Alabama's largest, had about 70,000 students. Almost 45% of the students were black. In 1970 about half of the district's black students were

enrolled in 16 schools that were 90% or more black. Only 18% of the black students were in schools with a white majority.

Under the new plan, about 8,000 students would be bused. Most of those would be black students transferred into white neighborhoods. In addition to the 10 nearly all-black schools, another five schools would remain more than 75% black.

Antibusing law voided—An Alabama law against mandatory school busing was ruled unconstitutional Dec. 3, 1971 by Federal Judge Sam C. Pointer. He cited the U.S. Supreme Court decision overturning a similar North Carolina law and said freedom of choice plans would be ruled out in Birmingham "at least until a unitary system has been in operation for a sufficient length of time to escape the tendency such option would have towards re-establishing a dual system."

The Alabama law, which a state judge, William C. Barbour, had invoked Oct. 18, required school boards to honor requests for transfer to schools of students' choice if parents determined that their children's health or education were endangered by busing.

Mississippi: *Governor defied in Jackson*—School officials in Jackson said Sept. 12, 1971 that they would continue to bus children to schools outside their neighborhoods despite an executive order by Gov. John Bell Williams directing that no state funds be used for busing.

In his executive order issued Sept. 11, Williams instructed the state auditor to withhold state funds from Jackson's public schools as the city moved to implement a federally-ordered desegregation plan that called for extensive busing. Williams said a 1953 Mississippi law prohibited the use of public funds for the busing of students who lived within the city limits of a "municipal separate school district."

In defying William's order, school officials in Jackson said it could not disregard the federal court order under which the desegregation was to be carried out. If the district disobeyed the order, Jackson officials explained, the Jackson district could be found in contempt.

U.S. Judge Dan Russell issued a permanent injunction Oct. 20 enjoining the

State of Mississippi from interfering with a desegregation plan for public schools in Jackson or withholding funds from the Jackson district because of busing.

Russell ordered the state tax commission, state auditor and attorney general not to interfere with implementation of a court-approved desegregation plan.

Jackson officials had sought relief from the federal court after Williams' action.

Massachusetts: *Conflict in Boston*—The Massachusetts Commission Against Discrimination directed the Boston school system June 23, 1971 to complete the integration of the city's public schools by the opening of the 1972 school year.

In ordering the integration, the commission said it had found that Boston's open enrollment arrangement was discriminatory against nonwhites and failed to eliminate racial imbalance caused by housing patterns. The commission, a state agency, directed the city's school committee to establish a central administration to eliminate the alleged discrimination.

In its 21-page report, the commission said Boston's system, which was drawn up to achieve school balance by the voluntary transfer of students, was not achieving the desired effect. According to the commission, statistics compiled by the school department showed that "only a small percentage of black students actually achieve admission to schools having a high white enrollment."

The commission attributed the arrangement's lack of success in part to the "lack of supervision and review," which encouraged "arbitrary and discriminatory decisions on applications for admission with the effect of intensifying racial imbalance in the schools."

The Boston School Committee Sept. 22 ended its attempts to integrate a new multimillion dollar school in a black neighborhood in the face of organized protests by parents.

Efforts at integrating the school had begun Sept. 8, but withered when black and white parents refused to send their children to the school. The attempt at integration had been part of a plan to racially balance three schools in the heart of Boston.

As a result of the committee's decision, the new school opened classes Sept.

22 with a ratio of four black students to each white student enrolled. The Lee School, an $8 million complex, had 1,200 students. The committee's action also meant that two other nearby schools would remain predominantly white and would be able to enroll children who up until the committee's decision had been attending without credit in defiance of the law.

Massachusetts withheld $14 million in operating funds from the Boston school system because of the abandonment of the integration plan. More than 78% of the city's nonwhite students were in majority nonwhite schools, although a 1965 state law required local officials to eliminate all such imbalance. While total white enrollment had declined in recent years, the number of all-white schools had increased to 15 by 1971.

The Department of Health, Education & Welfare (HEW) formally notified Boston school officials Dec. 1 that they were violating the 1964 Civil Rights Act by following policies that tended to create segregated school attendance patterns. Boston was the largest Northern school system to be so charged.

HEW noted that the Boston School Committee had maintained two types of intermediate school grade structures since 1965, when it had announced a plan to convert all junior high schools (grades 7-9) to middle schools (grades 6-8). The committee only implemented the plan in four schools, which had since become predominantly nonwhite, as had the elementary and high schools with meshing grade structures. While the resulting segregation may not have been deliberate, according to J. Stanley Pottinger, director of HEW's Office for Civil Rights, school officials "knew, or should have known, racial isolation was occurring. The burden is on them to do something about it."

Other examples of discriminatory policies in Boston which had been uncovered by earlier investigations by the Massachusetts Department of Education included cases of busing nonwhites past predominantly white schools with empty seats, nearly adjacent elementary schools totally segregated by race, and an all-white high school in a district that included large numbers of nonwhites.

The Massachusetts State Supreme Court Oct. 29, 1973 ruled in support of a new state plan to redraw Boston's school district lines to achieve racial balance by September 1974.

The plan, which would involve large-scale busing, had been drawn to conform with a state law limiting the number of black students in any school to 50%.

The same court ruled April 16, 1974 that a proposed binding referendum on a plan to use large-scale busing to integrate Boston schools would be unconstitutional. However, the court said a nonbinding "opinion poll" could be allowed on the ballot.

The ruling noted that the bill setting the referendum would prohibit assignment of students without parental consent, thus blocking enforcement of the state's earlier racial balance law. Gov. Francis W. Sargent, who had requested the court's opinion, vetoed the bill April 17.

Scarcely a month later, in a nonbinding referendum May 21, Boston voters rejected 30,789–2,282 the assignment of children to particular schools to achieve racial balance without parental consent. The 12% voter turnout was the lowest in the city's history.

U.S. Judge W. Arthur Garrity Jr. ruled June 21 that Boston had deliberately maintained a segregated public school system and ordered that the state racial balance plan be implemented in September.

Ruling in a suit filed by black parents and the National Association for the Advancement of Colored People, Garrity said school officials had knowingly carried out a system segregating both teachers and students through special attendance and grading patterns. Garrity ruled that the plaintiffs were entitled to every legal means of relief, including busing, no matter how "distasteful."

Under the state plan, the number of black-majority schools would be reduced from 68 to 40. At least 6,000 pupils, black and white (out of 94,000) would be bused.

Scattered violence and school boycotts marked the opening of Boston public schools Sept. 12, 1974 under the new plan.

Trouble was focused in the predominantly white South Boston area. At South Boston High, a boycott proclaimed by white parents and fear of violence kept attendance Sept. 12–13 at fewer than 100

pupils out of the 1,500 expected to be enrolled. Buses carrying black students were stoned as they left the school on both days, although Mayor Kevin White had ordered police escorts after the first incidents Sept. 12. In another neighborhood, a bus carrying white students was stoned as it passed through a black area.

The busing plan was carried out without serious incident in most other areas of the city, and system-wide attendance was about 65% of normal.

A referendum to end the independent Boston School Committee and replace it with a decentralized system of local advisory boards appointed by the city's mayor was defeated in Boston Nov. 5, 1975 by a recorded vote of 76,769 to 46,656. Mayor Kevin White had campaigned for passage of the measure, while a group of antibusing whites known by the acronym ROAR (Return Our Alienated Rights) had strongly opposed approval. The five-member School Committee, which was white and predominantly Irish-Catholic, had been the leader in the fight against forced busing and integration of Boston's schools.

U.S. Judge W. Arthur Garrity Oct. 30 had signed an order requiring the Committee to develop by Dec. 16 a city-wide school integration plan to replace the interim court-ordered program of busing for desegregation. The new plan, which would go into effect in the fall of 1975, would free several million dollars in emergency desegregation aid from the Department of Health, Education and Welfare (HEW). In his order, Garrity urged the Committee to draft plans that would achieve desegregation with a minimum of busing and reassignment of students.

In defiance of Judge Garrity's order, the School Committee, by a 3–2 vote Dec. 16, rejected a plan drawn up by the school system's attorneys and staff.

In disavowing the busing plan, John J. Kerrigan, chairman of the School Committee, said, "I can't in good conscience be an architect of a plan that would increase the bloodshed and hatred in the city of Boston." The other four members of the committee indicated full agreement with Kerrigan, but two voted to approve the citywide plan.

The program submitted to Garrity called for busing 35,000 pupils in all sections of the city. The city would be divided into six zones, each extending into the predominately black neighborhood of Roxbury.

As tension escalated, demonstrations by pro- and anti-busing forces became more frequent and grew larger than during initial weeks of the busing plan. Supporters of the court-ordered program marched through downtown Boston Dec. 14, protesting the chaos that accompanied implementation of the plan. The crowd, estimated by police at 15,000–20,000 persons, contained contingents from Washington, Chicago, Newark and other areas of the nation. Opponents of forced busing mounted a counterdemonstration Dec. 15 in the Boston Common.

Garrity Dec. 27 held three of the School Committee members in civil contempt of court for their refusal to approve a citywide busing plan for school integration. Garrity Dec. 30 ordered the committee members fined and barred from participating in school desegregation matters unless they endorsed a new integration plan by Jan. 7, 1975.

In a related development, the 1st U.S. Circuit Court of Appeals Dec. 19 unanimously upheld Garrity's finding June 21 that Boston had deliberately operated a segregated school system. The three-judge appellate panel ordered desegregation of the schools to continue.

The School Committee Jan. 27, 1975 submitted to Garrity a plan for desegregating the schools that fall. The plan provided for voluntary student enrollment in biracial classes.

The school committee's plan relied heavily on so-called "magnet schools" located in six different zones in the city. Children already attending integrated classes would be given the first chance to enroll in the varied learning programs at the magnet schools, and "an attempt then will be made to accommodate every student who applies for a citywide magnet school," a summary of the plan said.

Based on the make-up of surrounding neighborhoods, the remaining schools would be designated either "predominately white" or "predominately minority." Pupils of the opposite category then would be allocated to these schools. Children attending schools that still failed to meet federal court guidelines for racial mixture would participate in compulsory

scholastic activities at a "neutral" site one day a week.

Four court-appointed law and education experts March 21 made public a fresh plan for desegregating Boston's public school system in the fall of 1975. The plan, which would radically revamp the city's educational boundaries, would require the forced busing of at most 14,000 pupils, compared to the 18,000 being bused under the current interim desegregation plan.

Under the proposal, Boston would be divided into nine "community school districts" drawn mostly along traditional ethnic and racial neighborhood dividing lines. A tenth district of 32 specialized "magnet schools" would draw racially balanced groups of students from all over Boston. The plan also called for the "pairing" of Boston area colleges and universities with individual high schools and community districts to improve curricula and instruction.

The four court-appointed experts were Francis Keppel, former U.S. commissioner of education; Edward J. McCormack, former Massachusetts attorney general; Jacob J. Speigel, a retired justice of the Massachusetts Judicial Supreme Court; and Charles W. Willie, professor of education at the Harvard University graduate school of education.

Garrity May 10 issued a superseding plan for Boston school integration. It called for busing 21,000 pupils.

In his 104-page order, Garrity rejected the traditional system of assigning children to neighborhood schools because it would not "achieve substantial desegregation in Boston due to the geography of the city and racial and ethnic distribution in the city."

Among the provisions of the new plan: Boston would be divided into eight districts, seven of them containing a portion of the city's predominantly black center. Twenty-two special "magnet schools" would draw students from throughout the city and reflect Boston's racial and ethnic make-up. Twenty schools would be closed to promote integration by consolidating their student bodies.

Under the new plan, predominantly white South Boston, a focal point of anti-busing sentiment, would continue to share its schools with neighboring black areas. South Boston High School, the scene of considerable violence during the first three months the interim desegregation plan was in effect, was to have a student body of 1,500 whites and 900 blacks.

Citywide busing to desegregate the Boston public school system began Sept. 8. An atmosphere of tension pervaded the city, but the day was free of widespread racial violence that many Boston officials had feared would erupt.

Boston school officials said that, six weeks after the start of large-scale court-ordered busing, nonwhites made up more than 52% of the system's student population, it was reported Oct. 22. This figure compared with 48% the year before and 43% in 1973.

A reported 3,500 white students transferred to private schools or, by using relatives' addresses, to suburban public schools. The number of transfers was close to that of previous years, but an additional 5,000 whites out of 40,500 enrolled were listed as "missing."

Department figures also showed that 2,600 blacks out of a projected 33,000 were unaccounted for and that 800 had transferred to other schools.

Garrity put South Boston High School in federal court receivership Dec. 9, removing the school from Boston School Committee jurisdiction. Charging the committee, an elected policy-making body, with obstructionism, Garrity stripped it of control over security in the schools and implementation of a court-ordered desegregation plan.

The U.S. 1st Circuit Court of Appeals Jan. 14, 1976 upheld the May 1975 ruling that ordered extensive busing of Boston school children.

The three appellate judges unanimously approved the lower court integration plan in all its features. The opinion, written by Chief Judge Frank M. Coffin, said: "The overriding fact of the matter is that the District Court in this case had to deal with an intransigent and obstructionist school committee majority . . . [who] engaged in a pattern of resistance, defiance and delay."

A new survey, conducted by the Boston Globe and reported in a Jan. 24 Associated Press release, found that 85% of Boston's schools did not have a racial mix in compliance with federal court guidelines. The study showed that, as of Dec. 31, 1975, out of 162 schools, 96 were clearly violating, and 41 violating to a lesser degree, the court-determined integration guidelines.

■ A Boston Schools Department report asserted that the quality of public instruction had deteriorated in Boston since the start of court-ordered desegregation, the Boston Herald American reported Jan. 16, 1977. The newspaper said the report was being submitted to the federal government in support of a request by the schools department for $8.4 million in federal aid under the Emergency School Aid act.

Minnesota: *Minneapolis pairing*—Minneapolis' board of education Sept. 18, 1971 began to offset school segregation fostered by neighborhood housing patterns by pairing two of its elementary schools as part of an integration plan.

Under the pairing program, all the children in the upper three grades of a virtually all-white school had been bused to a school nearby that was 56% black. All children from kindergarten through the third grade were bused from the predominantly black school to the formerly white school. The pairing gave each school an enrollment that was about 25% black or Indian. Blacks and Indians made up about 5% of the city's total population of 434,400. Since 1960, the black population in the city had risen by 61% with the minority enrollment in the school system increasing from 6.6% in 1963 to 13% in 1971.

Dr. John B. Davis, superintendent of schools, said the board "felt pairing was an excellent and proper first step toward achieving an ideal racial balance in as many schools as feasible." He said pairing enabled the school system to "preserve the sense of neighborhood schools."

Government as Employer

It was generally assumed that the federal, state and municipal governments would set the example for effective affirmative action in the employment of women and members of minority groups. It was frequently said, however, that the example set by government was not always a good one.

Equality let-up denied. The White House Feb. 28, 1970 denied published reports that the Nixon Administration had decided to relax its pressure on federal agencies to step up employment of minority group members. The allegations had been made by Robert E. Hampton, chairman of the Civil Service Commission, who said Feb. 26 that the Nixon Administration had ended the drive because it believed the pressures to increase minority employment amounted to discrimination in reverse.

(Hampton told newsmen Feb. 27 that his remarks had been misunderstood. "I want to make it clear," he said, "that there has been no lessening of the efforts to achieve true equal opportunity for minorities and women.")

Ronald L. Ziegler, Nixon's press secretary, restated Hampton's claim that the civil service chief's remarks had been misunderstood. Ziegler said the Nixon Administration "has taken no steps whatsoever to ease minority hiring opportunities."

U.S. exam challenged. Eight black federal employees charged in a suit filed Feb. 4, 1971 that the Federal Service Entrance Examination, the principal test that qualified college graduates for civil service posts, was "culturally and racially discriminatory."

The eight plaintiffs, employes of the Department of Housing and Urban Development's (HUD) Chicago Regional Office, alleged that the exam violated the equal opportunity guarantees of the Fifth Amendment. They also said it violated the 1964 Civil Rights Act, several executive orders and the regulations of HUD and the Civil Service Commission.

Named defendants in the suit were George Romney, HUD secretary, and three Civil Service commissioners. The class action suit was filed in U.S. district court in Washington.

The plaintiffs charged that the exam "has served systematically to exclude qualified blacks and members of other minority groups from obtaining managerial and professional level positions in the federal service, and has by other means denied plaintiffs and their class equal employment opportunities."

The suit asked the court to bar the use of the examination until its alleged discriminatory aspects were eliminated, and that the use of other testing procedures be stopped until a determination could be made of their relation to specific job requirements.

According to the plaintiffs, about 49% of the 100,000 persons who took the test in 1969 finished with scores above 70, with "a disproportionately low percentage" of blacks and other minority group members passing.

HUD job bias found—A federal hearing examiner ruled later that the HUD and its predecessor agencies had been guilty of systematic discrimination against blacks in hiring and promotion, at least until late 1970, it was disclosed Oct. 21, 1971.

Julia P. Cooper, an Equal Employment Opportunity Commission lawyer appointed examiner by the Civil Service Commission, recommended that HUD repay 106 employes who had lost a day's pay after an October 13, 1970 protest during work hours against alleged discrimination. Miss Cooper found that, at least until the time of the protest, HUD supervisory personnel had frequently kept blacks in low grade levels while whites advanced, hired blacks at grade levels beneath their qualifications, limited or denied training opportunities to blacks, and penalized those who complained of these practices.

HUD officials, who had asked the Civil Service Commission to investigate the charges, admitted that discrimination had existed in the past. But Secretary George Romney denied, after the examiner's report was disclosed, that the problem remained. He cited a rise in minority employment at the agency to 40.5%, including 19.6% of those in grades 7 and above.

Judge bans Alabama job bias. A federal judge in Montgomery July 29, 1970 ordered seven Alabama state agencies to stop discriminating against Negroes in their hiring practices and to give immediate job consideration to 62 Negro applicants turned away earlier.

District Court Judge Frank M. Johnson Jr. directed state authorities to take steps to eliminate all future racial discrimination in hiring practices. He ordered them to submit a report to the court within 30 days on what had been done to comply with his order.

In reviewing the case, which was brought into court by the Justice Department in 1968, Johnson noted that Alabama was the only state that had refused to adopt a regulation formally banning racial discrimination and providing for a system of redress in such cases. In his decision the judge said that the state "engaged in, and continues to engage in, a systematic practice of discrimination against qualified Negro applicants by preferring lower-ranking white applicants." He ordered the departments to offer to the 62 Negro applicants the first available positions in a classification and at a pay rate commensurate with what they would have been earning but for the discrimination. Johnson also directed the seven agencies to hire Negroes and appoint them to positions other than custodial, domestic or laborer, when such applicants were listed as qualified and eligible.

N.Y. City bias banned. Mayor John V. Lindsay of New York City Aug. 24, 1970 issued executive orders that prohibited discrimination on the basis of sex or age in city employment and in work contracted by the city.

Black Peace Corps official quits. A high-ranking black Peace Corps official resigned his job April 12, 1971, charging the agency with discriminating against women and minorities.

William L. Tutman, the corps' first director of minority affairs, also filed a formal complaint with the Civil Service Commission documenting what he described as cases of discrimination against women and blacks. Tutman had been a staff member of the Peace Corps for five years, the last six months as minority affairs director.

Tutman made his resignation known in a letter to Peace Corps Director Joseph H. Blatchford. Tutman said the agency had failed "to assign top priorities to the concerns of minorities and women."

In the complaint filed with the Civil Service Commission, Tutman included documents that, he said, showed that three blacks, one a woman, had been denied staff positions because of what he

described as subjective comments by federal interviewers. He also complained that openings within the corps' top ranks were not made known until senior "white males" had been able to "anticipate" the vacancies and make recommendations for filling them.

School jobs for blacks in South cut. Citing previously unpublished government statistics, the National Education Association disclosed March 18, 1971 that as Southern communities dismantled their dual school systems the number of black teachers and principals dropped while the number of white faculty and administrative personnel increased.

The data was given to the NEA by the government on unanalyzed computer tapes from which the organization compiled its information. The NEA made the final figures public in a friend-of-court brief supporting the Justice Department in a desegregation suit against the state of Georgia. The brief was filed with the U.S. Court of Appeals for the 5th Circuit in New Orleans.

With the brief, the NEA presented the analyzed computer data showing, district by district, how black educators had been dropped from their posts as Southern school systems desegregated. Most of the figures dealt with school systems in Alabama, Florida, Georgia, Louisiana and Mississippi. Incomplete statistics from Texas were also presented.

School districts in those six states that received federal funds were required by law to report the racial compositions of their faculty and administrative staffs to the Department of Health, Education and Welfare (HEW). Of the districts that reported, 69% said the ratio of black to white faculty members had declined the last two years. During the same period, the number of black principals in those districts decreased by 20%.

In the districts that submitted figures, 1,040 black teachers were dropped while the number of white teachers rose by 4,192. The data on administrative personnel in Alabama was not complete, but in the other four states 232 black principals lost their jobs while 127 white principals were added to school staffs.

The NEA said the figures "show that black educators, particularly black principals, have borne burdens incident to desegregation in measures greatly disproportionate to any burdens borne by white educators."

(The case to which the NEA brief was attached involved the Justice Department's contention that the federal circuit court did not set strict enough standards for desegregating facilities in its December 1969 order requiring 81 Georgia school districts to integrate.).

Spokesmen for an association of U.S. school principals told a Senate panel June 14 that hundreds of black school principals across the South were either losing their jobs or being demoted as a result of school desegregation in the area.

Members of the National Association of Secondary School Principals told the Senate Committee on Equal Educational Opportunity that federal agencies were doing little to help the ousted black administrators.

Sen. Sam J. Ervin Jr. (D, N.C.) said he was not surprised at what he called an unfortunate situation. He said that since the whites were a majority in the South, it was not unusual for a white principal to be chosen to run a desegregated school that combined a formerly white and a formerly black school.

According to the witnesses' figures, in 10 Southern states the number of black principals dropped over the last eight years. In Alabama, for example, the number of black principals dropped in the last three years from 250 to 50. In Mississippi, 250 black administrators were displaced.

In court cases in 1971, the Justice Department charged three school districts in South Carolina, Virginia, and North Carolina with discriminating against black faculty and staff members by dismissing, reassigning and demoting them.

In the South Carolina case, the Justice Department filed a motion for supplemental relief May 28 in the U.S. district court in Columbia against the Chesterfield County school district. The motion charged the district with violating a court order by discriminatorily terminating the employment of black professional staff members at the end of the 1969–70 school year and discriminatorily reassigning and demoting black faculty members for the 1970–71 school year.

The government asked the court to order the district to reinstate, with back pay where appropriate, all professional staff members who were not offered contracts for the 1970–71 school year due to racial reasons.

In the Virginia case, the government filed a motion in the U.S. district court in Norfolk June 1 charging the Nansemond County district with reducing the black teaching staff for the 1971–72 school year and making schools racially identifiable through faculty and staff assignments. In addition, the government papers said a 1970 court-approved desegregation plan had failed to dismantle Nansemond's dual school system.

The district court was asked to order Nansemond's school board to show that its employment practices were not racially discriminatory and to draw up an effective school desegregation plan for the 1971–72 school year.

The government filed papers in Charlotte, N.C. June 1 asking the district court to order the Anson County school district to adopt non-racial employment guidelines and to reassign the county's students to schools on a non-racial basis. The Justice Department had charged the Anson County school board with hiring white teachers in preference to black applicants with better qualifications and dismissing and demoting black teachers.

New faculty plan for Chicago. Chicago School Superintendent James F. Redmond unveiled in the week of June 7, 1971 a new plan designed to broaden the integration of the city's public school teachers.

The new plan would recast the city's public school faculties so that no Chicago school would have a staff more than 75% white or 75% black.

The plan was drawn up to meet a federal demand for greater integration of the city's public school teachers. The Department of Health, Education and Welfare (HEW) had recommended a 65–35 ratio of white to black teachers in predominantly white schools and the reverse in schools with a black majority.

Redmond said the new balance would be achieved by assigning all newly appointed teachers or teachers with temporary assignments to black or white schools in a manner that would achieve the integration intended by the plan.

Action Vs. Employment Bias

Discriminatory tests barred. The Supreme Court ruled 8–0 March 8, 1971 that employers could not use job tests that had the effect of screening out Negroes if the tests were not related to ability to do the work. The court held that the employment bias section of the 1964 Civil Rights Act involved the consequences of employment practices, not simply whether the practices were motivated by racial bias.

The court limited the use of general educational and aptitude tests and said that "any tests used must measure the person for the job and not the person in the abstract." Writing for the court, Chief Justice Warren E. Burger said, "If an employment practice which operates to exclude Negroes cannot be shown to be related to job performance, the practice is prohibited."

The case grew out of applications for promotion by 13 black laborers at the Duke Power Co. generating plant at Dan River in Draper, N.C. Jack Greenberg of the NAACP Legal Defense Fund Inc. contended that the plaintiffs could challenge employment practices on the basis of discriminatory impact and need not prove bad motive on the part of the employer. The Justice Department and the Equal Employment Opportunity Commission had sought the ruling.

Eased bar standards opposed. Vice President Spiro T. Agnew Feb. 1, 1971 opposed suggestions from several Pennsylvania lawyers that the state ease its bar examination standards to admit more blacks to the practice of law.

In a speech before the National Association of Attorneys General in Washington, Agnew said he could see no reasons to justify steps that might "lower our standards of justice." He added that the best solution was not to lower examination standards but to improve educational standards. He said any competitive disadvantage could be cured by hard academic work.

The vice president's comments were in response to some Philadelphia attorneys who called for the abolition of the bar examination. According to the Washington Post Feb. 1, the attorneys said the tests were "culturally biased" against Negroes, that a high percentage of them do not pass and suggested that all persons who received law degrees be licensed to practice law.

Agnew said an easing of the standards could lead to situations where "unqualified people are put into positions of responsibility that they can't handle."

In another development involving blacks and bar examinations, Edward F. Bell, president of the National Bar Association (NBA), a predominantly black lawyers' group, Feb. 5 asked other lawyers' organizations to study whether bar examinations should be done away with as racially discriminatory.

Bell said recent studies seemed to indicate that bar examinations discriminated against black law school graduates. Bell, a Detroit attorney, cited lawsuits that had been filed in several states by law school graduates seeking to abolish the bar examinations because they did not test a graduate's legal knowledge.

University bias reported. A survey by the American Association of University Women, released Nov. 23, 1970, indicated that women did not have equal status with men in the academic world. Questionnaires were sent to 750 colleges in January, and the report was compiled from the responses of 454 of the institutions.

Dr. Mabelle G. McCullough, assistant dean of students at the University of Minnesota who headed the committee that made the survey, said there were "clear indications that there are discriminations" against women in the practices if not the policies of universities.

The summary of the survey said 90% of the schools said their faculty promotional policies were the same for both sexes; however the mean number of women department heads in all schools was less than three, and 34 coeducational schools had no women department heads. Women who chaired departments were mostly in the fields of home economics, physical education, languages, nursing and education.

The report said women made up 22% of the faculty in all ranks in the nation's colleges and universities, but that the "percentage of women decreases . . . as rank increases, with less than 9%

holding the rank of full professor." The report said 21% of the schools surveyed had no women trustees.

A Health, Education & Welfare (HEW) Department spokesman had said Nov. 5 that the University of Michigan was one of a dozen colleges and universities at which HEW inquiries had found sex discrimination and at which HEW had begun blocking approval of new federal contracts through the department's contract compliance division.

The Michigan contract freeze resulted from an Oct. 6 HEW staff report of discrimination.

Utility bias charged. The Equal Employment Opportunity Commission (EEOC) Nov. 17, 1971, after three days of hearings, charged the nation's gas and electric utilities with "rampant discrimination" in hiring and promoting minority group members and women. EEOC Chairman William H. Brown III promised to use his largely advisory powers to help "break the grip of Anglo males on virtually every good job in this industry."

The EEOC reported that only 6% of the industry's work force was black, the lowest percentage among the 23 largest industries, and 1.6% had Spanish surnames compared with 3.6% of all major industry workers.

The commission contended that some utilities used "culturally biased" general hiring tests unfair to non-Anglos, despite court rulings barring tests not directly related to job openings.

Women, who constituted 34% of the major industry work force, held only 15% of the utility jobs, the report noted, and were traditionally relegated to clerical jobs with little management opportunity and relatively low pay.

Industry spokesmen claimed that efforts to upgrade blacks had uncovered few qualified for better positions, although black workers for Detroit Edison and Southern California Edison Co. offered evidence of under-utilization of blacks.

Low employe turnover and promotion from the ranks in the highly unionized industry were also cited by company executives and independent experts as major causes of continuing inequality.

The Federal Power Commission (FPC) ruled July 11, 1972, however, that it had no power under federal law or the "public interest" concept to enforce fair employment practices by utilities.

The ruling came after 12 civil rights groups petitioned the FPC June 23 to take such action, charging "rampant discrimination against blacks, women and Spanish-surnamed Americans" by gas and electric utilities. They cited a September 1971 letter to the FPC from David L. Norman, assistant attorney general for the Justice Department's Civil Rights Division, who said the agency could exercise such powers.

But the FPC said that Congress had relegated fair employment powers to the Equal Employment Opportunities Commission, and said its "public interest" regulatory functions no more covered employment practices than it covered securities, taxes, wages or advertising, all of which were regulated by other agencies.

Detroit Edison bias damages ordered— Federal District Judge Damon J. Keith Oct. 2, 1973 ordered the Detroit Edison Co. to pay $4 million in punitive damages to blacks who, he said, had been subjected to "deliberate" and "invidious" racial discrimination. Judge Keith also assessed a local of the Utility Workers of America for damages of $250,000 for abetting the company's discriminatory practices.

A class-action suit had originally been filed in 1971 by three black employes, who were joined as plaintiffs by the Justice Department in 1972.

Judge Keith ordered that the damages be paid to the court for later determination of distribution among plaintiffs. The court also directed the company to make restitution in the form of back pay to blacks who had been denied promotion or jobs for racial reasons.

The decision established a quota system for hiring and promotion designed to achieve an overall work force 30% black, with 25% of skilled jobs to be filled by blacks.

Pacific Gas & Electric settlement—The Equal Employment Opportunity Commission announced Oct. 16, 1973 that Pacific Gas and Electric Co. of San Francisco had voluntarily pledged to increase employment opportunities for women and minorities in its managerial, craft and technical categories.

The agreement called for the company to review all its 3,000 women and 5,000 minority employes for possible advancement or transfer. Recruitment programs were to be instituted with special emphasis on placing Asian-Americans in high-paying craft jobs. The accord also provided for special management training programs for all minority groups and women.

El Paso Gas agreement—The Equal Employment Opportunity Commission and the El Paso Natural Gas Co. agreed Jan. 8, 1974 on a company program for increased job opportunities for minorities and women.

The agreement provided back pay and salary increases for women and minority employes whose current pay was below the norm for white males "of similar background and training." In addition, the company would seek during the next seven years to hire specific percentages of women, blacks, Spanish-surnamed and American Indians, with the percentages varying according to population makeup in the company's geographically-defined operating areas.

Georgia utility loses suit—The Justice Department Jan. 31, 1974 obtained a final court decree in Atlanta ordering the Georgia Power Co. to pay retroactive wages and pension benefits of almost $2.1 million to black employes who had been denied equal job rights. The order settled a suit, originally filed in 1969, which an appeals court had remanded to federal district court Feb. 14, 1973 for determination of back benefits.

The order also required the company to increase black employment to 17% of the work force within five years. Currently, 9.3% of the company's 8,278 employes were black.

Trucking bias charged. The Equal Employment Opportunity Commission Dec. 3, 1971 asked the Interstate Commerce Commission (ICC) to prohibit hiring bias among 15,000 interstate trucking firms employing over 1 million workers, charging the trucking industry with discriminating against women, blacks and Spanish-Americans by giving them only the lowest-paying jobs.

The EEOC said the ICC's "life and death power to license truckers" could be used to end bias, but the American Trucking Association claimed "no lawful basis" for such ICC action.

The U.S. Department of Justice Oct. 30, 1973 gave formal notice to 514 trucking companies, their collective bargaining association and the International Brotherhood of Teamsters that an investigation of the industry had found a pattern of illegal employment practices discriminating against blacks and Spanish-surnamed Americans.

The department charged that the industry had assigned most minority members to lower-paying jobs and had refused transfers or promotions on an equal basis with whites. The discrimination was perpetuated by the national freight contract with the Teamsters, which required that employes transferring to higher-paying jobs give up accrued seniority rights.

The department March 20, 1974 obtained a consent decree under which seven large trucking companies would adopt percentage hiring goals for blacks and Spanish-surnamed persons.

The legal basis for the agreement was a discrimination suit filed the same day against the seven companies, 342 smaller truckers, the International Brotherhood of Teamsters, the International Association of Machinists, and Trucking Employers Inc., the industry's collective bargaining organization.

The accord provided that 50% of vacancies would be filled by black and Spanish-surnamed applicants in communities where the groups made up more than 25% of the work force. In areas where the groups made up less than 25% of the work force, the hiring goal would be 33 1/3%. The quotas would be subject to the availability of qualified applicants in any locality.

The agreement could be modified to include Indians or Asian-Americans in certain areas.

The seven companies were Arkansas-Best Freight System Inc., of Fort Smith, Ark.; Branch Motor Express Co. of New York City; Consolidated Freightways Inc., of Menlo Park, Calif.; I.M.L. Freight Inc., of Salt Lake City; Mason and Dixon Lines Inc., of Kingsport, Tenn.; Pacific Intermountain Express Co., of Oakland, Calif.; and Smith's Transfer Corp., of Staunton, Va.

AT&T charges & settlement. In a 20,000-page report to the Federal Communications Commission, the Equal Employment Opportunity Commission Dec. 1, 1971 charged the American Telephone & Telegraph Co. and its operating subsidiaries with systematic job discrimination against blacks and Spanish-Americans, and called AT&T, with nearly a million employes, "the largest oppressor of women workers in the United States."

The report was a documentation of charges originally submitted to the FCC by the EEOC Dec. 10, 1970, in opposition to AT&T's requested rate increase, which was still pending.

AT&T denied the charges Nov. 30 in a statement prepared before the report was released. Executive Vice President Robert D. Lilley claimed that nonwhites or persons with Spanish surnames constituted 13% of all employes and one quarter of those hired within the last four years, and that minority employment had risen 265% since 1963.

Lilley admitted that the 7,500 minority people in management jobs were "not enough," but said the number had doubled in three years. He said 55% of all AT&T workers were women, including one third, or 57,000 of those in management positions.

The EEOC contended that most of the female and minority workers were underpaid and denied advancement opportunity. Blacks were said to be "largely relegated to the lowest-paying, least desirable jobs in the companies," and were subject to unfair hiring standards and tests. Southern AT&T affiliates lagged behind "even the minimal efforts" made elsewhere, and most black employes nationally were female, and "suffer from a dual handicap of race and sex."

Spanish surnamed Americans were systematically excluded from jobs, the report charged, and denied equality once hired, the report charged.

As for women, the EEOC claimed that the phone company maintained recruitment and promotion policies that in effect created men-only and women-only categories. Telephone operators, 99.9% female, had "virtually intolerable" working conditions including "authoritarian" work rules, and pay ceilings of $5,000-$6,000 a year, with almost no advancement possibilities.

In a 10,000-page brief released Aug. 1, 1972, AT&T disputed the EEOC's charges of massive bias. It said that over the past three years minorities had accounted for one quarter of all new employes, so that blacks constituted 10% of the total work force, and the number of Spanish-speaking employes had nearly doubled.

One third of AT&T managers were women, the company said, more than half of whom earned over $10,000 annually, and the number of women at middle management and higher levels had increased seven times as fast as all management jobs in the three-year period. About 40% of all managers and officials were women, compared with a 15% figure for the nation as a whole.

Although most of the 53.5% of its employes who were women were operators or clerks, the company criticized the EEOC's "disparagement" of the operator job, which it called "a good one." AT&T said the commission had ignored the "realities of the labor market" and the company's responsibility to provide good services.

AT&T and the General Services Administration (GSA) Sept. 20 announced an affirmative-action agreement for AT&T to increase and upgrade the employment of women and minority group members. The Labor Department's Office of Federal Contract Compliance (OFCC) told the GSA Sept. 29 that it was "assuming jurisdiction" over the agreement.

The GSA accord would have required AT&T to promote 50,000 women and 6,600 minority group members into better jobs within 15 months, and to try to hire 6,600 women for jobs usually filled by men and 4,000 men to traditionally female jobs, for a goal of 10% women among new employes in outside craft jobs and 5% men among newly hired operators. All qualified persons who applied for the opposite-sex jobs would be hired, as long as positions were open.

AT&T pledged that minorities and women would constitute a percentage of all new employes in each affiliated company equivalent to one and one half times the percentage of that minority group in the local area. AT&T would conduct semiannual progress reviews, subject to GSA inspection.

The plan was immediately criticized by some civil rights groups. The National Organization for Women (NOW), the National Association for the Advancement of Colored People (NAACP) and the Mexican-American Legal Defense Fund filed formal objections Sept. 29. They said the plan violated federal law in failing to provide for back pay to victims of past discrimination, ignoring job test procedures that were unfair to women or minorities, and ignoring unfair transfer policies.

AT&T, the Labor Department and the EEOC Jan. 18, 1973 reached an agreement under which the company promised to pay $15 million to 15,000 women and minority male employes as compensation for past discriminatory hiring and promotion practices. The company also agreed to pay $23 million a year in pay increases to 36,000 women and minority workers who had moved to higher paying jobs without being credited with seniority gained in lower category jobs. In return, the EEOC agreed to drop its opposition to rate increases for AT&T.

AT&T also agreed to a set of percentage goals for women in craft jobs and for men in traditionally female operator and clerical jobs that were about twice as high as those provided in the 1972 accord with the GSA. (The OFCC had rejected the 1972 pact's terms as inadequate.)

In a departure from previous cases, women would receive back pay, upon moving into craft jobs, even if they had failed to apply for the jobs under the impression that the company would deny the request. The settlement was the largest job bias compensation ever awarded, although the EEOC said the total payments would be far less than what the employes would have earned if they had been promoted earlier.

AT&T agreed to develop programs at all its facilities toward a goal of 38%–40% women in inside craft jobs and 19% women in outside craft jobs, and set a hiring goal of 10% men in operator jobs and 25% men in clerical jobs. About 1,500 women college graduates would be moved into a rapid-advance management training program allegedly closed to women in the past.

EEOC Chairman William H. Brown 3rd said he hoped the agreement "would be used as a model for government's negotiations with companies." Labor Department assistant solicitor William J. Kilberg said the settlement showed that administration still supported numerical goals and timetables as a means to end job discrimination. But the National Organization for Women criticized the plan for failing to set specific timetables for the numerical goals.

More than a year later, AT&T and the federal government May 30, 1974 reached an additional agreement providing almost $30 million in back pay and future salary adjustments to compensate for pay discrimination against managerial employes.

The majority of those receiving pay adjustments would be women, but the government had charged that in some cases sex discrimination worked in both directions, and that there were instances of racial discrimination.

The settlement provided salary adjustments of $14.9 million in the upcoming fiscal year for 17,000 workers (10,000 women) who had been promoted into the management category but who were paid less than the average white male. The government had charged that pay inequities were built into the promotion system, since increases were typically granted on a straight percentage basis, and white males had generally been paid more at the nonmanagement level. Under the agreement, newly-promoted workers would be paid no less than the average salary of "the most favored sex."

Back pay of about $7 million would go to 7,000 employes who had received less than the average after their promotions.

The company estimated that an additional 8,400 workers (5,000 women) would be promoted into the affected categories within the coming year and would receive about $7.5 million more than would have been paid without the settlement.

The pact covered the two lowest management categories, but a Labor Department spokesman said exclusion of higher-ranking employes from the current action did not foreclose future action on their behalf.

In a supplemental settlement with the Labor and Justice Departments, the GSA and the EEOC (reported May 14, 1975), AT&T agreed to "priority" hiring and promotion of women and minority workers in cases in which the company had fallen short of the goals specified in the 1973 agreement.

Sex Roles & AT&T

Equal Employment Opportunity and the AT&T Case. Edited by Phyllis A. Wallace. Cambridge, Mass., The MIT Press, 1975. 355 pp. $16.95.

In November 1970, the American Telephone and Telegraph Company (AT&T) asked the Federal Communications Commission to approve an increase in long distance rates. The events covered by this book began a month later when the Equal Employment Opportunity Commission petitioned the Federal Communications Commission (FCC) to intervene on the grounds that the company had been discriminating against women and blacks, Hispanic Americans, and other minorities in violation of the Federal Communications Act, Title VII of the Civil Rights Act of 1964, and other statutes. These events culminated in agreements between AT&T and the government which were embodied in consent decrees in January 1973 and May 1974, and which have had far-reaching implications for all of industry. · · ·   While the case was based on discrimination against minorities and women, the greatest emphasis was placed on sex-segregation of jobs and even entire departments. The operator and clerical jobs were predominantly female, and the craft jobs were predominantly male. This chapter also gives a partial presentation of the company's position, the only chapter to do so. Significantly, an AT&T spokesman complained that the company's past policies and practices were being measured by 1971 standards, whereas definitions of discrimination had changed considerably since the passage of the act.

It is important that the consent decrees played a key role in changing public perceptions of what constitutes sex discrimination in jobs. They set goals and timetables for employment of women in previously all-male craft jobs, and for men in operator and clerical jobs. ...

—From a book review by Herbert Hammerman in Monthly Labor Review (September 1976)

Under the 1975 agreement, AT&T promised back pay ranging from $125 to $1,500 to "an undetermined number of employes whose promotions may have been delayed." Under the new agreement, an AT&T spokesman said, an estimated 5,000 workers who should have been hired or promoted under the original decree would be given special attention.

The supplemental agreement remedied "the failure of a number of Bell System [AT&T] companies to fully implement the 1973 consent decree in a timely manner," said William J. Kilberg, solicitor for the Labor Department. This failure, Kilberg said, meant that persons "who should have benefited by that decree in fact experienced no improvement in their employment." The new order provided "a mechanism for these persons to catch up to where they should be and to compensate them for the delay," he said.

The affirmative action agreements, however, created new problems for AT&T. U.S. District Court Judge Gerhard A. Gesell ruled June 9, 1976 that AT&T must pay damages to a white male employe who had been passed over for a promotion. The promotion had gone to a woman with a lower seniority and experience rating. AT&T said that it had promoted the women to comply with a court-ordered affirmative-action plan. The company argued that it could not be "simultaneously in compliance and in violation of the same [civil rights] act by promoting the lesser qualified person." Gesell's ruling, AT&T said, had the effect of putting AT&T in that position.

Shortly thereafter, Judge A. Leon Higgenbotham Jr., in a decision in federal district court in Philadelphia, upheld the AT&T compensatory promotion plan. Three telephone employes unions had objected to the bypassing of the seniority system for some promotions, contending that it constituted reverse discrimination.

A "final" report on AT&T's compliance with the 1973 affirmative action decree was submitted by federal officials in U.S. District Court in Philadelphia Jan. 17, 1979. The report said that the company was in "substantial compliance" with U.S. orders to end job discrimination against women and minorities.

The report cautioned that "the government does not believe that all equal-employment opportunity problems have been remedied and forever put to rest."

But it said the decree "was not intended to be the instrument" to solve all the company's equal-employment problems.

AT&T employed 980,000 persons.

As evidence of "substantial progress" by AT&T in reducing job discrimination, the report said that:

■ Women held 28.5% of all management jobs in the Bell system, compared with 22.4% in 1973.

■ Women held 6.9% of top management jobs, compared with 2.1% in 1973.

■ Employment of blacks by the Bell system increased to 12% from 10.6% in 1973. Black representation in management jobs increased to 5.5% from 2.2%.

■ Hispanic employment rose to 3.9% of the Bell system's total from 2.5% in 1973. Hispanics' share of management posts increased to 2.1% from .7%

Hardening Positions

Focus on Busing

The struggle over quotas and affirmative action in education resulted in a hardening of positions by 1972. Much of the controversy centered on the issue of busing, and the Nixon Administration was defeated in an effort to legislate a ban against court-ordered busing for racial balance.

Nixon urges anti-busing bill. After weeks of Administration discussion and planning, President Nixon presented his anti-busing arguments to the nation in a television and radio address March 16, 1972 and then sent a special message to Congress March 17. He called for legislation to deny courts the power to order busing of elementary schoolchildren to achieve racial integration. He asked for a moratorium on all new busing orders.

(White House Press Secretary Ronald Ziegler had said March 13 that Nixon made his decision at Camp David, Md. over the March 11-12 weekend, but would postpone publication until after the primary, to avoid influencing the voters. The President had received final recommendations March 10 from a Cabinet-level committee he had designated Feb. 14.)

Broadcast reveals proposals—In his broadcast March 16, Nixon said he was acting to enforce his "well known" position, expressed "scores of times over many years" against "busing for the purpose of achieving racial balance." Urgent action was necessary because in several cases the "courts have gone too far," creating "confusion and contradiction in the law; anger, fear and turmoil in local communities," and "agonized concern" among parents "for the education and safety of their children."

The President repeatedly claimed support for his position among blacks as well as whites, since, he said, "the great majority' of Americans—white and black" opposed busing children out of their own neighborhoods.

Nixon cited "thousands of letters" he had received from all sections of the country complaining of inconvenience, fear and frustration, including the loss by children bussed out of poor neighborhoods of "the extra personal attention and financial support in his school that we know can make all the difference."

To meet these complaints, the President promised to submit legislation to Congress, order "all agencies and departments of the federal government at every level to carry out the spirit as well as the letter" of his position, and direct the Justice Department to intervene where lower courts had "gone beyond the Supreme Court requirements in ordering busing." He urged listeners to drum up Congressional support for his proposals.

The President also called for a new commitment that "the children currently attending the poorest schools in our cities and rural areas be provided with education equal to that of good schools in their communities."

Message to Congress—Nixon began his message by asserting that the dismantling of "the old dual-school system in those areas where it existed" was "substantially completed." Therefore, efforts to meet the "constitutional mandate" laid down in the 1954 Supreme Court's *Brown v. Board of Education* desegregation ruling, which Nixon defined as a requirement "that no child should be denied equal educational opportunity," should "now focus much more specifically on education: on assuring that the opportunity is not only equal but adequate, and that in those remaining cases in which desegregation has not yet been completed it be achieved with a greater sensitivity to educational needs."

Nixon approached the busing issue from that emphasis on education rather than desegregation:

"In the furor over busing, it has become all too easy to forget what busing is supposed to be designed to achieve: equality of educational opportunity for all Americans."

The President conceded that some opponents of busing were motivated by racial prejudice, but claimed that "most people, including large and increasing numbers of blacks and other minorities, oppose it for reasons that have little or nothing to do with race. It would compound an injustice to persist in massive busing simply because some people oppose it for the wrong reasons."

In many communities, Nixon said, busing was seen as "a symbol of helplessness, frustration and outrage," as parents were denied the right to choose their children's school, were forced to suffer inconvenience, and felt they were subjected to "social engineering on an abstract basis."

Among black parents, the President contended that the "principal emphasis" of the concern for quality education had shifted from desegregation, and now rested on "improving schools, on convenience, on the chance for parental involvement—in short, on the same concerns that motivate white parents—and

in many communities, on securing a greater measure of control over schools that serve primarily minority-group communities."

In addition, Nixon charged that advocates of "system-wide racial balance" would condemn blacks to a permanent "minority status" in most schools, which would be "run by whites and dominated by whites," while those black students in densely populated central cities could never be reached by busing plans in any case.

One of the "historical" factors leading courts to order large-scale busing, Nixon wrote, had been "community resistance" against a unitary school system. This, according to Nixon, the courts "sometimes saw as delay or evasion." But "the past three years" had brought "phenomenal" progress toward unitary systems and toward a "new climate of acceptance of the basic constitutional doctrine."

The President called this "a new element of great importance: for the greater the elements of basic good faith, of desire to make the system work, the less need or justification there is for extreme remedies rooted in coercion."

Finally, Nixon implied that plans for massive busing imposed over community resistance would not be likely to achieve their objectives. The schools, he said, should assume a more modest burden, since they could not by themselves bring about "the kind of multiracial society which the adult community has failed to achieve for itself," and might only risk imposing "lasting psychic injury" on children by trying.

Without Congressional intervention, the President warned, busing would continue to be ordered by some courts to a degree "far beyond what most people would consider reasonable" and beyond Supreme Court requirements. He cited a "maze of differing and sometimes inconsistent orders" which have caused "uncertainty" and "vastly unequal treatment among regions" and districts.

As authority for Congressional action to substitute "statutory law" for "case law" as a guide to the courts, Nixon cited the enforcement clause of the 14th Amendment (the basis for desegregation rulings). The clause gives Congress "power to enforce, by appropriate legislation, the provisions" of the amendment.

Besides, Nixon wrote, "the educational, financial and social complexities of this issue are not, and are not properly, susceptible of solution by individual courts alone or even by the Supreme Court alone."

The President's legislative program consisted of two separate bills. The first, on which he requested immediate action, would impose a temporary freeze on all new busing orders by federal courts, "while the Congress considers alternative means of enforcing 14th Amendment rights." The second, an "Equal Educational Opportunities Act," would specify those alternative means, and would attempt through federal aid to improve education for poor and minority children.

Busing moratorium—The Student Transportation Moratorium Act would prohibit all new court busing orders immediately on passage until July 1, 1973, or until Congress passed appropriate legislation, but "would not put a stop to desegregation cases." Where "lower courts have gone beyond the Supreme Court" in ordering massive busing, Nixon promised "intervention by the Justice Department in selected cases."

This "unusual procedure" by Congress would provide a "calm and thoughtful" atmosphere for further deliberation, and would "relieve the pressure on the Congress to act on the long-range legislation without full and adequate consideration." Since Nixon found it "abundantly clear" from "the upwelling of sentiment" against busing that some curb was inevitable, he asked that "while the matter is being considered in Congress" the courts should "not speed further along a course that is likely to be changed."

Equal Opportunities Act—The second Nixon proposal would define the responsibilities of school districts concerning integration and minority opportunities, specify remedies for violations, and stimulate improvements in poorer schools.

Deliberate segregation would be prohibited, and previously dual school systems would "have an affirmative duty to remove the vestiges" of segregation.

No student could be assigned to a school other than the one nearest his home, or allowed to transfer to another school, if greater racial segregation would result. Voluntary transfers to promote integration would be encouraged.

But "racial balance" would not be required, and "the assignment of students to their neighborhood schools would not be considered a denial of equal educational opportunity," unless the schools had been located for purposes of segregation.

Faculty and staff employment and assignment bias would be banned.

School authorities would have to "take appropriate action to overcome whatever language barriers might exist," especially among Mexican-Americans, Puerto Ricans and Indians.

If a court found violations, it could only impose remedies "to correct the particular violations," and it could not change or ignore district lines unless they had been deliberately drawn to prevent integration. All desegregation orders would expire after 10 years, or five years if busing were involved, and subsequent orders could be imposed only if new violations were found.

Courts would have to choose from a list of preferred remedies, using the least severe that could correct the situation. The remedies would be:

(1) Assigning students to the school nearest their homes, taking "natural physical barriers" into account; (2) assigning students to the nearest school regardless of physical barriers; (3) permitting voluntary transfers to promote integration; (4) revising attendance zones or grade structures without new busing; (5) building new schools and closing inferior schools; (6) establishing "magnet schools" or educational parks; and (7) any other feasible plan, excluding any new busing of sixth grade or younger students, and allowing busing of older children only on a temporary basis where no health or educational risk was involved, and provided the order was stayed until approved by an appeals court.

Congressional action begun—Senate and House committees began scheduling hearings on the President's proposals March 17, amid reports that the Administration hoped to attach the busing moratorium to the higher education bill in a Senate-House Conference. Both the Senate and House versions of the bill had included various measures to curb busing short of a moratorium. Senate leaders Mike Mansfield (D, Mont.) and Hugh Scott (R, Pa.) both suggested March 18 that the conference consider the President's proposal.

The proposals ran into opposition from Democratic committee chairmen whose committees would normally handle them. Chairman Carl D. Perkins (D, Ky.) of the House Education and Labor Committee March 22 called Nixon's plan "superficial, confusing and unnecessary."

Rep. Emanuel Celler (D, N.Y.), chairman of the House Judiciary Committee called the moratorium "an unconstitutional interference with the judicial power." His Senate counterpart, James Eastland (D, Miss.) said March 20 that the moratorium would allow "separate but equal schools in the North," yet ignore substantial busing already ordered in the South.

Among other congressmen commenting, Sen. Edward Kennedy said Nixon's two proposed bills "would combine to perpetuate segregated educational systems where they may continue to exist." Kennedy said busing was often "the only possible device to end outright segregation."

Candidates react. Nixon's message was roundly criticized by all the leading Democratic presidential candidates, although Sen. Hubert Humphrey at first claimed the President had adopted his own views.

Humphrey said March 17 of Nixon's TV address that "at long last the President has been able to get his finger up in the air and sense what's going on and has decided that he would say amen to some of the things that some of the rest of us have been trying to do."

But after reading "the fine print" of the message to Congress, Humphrey said in Milwaukee March 20, he decided the proposals were "insufficient in the amount of aid needed for our children, deceptive," and "insensitive to the laws and the Constitution."

Sen. Edmund Muskie, campaigning in Illinois March 17, repeated his view that

busing for desegregation "has value if used with common sense," while Sen. George McGovern, Rep. Shirley Chisholm and New York Mayor John Lindsay sharply criticized the President's stand, which McGovern called "a frantic effort to capitalize on this emotional issue" in order to distract attention from Vietnam, taxes and unemployment. Mrs. Chisholm said Nixon had shown "final evidence of his desire to shut the door to real equality," and Lindsay called the proposals a "cave-in" to the views of Alabama Gov. George Wallace.

Sen. Henry M. Jackson, who had favored an antibusing constitutional amendment, called Nixon's plan "intellectually dishonest" and "an attack on the Bill of Rights itself."

Alabama Gov. George Wallace said March 17 that the President didn't go far enough in his proposals. He said Nixon should use his executive powers to instruct the Justice Department to reopen all schools under a freedom of choice plan. "People want action now and not talk," Wallace said.

Nixon news conference. President Nixon held an impromptu, untelevised news conference in his office March 24. The President discussed his school busing views. He said the Constitution gave Congress the power "to set up the remedies to accomplish the right of equal protection of the law." And while he agreed with the Supreme Court's position "that legally segregated education was inherently inferior education," the question was:

"How do we desegregate and thereby get better education?" Busing "for the purpose of achieving racial balance not only does not produce superior education," he said, "it results in even more inferior education."

Therefore, his proposals dealt with the issue "by saying we can and should have desegregation but we should not compound the evil of a dual school system, of legal segregation, by using a remedy which makes it even worse."

In his opinion, a moratorium on busing was constitutional and the court would so hold because "it deals with a remedy and not a right."

Even if a course of maximum busing were pursued, Nixon said, "it would still leave the vast majority of black school-children living in central cities going to what are basically inferior schools."

In general, his Administration had made "great progress in desegregation," Nixon said. "There are more black students that go to majority white schools in the South than in the North at the present time. The dual school system has been virtually eliminated."

He told the newsmen, "we cannot put the primary burden for breaking up these patterns [of inner-city segregation] on the educational system . . . Whenever a device is used to desegregate which results in inferior education, we are doing a grave disservice to the blacks who are supposed to be helped."

Blacks oppose Nixon move. Prominent black spokesmen, including the Congressional Black Caucus, the Council of Black Appointees of the Nixon Administration and leaders of black organizations spoke out against plans to limit busing March 15-28.

The 13 Black Caucus members issued a statement March 15 saying "we strongly reaffirm our support of busing as one of the many ways to implement the constitutional requirement of equal opportunities in education," although "massive busing" would usually not be required. They criticized "those who would exploit this issue for personal, political or monetary gain."

The same day, Gary, Ind. Mayor Richard G. Hatcher, who had helped chair the National Black Political Convention in that city March 10-12, reported that the convention, after passing a resolution against busing, went on and approved a supplementary resolution supporting the practice "in cases where it serves the end of providing quality education for black people."

The Council of Black Appointees of the Nixon Administration said in a March 20 statement it was studying ways to amend Nixon's legislative proposals "to safeguard the rights of black Americans," since the bills posed "grave constitutional questions" which "unintentionally, may adversely affect" blacks.

Clarence Mitchell, Washington office director of the National Association for the Advancement of Colored People, said March 28 his organization would challenge Nixon's proposals in the courts "before the ink is dry" if passed by Congress. He called the bills "the most blatant products of racism that I have seen in the federal government."

Dissent in Administration. In two separate moves April 25-26, 1972, two-thirds of the Justice Department's civil rights lawyers and the chief black officeholders of the Nixon Administration expressed strong reservations about the Administration's proposals to curb the use of busing for school integration.

A letter signed by 95 of the 148 lawyers in the Justice Department's Civil Rights Division and sent to Congressional leaders and committees April 25 opposed any legislation "which would limit the power of federal courts to remedy, through busing, the unconstitutional segregation of public school children." The letter did not specifically cite Nixon's proposals. The signers called such legislation of doubtful constitutionality, and inconsistent "with our national commitment to racial equality."

Ten black lawyers in the department, seven of whom signed the letter to Comgress, issued a separate public statement calling the busing issue a "sham" that could undo "much of the progress that has been made in the desegregation area in recent years."

Acting Attorney General Richard Kleindienst responded to the statements April 25 by suggesting that the lawyers resign if the bills were passed and if the lawyers could not in conscience enforce them.

The White House released a report April 26 by the Council of Black Appointees criticizing the proposed bills and the intervention by the Justice Department in pending desegregation cases. The Council called for changes in the bills to allow greater flexibility by courts in drawing up desegregation plans. The report said that intervention in the court cases had had "a chilling effect on black people," who believed the federal government had decided to use its power and influence to aid "those who stand in opposition to the constitutional rights of minority school-children."

Busing compromise. A compromise curb on school busing, attached to a higher education bill, became law after the omnibus measure was approved by House-Senate conference committee May 17, 1972, passed by 63–15 Senate vote May 24, adopted by 218–180 House vote June 8 and criticized but signed by President Nixon June 23.

The busing provision would delay all new court busing orders until appeals had been exhausted, or until Jan. 1, 1974. The House bill had set no deadline, while the Senate bill had limited the delays to cases crossing local district lines and to June 30, 1973.

Federal funds could not be used to finance busing for desegregation unless requested by local authorities, nor could federal officials order or encourage districts to spend state or local funds for busing, in cases in which busing endangered pupils' health or education, "unless constitutionally required." This was similar to provisions in the Senate bill, but milder than the House bill's total prohibition against federal funds or encouragement for busing.

Passage of the bill, which included major new programs of aid to colleges and needy college students, was endangered by opposition from House members to any watering down of their tough antibusing provisions. The House had voted May 11 a second time by a 275–124 vote to instruct its conferees not to compromise on the issue.

Rep. Edith Green (D, Ore.), who had helped write the education provisions, refused to sign the conference report, saying the "integrity of the House" was at stake. Sens. Jacob Javits (R, N.Y.) and Walter Mondale (D, Minn.) did not sign the report, which they thought had gone too far in restricting the courts. The final vote on busing in conference had been 11-9 among representatives and 7-5 among senators in favor of the compromise, according to conference committee chairman Rep. Carl Perkins (D, Ky.).

Later May 17 House Democrats defeated in caucus by a 125–87 vote a resolution backed by Joe Waggoner Jr. (La.), which would have put Democrats on record against busing, and would have instructed Democrats on the Judiciary and Education Committees to report out antibusing legislation and an antibusing constitutional amendment.

Voting against the measure when the Senate took action May 24 were several Northern liberals led by Javits and Mondale, who said they objected to the provisions limiting the use of busing for school integration. Liberals had succeeded by a 44-26 vote the previous day in tabling a motion by Minority Whip Robert Griffin (Mich.) to send the bill back to conference with instructions to accept the tougher House antibusing provisions.

Sens. Hubert Humphrey (D, Minn.) and George McGovern (D, S.D.), both campaigning in the California presidential primary, announced they would have voted for the bill.

President Nixon's chief assistant for domestic affairs John Ehrlichman said May 19 that Nixon believed the compromise busing provisions fell "far short" of his own proposed bills, and were "no substitute for the necessary busing legislation." Ehrlichman noted that the compromise would only delay court ordered busing until appeals had been exhausted, which would already have happened in some districts by fall. In addition, he said, the bill set no "final, clear public policy" on busing limits when it expired Jan. 1, 1974.

When the House voted on the bill June 8, a majority of Democrats and Republicans accepted the conference committee's busing compromise despite two earlier House votes instructing the conferees not to water down the tougher provisions approved by the House.

Voting against the measure were foes of busing who thought the compromise gave only an "illusion of relief," in the words of Democratic Rep. Edith Green; also in opposition were liberals, including members of the Congressional Black Caucus, who questioned the constitutionality and segregationist implications of the provision limiting court desegregation powers.

On signing the bill June 23, President Nixon criticized the anti-busing provisions as an "inadequate, misleading and entirely unsatisfactory" response to "one of the burning social issues of the past decade."

Nixon noted that the bill's moratoriuʌn on court busing orders was only temporary, while his own proposals had included a set of uniform national guidelines for any future desegregation orders, with a permanent ban on most busing for integration. Furthermore, Nixon said, the bill's language only barred orders requiring busing "for the purpose of achieving a balance among students with respect to race," and he predicted that "an adroit order-drafter may be able to prevent any effective application of this law."

Nixon said he would have vetoed the busing provisions if they had not been attached to the higher education-desegregation aid bill, which incorporated several Administration proposals.

Presidential domestic adviser John Ehrlichman said at a news conference the same day that Nixon would "go to the people" to seek an antibusing constitutional amendment if Congress failed to pass his proposals.

Rep. Carl Perkins (D, Ky.), whose House-Senate conference committee had drafted the final bill, said June 23 that the busing provisions would "bring uniformity of legal procedures on this issue for the first time," and said Nixon "just wants to keep the busing issue alive. He played politics with it as far as he could and he's still trying to keep it up."

Prior action—The Senate April 21, 1971, by 51–35, rejected a proposal to force suburban communities to integrate their schools with neighboring inner-city public schools within 12 years.

Discussion on the proposal was marked by exchanges between Sen. Abraham A. Ribicoff (D, Conn.), the proposal's sponsor, and Sen. Jacob K. Javits (R, N.Y.), who spoke against it.

At one point, Ribicoff charged Javits with "hypocrisy" for being "unwilling to accept desegregation for his state, though he is willing to shove it down the throats of the senators from Mississippi." Looking directly at Javits, Ribicoff said: "I don't think you have the guts to face your liberal constituents who have moved to the suburbs to avoid sending their children to school with blacks."

Ribicoff had introduced his proposal March 16 as an amendment to a $1.4 billion bill designed to assist school districts in desegregating.

Javits said the "essential basis" for his opposition to the amendment was that if it was accepted it might jeopardize the bill which he was instrumental in drawing up. Javits said April 20 that the plan to integrate suburban schools "is Senator Ribicoff's idea. It may be a good one, and it may be a bad one, but I think it will sink this bill, and my people sent me here to achieve results."

There was no ideological pattern discernable in the Senate vote. Southerners and Northerners voted on both sides of the measure. Of the 51 senators who voted against the proposal, 19 were Democrats including some leading civil rights advocates. Twenty-eight Democrats and seven Republicans voted for the measure.

Ribicoff's amendment would have required all schools within a metropolitan area to have a percentage of minority students at least equal to half the percentage of minority students in the entire metropolitan area.

Opposition to the proposal was supported by Elliot L. Richardson, secretary of the Department of Health, Education and Welfare (HEW), who said adoption of the amendment could kill the entire bill, and Clarence Mitchell, director of the Washington bureau of the National Association for the Advancement of Colored People (NAACP).

In a speech inserted in the Congressional Record, Ribicoff deplored "the seemingly inexorable march toward apartheid in the North as well as the South." Citing U.S. figures showing that Northern schools as a whole were more segregated than schools in the South, he said "racial isolation is now just as pervasive in the North as it is in the South."

(The figures cited by Ribicoff, compiled by the Department of Health, Education and Welfare (HEW), showed that 27.6% of black students in the North attended schools where a majority of students were white, while 38% of black students in the South attended predominantly white schools.)

The revised bill was later accepted by 74–8 senate vote April 26 and sent to the House. As passed, it authorized $1.4 billion in federal aid to help school districts integrate their schools, and it would give communities broad discretion over use of most of the funds allotted. In applying for grants, however, school districts would be required to have a broad plan for eliminating segregation and use a portion of their grant to create at least one "stable, quality, integrated school."

According to the measure, the model schools would have a "substantial portion of children from educationally advantaged backgrounds" but would be substantially representative of the racial makeup of the community.

School districts that were under U.S. court orders to desegregate could be exempted from the requirement to set up a model school.

During the week the bill was debated, Southern senators proposed a number of amendments, all but one of which were turned down.

The only one to get the Senate's backing was authored by Sen. John C. Stennis (D, Miss.) and approved April 22 by a 44–34 vote. The amendment put the Senate on record as declaring that it was "the policy of the United States" to enforce federal school desegregation laws in communities where the segregation resulted from housing patterns as well as in areas where the segregation had been sanctioned by law.

Stennis said his amendment would eliminate the "dual standard" of enforcement under which he said Southern schools were threatened with forfeiture of federal funds if they failed to desegregate while schools in Northern cities and suburban areas remained segregated.

Other efforts to attach Southern-sponsored amendments to the bill were rejected. The Senate turned down April 26 a series of amendments put forward by Sen. Sam J. Ervin Jr. (D, N.C.) designed to relax some of the U.S. desegregation guidelines. One amendment would have permitted communities with "freedom-of-choice" school plans, under which a student could enroll in any school in the district, to be exempt from further desegregation efforts.

Another Ervin amendment would have prohibited a U.S. judge or official from ordering a desegregation plan that called for the busing of schoolchildren for racially balanced schools. A third would have prohibited the federal government from stopping a child from attending the public school nearest his home.

More than six months later the House voted overwhelmingly Nov. 5 against busing for racial integration. It then approved, 332–38, a $1.5 billion program of aid to school desegregation. The major action was on the three antibusing amendments which made it clear that the House agreed with the President in its opposition to busing.

The key antibusing amendment would prohibit the use of the $1.5 billion to pay for buses, drivers or any other cost of transporting children out of their neighborhood schools for the purpose of racial integration. Dozens of liberal Democrats voted with nearly all Republicans and Southerners to pass that amendment by a 233–124 vote.

Another amendment would not allow federal court orders requiring busing to go into effect until all appeals had been exhausted or until the time for appeal had passed. That amendment passed 235–125.

A third amendment, adopted by a vote of 231–126, would forbid U.S. education officials from requiring, or even encouraging, communities to institute busing plans.

The antibusing bandwagon hit full stride near midnight when Rep. Edith Green (D, Ore.), a foremost House education expert and mother of two sons, took the floor.

Rep. Green said "we cannot go back 100 years to make up for the errors of our ancestors. The evidence is very strong that busing is not the answer to our school problems. I never bought a home without looking first to find out about the schools my boys would attend. If the federal government then is going to reach its long arm into my house and say, 'Well, we are sorry you bought your home here, but your children are going to have to be bused 30 miles,' I say the government has gone too far."

With the legislation still pending, the Senate Feb. 24, 1972 approved a compromise on the busing issue.

The Senate plan, offered by party leaders Mike Mansfield (D, Mont.) and Hugh Scott (R, Pa.) was in the form of three amendments to a combined higher education and desegregation aid bill, and was designed to put an outer limit on the use of busing, yet retain it as a desegregation tool in some cases.

The amendments were passed by votes of 51–37, 50–38 and 79–9, the negative votes coming mostly from Southerners and conservative Republicans.

The first provision would bar the use of federal funds for busing unless voluntarily requested by "local school officials."

The second provision would prohibit federal aides from requiring or encouraging local officials to bus children "where the time or distance of travel is so great as to risk the health" or education of the child, or where the receiving school was "substantially inferior" to the neighborhood school. The provision would thus adopt as federal regulation the guidelines issued by the Supreme Court in its April 1971 Charlotte, N.C. desegregation decision.

A third proviso would delay enforcement of court-ordered busing pending all appeals, but only in cases crossing local district lines, and only until June 30, 1973.

After temporarily reversing itself, the Senate approved the amended bill by 88–6 vote March 1 and sent it to joint conference committee.

Antibusing bill dies. The Senate Oct. 12, 1972 again failed to end a filibuster by Northern liberals against a House-passed bill to limit school busing for integration. It put to rest for the session President Nixon's program to deal with school integration.

The bill would have prohibited federal courts and executive departments from ordering the assignment of elementary or secondary school students to any school other than the school within his district "closest or next closest" to his home, unless district lines had been drawn for deliberate segregation purposes. The bill would have prohibited all federally-ordered crosstown or interdistrict busing, although permitting school pairings.

Districts already operating under desegregation orders could have reopened their cases in the courts to conform with the bill's criteria. The less specific antibusing provisions enacted in June in combination with the higher education bill had not prevented most court busing orders from taking effect.

Senate debate on the bill had begun Oct. 6, after Sen. James B. Allen (D, Ala.) had succeeded through parliamentary maneuvers to get the House bill directly on the floor without committee consideration. Supporters claimed the backing of a majority of Americans, while opponents, seeking to block passage by extended debate in the last scheduled week of the 92nd Congress, charged the bill would have unconstitutionally interfered with court powers to enforce civil rights and would have undone recent progress in desegregation.

Cloture motions were defeated Oct. 10 by a 45–37 vote, Oct. 11 by a 49–39 vote and Oct. 12 by a 49–38 vote, nine short of the necessary two-thirds of those present and voting. The Senate then agreed by a 50–26 vote to go on to other legislation.

In an earlier development, the House Rules Committee decided Aug. 1 by a 9–6 vote to discharge the Judiciary Committee from further responsibility for a proposed antibusing constitutional amendment, which the committee had had under consideration for over a year. The amendment was sent to the floor, where it was opposed by Democratic leaders Carl Albert and Hale Boggs. It was only the fifth bill in 20 years to be so treated.

Nixon Administration enters 5 cases. In line with President Nixon's new school desegregation policies, the Justice Department asked to intervene in five appeals against court-ordered busing—in Richmond, Va. March 31, Tennessee April 10, Dallas April 14, Oklahoma City April 27 and Fort Worth April 28.

In the Richmond case, in which U.S. District Court Judge Robert R. Merhige had ordered a merger of city and suburb school districts, the Justice Department asked the U.S. Court of Appeals for the 4th Circuit to accept a friend-of-the-court brief in the Richmond School Board's appeal since "the outcome of this case will affect" the government's desegregation "enforcement responsibilities."

In Tennessee, the Justice Department asked to intervene in an appeal by the Metropolitan County Board of Education of Nashville and Davidson County, filed in the U.S. Court of Appeals for the 6th Circuit in Cincinnati, of a federal district judge order, which required the busing of 28,000 additional students.

In the Dallas case, the Department asked the 5th U.S. Circuit Court of Appeals in New Orleans to consider the guidelines recommended by President Nixon's proposed Equal Educational Opportunities Act, which would bar any further elementary school busing for integration and use busing only as a last resort in other schools.

The department asked the 10th U.S. Circuit Court of Appeals in Denver to accept a brief in favor of the Oklahoma City School Board appeal of a federal district court order requiring increased busing. The brief asked the court either to delay a decision until the Supreme Court ruled on a similar Denver case, or to order the district court to reconsider whether some school segregation had been caused by changing neighborhood racial composition rather than by government discrimination.

In the Fort Worth case, the department asked to intervene in an appeal brought in the 5th U.S. Circuit Court of Appeals by black parents objecting to a federal district court desegregation plan.

Moratorium stays denied. In the first court test of the June antibusing provision, the only antibusing measure to win Congressional approval, stays of desegregation orders were denied later in 1972 for schools in Oxnard, Calif., Augusta, Ga., Las Vegas, Nev., Nashville, Tenn. and Oklahoma City, but granted for Chattanooga, Tenn.

The Ninth U.S. Circuit Court of Appeals in San Francisco rejected a plea Aug. 22 by the Oxnard school board and the Justice Department to suspend a busing plan begun in the 1971–72 school year. The court ruled that the new legislation could not be applied retroactively, despite Justice Department arguments that the moratorium was intended to apply in all cases in which appeals had not been exhausted.

Supreme Court Justice Lewis F. Powell refused Sept. 1 to stay a busing plan for Augusta, on the grounds that the bill applied only to orders issued for the purpose of achieving racial balance. The Augusta plan, he wrote, had been ordered to correct unlawful segregation. A Justice Department appeal Sept. 5 that the entire court provide an "immediate interpretation" of the law was rejected Sept. 8 by Chief Justice Warren E. Burger.

Justice William O. Douglas rejected a plea Sept. 12 by Las Vegas school officials, supported by Justice Department lawyers, to stay a busing plan. The schools involved in the plan, which clustered predominantly black and predominantly white schools, had remained closed during the appeal. Justice William Rehnquist had ruled in the Nashville and Oklahoma City cases that the amendment did not apply, according to the Washington Post Sept. 7.

In Chattanooga, U.S. District Court Judge Frank Wilson Jr. ordered a delay Aug. 11 of a busing order he had issued earlier for the lower grades, although leaving in effect a high school integration plan. Wilson said he did not think his order required "a racial balance," as specified in the bill, but approved the delay requested by the school board since he could not "ignore the popular use of the English language," which equated busing for desegregation with racial balance. The stay would remain in effect only during the 18-month lifetime of the bill.

Integration gains denied. A study of school integration programs involving busing in six Northern cities, reported May 21, 1972, found no improvement in academic achievement among black students or racial cooperation.

The study was conducted by Harvard University professor David J. Armor, and included programs in Boston, White Plains, N.Y., Ann Arbor, Mich., Riverside, Calif. and Hartford and New Haven, Conn. While no significant academic differences were found between black students bused and control groups which remained in ghetto schools, the first group tended to show declines in self-esteem and in educational and job aspirations. Armor recommended, however, that voluntary busing programs be continued, since the bussed students tended to get better opportunities for higher education.

Armor emphasized that his study involved only short-term effects, but wrote "it appears that integration increases racial identity and solidarity," and "at least in the case of black students, leads to increasing desires for separation."

Prince Georges busing starts. A busing desegregation plan involving 33,000 students was implemented without serious incident Jan. 29, 1973 in Prince Georges County, Md., as a boycott threatened by white parents' groups seemed to falter.

The plan had been ordered in 1972 by U.S. District Court Judge Frank A. Kaufman, who ruled that the county school board had failed to meet its constitutional requirements to desegregate the 162,000-student system. One-fourth of the system's students were black, concentrated in communities bordering on Washington.

The U.S. 4th Circuit Court of Appeals upheld the ruling Jan. 23, over an appeal by the county government, Gov. Marvin Mandel and the Justice Department. Chief Judge Clement Haynsworth called the case "routine" and "the same kind of case we had in the cases to the south of here." All six justices of the Supreme Court present in Washington Jan. 26 refused a plea for a stay.

The plan increased the percentage of students being bused from 48 to 56.

Majority vs. busing. The Gallup Poll reported Sept. 8, 1973 that while a large majority of the nation favored integration of public schools, only 5% (9% of the blacks and 4% of the whites) favored busing as a means of achieving integration.

Offered two alternative methods of integration, 27% of those polled favored changing school boundaries to allow persons from different economic and racial groups to attend the same schools, and 22% chose creation of more housing for low-income groups in middle-income neighborhoods. The poll found 18% (19% of the whites and 9% of the blacks) completely opposed to integration.

Other questions found that opposition to busing was based more on fears of infringement of personal liberties and higher school taxes than on racial animosities.

While only 27% of Northern white parents said they would object to sending their children to schools where as many as half the students were black, 63% said they would object if more than half the students were black. The latter figure was an increase from 51% in 1970. Corresponding figures for Southern white parents were 36% and 69%, the latter figure unchanged from 1970.

Supreme Court splits on district lines. In the first non-unanimous decision in a modern school desegregation case, the Supreme Court June 22, 1972 ruled, by 5–4, that the town of Emporia, Va. could not constitutionally remove its schools from the Greensville County school system, which had a higher percentage of blacks. All four Nixon appointees dissented, although they joined the majority in a companion case to prevent Scotland Neck, N.C. from leaving the Halifax County school system.

Writing for the majority, Justice Potter Stewart said the 4th U.S. Circuit Court of Appeals had erred in trying to determine the "dominant purpose" of Emporia in seceding from the county district. The appeals court had found that purpose to be educational quality and local control, but Stewart said "inquiry into the 'dominant motivation' of school authorities is as irrelevant as it is fruitless."

School desegregation decisions must be based, he wrote, "on whether actions by school units are effective in actually dismantling former dual school systems." Stewart supported the rule enunciated by the district court that originally invalidated Emporia's secession, that "a new school district mayn't be created where its effect would be to impede" desegregation.

Emporia had decided to operate its own school system in 1969, when the county was under a court order to "pair" its largely segregated schools to increase integration. The new Emporia district would have been 48% white, while the remaining rural schools would have been only 28% white, although each system would have been in itself integrated. A single Greensville County district would be 34% white.

Stewart said Emporia's action resulted in a situation in which "one of the two new systems is, in fact, 'white' and the other is, in fact, 'Negro,'" especially since the better equipped formerly all-white high schools were located in Emporia. He said the 1969 Emporia move, coming after 15 years of noncompliance with Supreme Court desegregation rulings, would have been a "message" to local blacks.

In the dissenting opinion, Chief Justice Warren Burger wrote "the goal is to dismantle dual school systems rather than to reproduce in each classroom a microcosmic reflection of the racial proportions of a given area." Once local authorities had eliminated segregation by establishing unitary districts, he wrote, judges should not impose their own plans merely to correct "discrepancies" in racial attendance ratios.

Burger said, however, that he might take a different view in districts facing desegregation "where ostensibly neutral attendance zones or district lines are drawn where none have existed before."

In a concurring opinion in the related North Carolina case, the chief justice, joined by his fellow dissenters in the Virginia case—Justices Lewis Powell, Harry Blackmun and William Rehnquist—explained that the apparent segregationist motives of Scotland Neck officials led him to invalidate their actions, as did the substantial difference in racial attendance figures. The Scotland Neck district would have been 57% white, while the unified Halifax County system was 22% white. A Halifax system without Scotland Neck would have been only 11% white, leading in Burger's opinion to the creation of too many all-black schools.

All nine judges joined in reversing the 4th Circuit Court in the case. The court's opinion stated that Scotland Neck would have become a "refuge" for whites.

The North Carolina legislature had passed special enabling legislation to permit the Scotland Neck withdrawal. The Department of Justice had intervened in both the Virginia and North Carolina cases on the side of the plaintiff black parents. Emporia and Scotland Neck officials both argued that countywide districts would merely drive white students into private schools, thereby increasing segregation, but none of the justices accepted the argument as a justification for avoiding desegregation.

Bias fund cuts ordered. A federal judge in Washington ordered the Department of Health, Education and Welfare (HEW) Feb. 16, 1973 to begin proceedings to deny federal funds to school districts and state college systems that had not complied with desegregation requirements.

U.S. District Court Judge John H. Pratt had ruled in November 1972 that HEW had violated the law in refraining from any fund cutoffs since early 1970. Pratt set timetables for HEW action in several categories of cases, and ordered the department to submit detailed progress reports every six months to the NAACP Legal Defense and Educational Fund, which had filed the suit. HEW was ordered within 120 days to begin cutoff procedures, which included notification of districts, hearings, and notification of Congress, against 10 states which operated racially segregated systems of higher education, and had either failed to submit desegregation plans or submitted plans rejected by HEW. Proceedings within 60 days were ordered for 74 school districts that had been found by HEW by 1970–71 to be out of compliance with submitted desegregation plans.

Sixty-day limits were set for 42 districts found by HEW in violation of a 1971 Supreme Court ruling by maintaining schools with "substantially disproportionate" racial ratios without justification, and for 85 other districts, which had not yet been required by HEW to justify disproportionate enrollments.

Pratt ordered HEW to begin "without unreasonable delay" an enforcement program in vocational schools and schools for the handicapped in 17 states, many of which the court found "obviously segregated."

HEW was ordered to begin monitoring 640 districts under court desegregation orders "to the extent that resources permit" and report the findings to the court involved. But Pratt agreed that HEW could not cut off funds for "continuing" programs during enforcement proceedings, and could not require repayment of funds granted during the proceedings.

Joseph L. Rauh Jr., one of the plaintiff's lawyers, said about three million students were involved in the cases under the court's order. The systems were scattered in Pennsylvania and 16 Southern and Border states.

Acting under the ruling, the HEW's Office for Civil Rights ordered 25 school districts in 12 states March 24 to submit new plans by April 10 that would "eliminate the vestiges of" their "former dual school systems" by the fall of 1973, and warned that failure to comply might lead to legal action and a cutoff of federal aid.

The civil rights office also requested 10 states to submit higher education desegregation plans by April 23, in accordance with the court order.

The court order was upheld June 12, 1973 by the Circuit Court of Appeals for the District of Columbia.

In upholding District Court Judge John H. Pratt's order as "unassailable," the court said HEW was "actively supplying segregated educational institutions with federal funds, contrary to the expressed purpose of Congress."

The only change in Pratt's order was to allow an additional 120 days for 10 state college systems to submit desegregation plans and another 180 days for HEW to initiate compliance procedures. The court noted the problems of statewide planning to provide minority access to college programs and cited a brief filed by a group of 110 Negro colleges asking for a delay in Pratt's order.

The more than 200 school districts affected were in Pennsylvania and 16 Southern and border states.

Northern schools warned. The Supreme Court ruled June 21, 1973 that Northern school systems with substantial areas of segregation would be treated the same way as had Southern school systems with de jure patterns of segregation.

In a case involving Denver, the court said school board policies that fostered segregation even in limited parts of a metropolitan area might affect the whole system, and the whole system required desegregation, "root and branch."

Black and Mexican-American parents had sued the Denver school board, charging it with the creation of segregated schools through manipulation of attendance zones, school site selection, and a neighborhood school policy.

Justice Rehnquist dissented, and White, a native Coloradan, did not participate.

The Denver ruling was the high court's first decision dealing with the question of de facto segregation. While the court stopped short of eliminating the distinction between de jure and de facto segregation, it said "proof of state-imposed segregation in a substantial portion of the district will suffice to support a finding by the trial court of the existence of a dual system. . . . Where the finding is made, as in cases involving statutory [de jure; Southern] dual systems, the school authorities have an affirmative duty to effectuate a transition to a racially nondiscriminatory school system."

The court ordered the case returned to the federal district court in Denver to allow Denver school authorities to prove they did not intend to provide racial separation.

Indianapolis orders. U.S. District Court Judge S. Hugh Dillin July 20, 1973 found the State of Indiana guilty of maintaining segregated school systems and ordered the state legislature to devise a permanent integration plan for the Indianapolis metropolitan area. For the 1973–74 school year, Judge Dillin ordered an interim plan under which almost 6,000 black students from Indianapolis would be bused to 18 suburban districts.

Judge Dillin said if the legislature did not act within a reasonable time, the court would devise its own plan.

Under the interim order, suburban districts were required to accept black students from the city in numbers equal to 5% of total enrollment. City schools were ordered to reassign pupils so that no school had less than 15% black enrollment. Dillin said schools in the metropolitan area should eventually reflect the 19.5% black enrollment in the area, but added that "perfect racial balance . . . is not required by law, and will not be ordered."

Dillin June 11 had rejected a final desegregation plan submitted by the Indianapolis school board to integrate the city's schools without involving suburban districts. Dillin's decision set the stage for trial of a suit, filed by the National Association for the Advancement of Colored People, seeking a merger of the 95,000-pupil Indianapolis system with the schools of 19 suburban counties.

Dillin Aug. 1, 1975 ordered the transfer of 6,533 black Indianapolis pupils to eight suburban school systems that he said had "consistently resisted the movement of black citizens or black pupils into their territory." A desegregation plan that was confined to the city system would only prompt the flight of more whites to the suburbs and was undesirable, he said.

Dillin's order called for the one way busing of students from the Indianapolis system, which was 42% black, to achieve a black student population of about 15% during the next three years in all suburban districts.

The eight suburban districts, all autonomous corporations, were located within the civil city boundaries of Indianapolis. Although the Indianapolis city government was merged with the Marian County government in 1970, school boundaries and taxing authorities were left intact.

Dillin also enjoined the Indianapolis City Housing Authority from building any additional public housing within the boundaries of the Indianapolis Public Schools System.

The 7th U.S. Circuit Court of Appeals upheld Dillin's order in July 1976. It found Indianapolis and the state of Indiana in violation of the 14th Amendment, which guaranteed equal protection of the law. The appeals court cited the "confinement" of public housing to the city as one violation and an aspect of a 1969 Indiana law as another. The law, called Uni-Gov, had consolidated all parts of the Indianapolis and Marion County governments except their school districts. (The proponents of Uni-Gov had argued that a consolidated school district would be too large for citizens to control and would raise taxes.)

The appeals court ruling was vacated Jan. 25, 1977 by a 6–3 Supreme Court decision.

The Justice Department, the suburban school districts in question and others had asked the Supreme Court to review the appellate decision.

The Supreme Court overturned the appeals court, ruling that proof of intent was necessary to demonstrate a constitutional violation in racial discrimination cases. Justices Thurgood Marshall, William J. Brennan Jr. and John Paul Stevens dissented without comment.

College & University Problems

Wellesley rejects coed plan. Wellesley College announced April 16, 1971 that its trustees had rejected a plan to admit men as degree candidates. The plan was a recommendation of a Commission on the Future of the College, whose members had been appointed by the trustees.

The trustees, however, reaffirmed support for a cross-registration program with Massachusetts Institute of Technology and for student exchange programs with 11 colleges.

Seminary for more minorities & women. Union Theological Seminary's board voted May 31, 1972 to require that ratios at the seminary for all students, faculty, staff and directors be one-third black and representatives of other minority groups and one-half be women.

Mrs. Beverly Harrison, a seminary professor and head of the planning group which proposed the change, acknowledged that the seminary would have initial difficulty in placing 50 women graduates a year.

Jews denounce quotas. The leaders of two major Jewish civil rights organizations criticized the use of preferential quotas for admission and employment of minority group members by educational institutions. The remarks were made June 29, 1972 in speeches before the National Jewish Community Relations Advisory Council.

Benjamin R. Epstein, national director of the Anti-Defamation League of B'nai B'rith, asked the Department of Health, Education and Welfare to revise its guidelines and discourage "preferential treatment" for some minority groups, which Epstein said resulted in discrimination against other qualified individuals. He suggested expansion of university facilities as part of affirmative action programs to rectify past discrimination.

Naomi Levine, acting executive director of the American Jewish Congress, said universities had violated the law by setting "fixed quotas" to protect "sorely needed federal funds," while the law only required "good faith efforts" to reach attendance and employment goals. The council approved a resolution supporting "specific goals and timetables not determined by population percentages" as long as no "rigid requirements" were set.

In early 1973, six national Jewish organizations sent 19 cases of alleged discrimination in hiring or admissions by colleges against white males to the Office for Civil Rights, which they urged to "prevent or eliminate preferential treatment."

The groups, it was reported Jan. 14, said the cases, which they added to 33 other examples previously submitted, usually reflected "college and university policy." They cited new guidelines issued by the Department of Health, Education and Welfare in 1971 in response to an earlier complaint as the basis for action to correct the alleged violations.

The groups were the Anti-Defamation League of B'nai B'rith, the American Jewish Committee, the American Jewish Congress, the Jewish War Veterans, the Jewish Labor Committee and Agudath Israel of America.

College integration plans rejected. The Department of Health, Education and Welfare Nov. 13, 1973 rejected public college desegregation plans that had been filed by nine states in compliance with a federal court order upholding HEW's right to withhold aid from segregated systems.

The states—Arkansas, Florida, Georgia, Louisiana, Mississippi, North Carolina, Oklahoma, Pennsylvania and Virginia—were given 90 days to submit revised plans.

Louisiana and Mississippi submitted documents, HEW said, which asserted that the states were already in compliance with integration orders. The other seven states, according to HEW, had failed to be specific enough in their proposals as to costs, the extent of minority involvement in preparing the plans and means for upgrading black colleges to attract whites. Maryland, the 10th state affected by the court order, had filed a partial plan which HEW said indicated a "positive and constructive" approach to desegregation.

(Louisiana filed suit in Baton Rouge Dec. 10, charging HEW with issuing "unsound" and "ill-conceived" desegregation orders which exceeded federal guidelines. Gov. Edwin W. Edwards (D) had said June 8 he would defy the order to desegregate predominantly black Grambling College and Southern University and accept a cutoff of federal funds, rather than

"make a chocolate milk facility" out of the state's universities. He said both blacks and whites favored maintaining the current status of Southern and Grambling.)

Revisions accepted—After revisions were submitted by most state college systems whose proposals had been found unacceptable, HEW June 21, 1974 accepted desegregation plans for state-controlled colleges submitted by eight of 10 states faced with a cutoff of federal funds because of failure to comply with HEW guidelines.

The eight states filing "acceptable" plans were Arkansas, Florida, Georgia, Maryland, North Carolina, Oklahoma, Pennsylvania and Virginia. Mississippi submitted a "good" plan for its four-year colleges but refused to comply for the two-year institutions.

HEW officials said a major goal of the plans was the upgrading of faculty and course offerings in predominantly black schools to make them attractive to all races, rather than elimination of the schools.

Employment Bias Policy

Job rights bill passed. A bill to give the Equal Employment Opportunity Commission (EEOC) power to seek court enforcement of its findings of job discrimination and to expand its jurisdiction was approved by the Senate March 6, 1972 by 62–10 vote and by the House March 8 by 303–110 vote. President Nixon signed it March 24.

The bill as approved by a Senate-House conference Feb. 29 followed the more liberal Senate version in extending EEOC coverage to 10.1 million state and local government workers, all employes of public and private educational institutions and all companies and unions with at least 15 workers, instead of the previous minimum of 25.

Two House provisions were dropped that would have curbed class action suits and made the EEOC the only federal agency with job bias authority.

The conferees gave the EEOC, rather than the Justice Department, power to bring suits against a "pattern and practice" of union or employer bias. An independent EEOC general counsel was provided for, appointed by the President and subject to Senate confirmation, but acting only under orders of the commission.

Debate on quotas. Administration leaders denied Sept. 3–7, 1972 that they were planning to drop the Philadelphia Plan designed to increase minority employes on federal construction projects.

Nevertheless, the Labor Department said that the programs were undergoing reviews in light of President Nixon's statements opposing job quotas for minority groups.

The New York Times reported Sept. 3 that Arthur A. Fletcher, former assistant secretary of labor, and others who were still in the Labor Department had said the Philadelphia Plan would be dropped, partly to attract support from union members who had opposed the plan. The plan, begun in 1969, required building contractors in the Philadelphia area to set percentage goals for minority employment, ranging up to 26% by 1973.

About 55 other cities had adopted similar programs, often called "home town" plans, geared to the minority proportion of the general population, although all but four had been voluntarily adopted. Contractor associations and labor unions had frequently opposed the plans, while civil rights groups charged lax federal enforcement.

Labor Secretary James D. Hodgson said in a Sept. 3 statement that no decision had been made to drop the program, although all programs that might involve quotas "were being reviewed." He denied that the Philadelphia Plan was a "quota system." He called it a system of "goals and timetables," which contractors must make a "good-faith effort" to achieve. White House Press Secretary Ronald Ziegler made the same distinction Sept. 4, and said the Times story was "without substance."

Secretary of Health, Education and Welfare (HEW) Elliot L. Richardson reinforced the denial Sept. 7. He said a team of Labor and HEW experts would be sent to Philadelphia to review recent progress. But the Sept. 5 Wall Street Journal cited one Labor Department official as saying that since "it's possible

to apply" goals and timetables "in a quota form," all programs of the Office of Federal Contract Compliance, which administers the plan, would be reviewed.

Nixon had stated his opposition to job quotas in an Aug. 11 letter to the American Jewish Committee (AJC), in his Presidential nomination acceptance speech at the Republican National Convention and in a Labor Day speech Sept. 3, in which he called quotas "a dangerous detour away from the traditional value of measuring a person on the basis of ability." Democratic presidential candidate George McGovern, in an Aug. 14 letter to the AJC, had also opposed quotas as "detrimental to American society."

In an Aug. 18 letter released Aug. 24 Nixon had ordered all executive departments not to interpret minority job goals as quotas.

Civil rights groups charged that a memorandum dated Sept. 15 from Labor Secretary James D. Hodgson to "all heads of agencies" in the federal government had nullified minority hiring plans.

The memo stated that the Office of Federal Contract Compliance did not require "quotas or proportional representation" of minorities, although "the goals required of government contractors" may have been "misinterpreted or misapplied." Hodgson said the goals were merely "targets," and failure to reach them "is not to be regarded as, per se, a violation."

In a Sept. 25 NAACP-NOW conference, Herbert Hill, NAACP labor director, said the memo implied abandonment of the Philadelphia Plan and similar programs, since it removes the "major standard for measuring good-faith efforts in all previous minority hiring plans." He charged that the Administration "retreat" on the issue was "in large part, part of a political payoff to the AFL-CIO" for its neutrality in the presidential election.

Hill criticized the Administration, contractors and building trades unions for hindering enforcement of the Philadelphia Plan, the first federal minority hiring agreement, but admitted that more blacks were employed in the Philadelphia building trades than when the plan was begun in 1969, and said it should be retained.

Secretary of Housing and Urban Development George Romney Sept. 28 ordered a Philadelphia construction contractor barred from further federal building work after determining that the firm, Russell Associates, had not complied with provisions of the plan. The firm had held a $225,000 plumbing contract on a 1970–71 housing project, and was the third company to be debarred under the plan.

New Chicago job plan. Nine Chicago building contractor associations and 15 building trades unions signed a voluntary agreement to employ 9,820 additional minority workers by 1976, with specific yearly hiring goals for each trade, the Labor Department announced Oct. 18, 1972. (But the plan failed within a year.)

The Chicago Urban League was to run a $1.7 million recruitment and training program with funds supplied by the Labor Department's Manpower Administration. But no minority representatives actually signed the agreement, a reflection of disputes in some of the 52 minority hiring plans in the country over who would represent minority groups.

Donald M. Irwin, Chicago regional director for the Labor Department, called the plan "the most extensive" ever signed. The participating unions had current memberships of 41,000. Irwin said locals of roofers and ironworkers, which had not signed the plan, would be restricted in bidding for federal contracts.

An earlier Chicago plan, begun in 1970 but which had placed only 150 minority workers by May 1971, was disbanded at that time, when its director, Fred Hubbard, disappeared. Hubbard was arrested in Los Angeles in September and charged with embezzling $100,-000.

The 1972 plan also collapsed, on Oct. 18, 1973, when the Labor Department finally announced it was withdrawing support because of poor performance.

Conceding that Chicago was "just not susceptible to a voluntary solution," the department noted that only about 200 minority workers had been hired under a first-year federal grant of $1.7 million, compared with a goal of training and qualifying 1,700 such workers. The Chicago Urban League, which had administered the program, accused both unions and contractors of intransigence.

The Labor Department's announcement that it would impose its own hiring plan was greeted with skepticism by Herbert Hill, labor director of the National Association for the Advancement of Colored People, who said compulsory plans in other cities had "invariably" been based on "less than what the law requires."

The Labor Department announced Dec. 20 that it had imposed its Chicago plan.

The plan set "goals and timetables" and provided penalties of contract cancellations and ineligibility for future contracts if companies failed to demonstrate "good faith" efforts to comply.

'Good faith' job plan set. Representatives of construction employers and unions and minority groups signed a three-year pact April 6, 1973 to make a "good faith effort" to achieve 6% black membership in each local construction union in New York's Nassau and Suffolk Counties.

It was the first "hometown plan" to be approved by the Office of Federal Contract Compliance of the U.S. Department of Labor since President Nixon emphatically rejected the "quota" concept of minority job advancement in 1972

The plan had been delayed for nine months because of Administration insistence that the phrase "good faith effort" be inserted before mention of the 6% goal. The agreement could be canceled after each year, 60—90 days after written notification by any of the participant groups.

Delta job pact approved. An anti-discrimination agreement between the federal government and Delta Air Lines was approved by Federal District Court Judge Charles A. Moye in Atlanta, it was reported May 3, 1973. The consent order followed a suit filed April 16 by the Departments of Justice and Labor.

The agreement, effective for five years, would allow women and minority employes the opportunity to transfer to higher level jobs, held predominantly by white males. Delta said such applicants would be allowed to transfer only if qualified and when positions were actually open.

Under terms of the pact, the first 1,000 persons transferred would be eligible for $200–$1,000 in back pay based on job classification and $100 for each year of employment.

LBJ asks compensatory aid. Former President Lyndon B. Johnson told a two-day civil rights symposium in Austin, Tex. Dec. 12, 1972 that compensatory programs would be needed to enable blacks and other minorities to "overcome unequal opportunity."

The symposium was sponsored by the Lyndon Baines Johnson Library and the University of Texas to celebrate the public availability of the Johnson civil rights papers, and attracted several hundred black and white civil rights leaders.

Johnson criticized the "language of evasion" that labeled programs to enhance equal opportunity as special consideration for some groups. He said "to be black in a white society is not to stand on level ground." Although he conceded that "individuals and groups who had struggled long to gain advantages for themselves do not easily yield the gains," he warned whites that "no advantage is safe, no gain is secure in this society unless those advantages and gains are open to all alike."

Johnson called for more scholarships for minority youths, more minority labor union trainees, and a greater effort by businessmen and professionals "to make certain that blacks qualify for advancement up the promotion ladder."

U.S. unit scores Administration. The U.S. Commission on Civil Rights charged in the fourth of a series of reports to Congress Feb. 9, 1973 that most federal agencies were failing to enforce adequately the nation's civil rights laws, and lacked commitment or leadership to change the situation.

The commission laid much of the responsibility for the government's poor record on a lack of "Presidential leadership." It predicted that without such leadership "a steady erosion of the progress toward equal rights" would take place, because of the historically crucial role of the President as a moral and political leader. The Administration had "no government-wide plan for civil rights enforcement," the report charged, and even agencies with related civil rights responsibilities, such as the Civil Service Commission, the Equal Employment Opportunity Commission (EEOC) and the Office of Federal Contract Compliance (OFCC), did not work together effectively.

The 425-page report by the independent, Congressionally created agency was the last prepared under the direction of the Rev. Theodore M. Hesburgh, who had resigned in November 1972.

Even when civil rights agencies recognized their duties and initiated action, the report said, "enforcement proceeds at a snail's pace." The commission warned that "the long-term stability of this nation demands an end to discrimination."

With respect to school integration, the report said the Administration's decision to stop the cutoff of funds for uncooperative districts in favor of voluntary negotiations had not brought greater compliance, especially since the Department of Health, Education and Welfare (HEW) did not require the use of "all available techniques" of desegregation, including "transportation." In addition, there had been "virtually no effort to prevent the flow of federal funds to non-public schools which are enjoying in discriminatory practices," or to end tax exemptions for them.

In the job rights area, the report charged the OFCC had been downgraded. It said the agency had "no adequate procedures to resolve compliance problems" on hiring agreements with contractors. The EEOC, while it had made "potentially effective" procedural changes, had an ever-growing backlog of complaints, expected to reach 70,000 by June, 1973, and assigned low priority to enforcing agreements. The Civil Service Commission, while it had "improved" its complaint handling mechanisms and now required federal agencies to adopt hiring goals and timetables, had failed to change the "pronounced disparate treatment" of minority employes in federal departments. Though minorities constituted 15.2% of federal employes in 1972, up from 14.7% in 1970, they still made up less than 3% of those in policy-making positions, the report said.

The Department of Housing and Urban Development was praised for new regulations requiring affirmative action to assure minorities access to new projects before they were approved, but the report said the rules had not been applied to existing projects despite evidence of extensive segregation.

Most regulatory agencies, the report charged, continued "to deny the full scope of their civil rights responsibilities." Despite an opinion by the Justice Department that the Federal Power Commission had authority to enforce fair hiring practices in the power industry, the commission said, the agency refused to take action, as had the Interstate Commerce Commission. The Federal Communications Commission had failed to enforce fully the hiring plans submitted by broadcasters, while the agencies responsible for the financial community had not even begun "to collect racial and ethnic data," including the Federal Reserve Board, the Comptroller of the Currency, the Federal Deposit Insurance Corporation and the Federal Home Loan Bank Board." The Civil Aeronautics Board and the Securities and Exchange Commission were also criticized, as were the Interior Department, the Law Enforcement Assistance Administration and the Civil Rights Offices of the Departments of Justice and HEW.

Some progress was noted in the Office of Management and Budget, the Department of Agriculture, and HEW, which the Commission praised for conducting special studies on health and social services.

EEOC charges company, union bias. The Equal Employment Opportunity Commission (EEOC) notified four large corporations and several major unions that charges of job discrimination on the basis of race, sex and national origin had been filed against them, it was reported Sept. 18, 1973. This move was intended as warning that EEOC intended to require affirmative action of those notified.

Since the filing was only the first step in the EEOC's conciliation and investigation process, it was legally prohibited from revealing the names of those charged. But news reports (later confirmed by the companies and unions) identified the firms as General Motors Corp., Ford Motor Co., General Electric Co. and Sears, Roebuck & Co. The unions identified included the United Auto Workers, the United Electrical Workers and the International Union of Electrical, Radio and Machine Workers. (The National Electrical Contractors Association and the International Brotherhood of Electrical Workers confirmed Sept. 20 that they had been notified by the EEOC of similar charges.)

A commission spokesman said that if the preliminary out-of-court negotiations failed to resolve the issues, the complaints could be taken to court. The commission was reportedly seeking a settlement along the lines of the one reached earlier in 1973 with the American Telephone & Telegraph Co.

The action was the first taken by the EEOC's new National Programs Division, which was created to deal with discrimination cases involving large numbers of workers on a company-wide basis. The charges involved wages, benefits, terms and conditions of employment, promotion, training and testing programs, layoff and seniority procedures.

The companies and unions reacted to the charges with surprise, and a spokesman for the United Electrical Workers noted that his union had been trying to get the EEOC to "end its lethargy and enforce the anti-discrimination laws."

Herbert Hill, labor director for the National Association for the Advancement of Colored People, said his organization had previously filed complaints with the EEOC against the four companies. Hill called the commission's action significant because it recognized that discrimination was not merely "random acts of bigotry" but part of "broad patterns that are codified in collective bargaining agreements."

Xerox, others sued—The EEOC announced Aug. 29 that it had filed a suit charging the Xerox Corp. with engaging in "policies which exclude Spanish-surnamed persons from employment" in California. The suit asked for a permanent injunction against the company to prevent discrimination based on national origin.

Two other suits announced Aug. 29 accused Avondale Shipyards Inc. of New Orleans and the Red Arrow Corp., a St. Louis trucking company, of job discrimination against blacks.

The commission had announced July 19 its first suit against a television station. WREC-TV in Memphis, owned by the New York Times, was accused of discriminating against women and blacks in hiring, recruiting and job classification. Another suit announced the same day accused the Seattle Post-Intelligencer—a Hearst Corp. newspaper—and locals of the Newspaper Guild and the International Typographical Union of discrimination against blacks in hiring and apprenticeship programs, against women by hours restrictions and pregnancy-leave policies, and against men by denying them lounges and rest periods, which were provided for female employes.

PUSH for 15% commitment. People United to Save Humanity (PUSH), a black civil rights organization, began a drive Dec. 30, 1972 for agreements with Miami Beach hotels to hire blacks to fill 15% of their jobs, and to give 15% of their bank, laundry and other service business to black-owned businesses.

PUSH had held the fourth annual Black Expo in Chicago Sept. 27–31.

The exposition of black business and cultural efforts drew over 700,000 visitors and grossed about $500,000 to help PUSH's economic programs.

PUSH leader Rev. Jesse L. Jackson, according to a Sept. 27 report, said the group's boycott and picketing tactics had obtained over $100 million in concessions from major corporations and banks in the form of hiring and promotion, deposits in black banks and contracts with black suppliers. Some 500 companies, black and white, exhibited.

Amex job plan. The American Stock Exchange (Amex) announced in New York Jan. 15, 1973 that it was preparing an affirmative action program to recruit and upgrade women and minority group members at Amex, and urged the Securities and Exchange Commission to develop equal employment programs in the entire securities industry.

Government Employment

Nixon bans job quotas. President Nixon banned minority employment hiring quotas in the federal government Aug. 24, 1972.

The order, transmitted by Civil Service Commission (CSC) chairman Robert Hampton, was in response to a letter sent Aug. 4 by the American Jewish Committee (AJC) to President Nixon and Democratic presidential nominee George McGovern expressing concern over the use of job quotas.

Hyman Bookbinder of the AJC said Aug. 25 that quotas had become "particularly serious in our government education programs." Bookbinder said the AJC's position was not intended to "mean we should reduce efforts to increase the number of blacks, women and Chicanos [in jobs]. But we mustn't do it on a quota basis."

The CSC had asserted that no quota practices existed, but according to the Washington Post Aug. 25, the government's "affirmative action" hiring programs were, in effect, de facto quota systems.

In his reply to the AJC, McGovern also opposed the use of quotas; however, he had also often promised jobs to blacks in his administration in proportion to their number in the population, the Post said.

Blacks gain in top U.S. jobs—The Civil Service Commission said Dec. 18 that a survey of government workers taken in May showed that the number of blacks and other minority group members in general schedule grades 12–18, earning $15,000–$36,000 a year, had increased 12.5% over a year earlier, and that minority group members had accounted for about 25% of the increase in personnel in those grades. But the nearly 16,000 high-level minority workers still accounted for only 5% of the work force in those grades.

Overall, blacks, Spanish-surnamed people, Orientals and Indians held 505,-568 federal jobs as of May 31, 19.6% of the total.

Irrigation job order—A U.S. district court judge in San Diego ordered Sept. 8 that the Imperial Irrigation District hire blacks or Mexican-Americans to fill two-thirds of all new vacancies until the minority proportion of the district work force, then 15.2%, rose to the minority percentage of the Imperial County population, 49.5. According to California Rural Legal Assistance, which had filed the suit, the two-thirds hiring ratio was the highest ever ordered by a federal judge.

EEOC aide charges bias. A white senior investigator in the Equal Employment Opportunity Commission's (EEOC) New York district resigned June 5, 1972 after filing formal charges that EEOC "discriminates in favor of Negroes and Spanish-surnamed Americans in hiring, promotion and terms and conditions of employment."

Carl Shiffman, who had worked for two years at the EEOC, said he had been denied a promotion because he was white and Jewish, and because he had opposed the firing of another white employe who had made similar charges in 1971.

EEOC guilty of bias—U.S. District Court Judge Gerhard Gesell ruled in Washington Sept. 23, 1975 that the EEOC had discriminated against George Rogers, a black who was deputy director of the EEOC's district office in Philadelphia.

Rogers had charged that he had been passed over for promotion to director because of race. The commission countered that even if race had been considered in the selection, Rogers had not been the best qualified candidate for the job.

Gesell ruled that since "race played a part" in the hiring decision, it was enough to "taint" the selection.

Indian preference. Supreme Court Justice Thurgood Marshall Aug. 16, 1973 stayed a lower court ruling which had nullified employment preference for Indians in the BIA. A federal district court in Albuquerque, N.M. had ruled June 1 that the policy violated U.S. civil rights laws.

Marshall issued the stay at the request of the government, which said the bureau was caught between conflicting court rulings and faced contempt citations no matter which choice was made between Indian and non-Indian job applicants.

Women & government jobs. President Nixon reported April 28, 1972 that the number of women in federal policy making jobs earning over $28,000 had risen from 36 in April 1971 to 105 currently. Over 1,000 additional women held middle management positions earnings $17,700–$24,200 a year.

In a Washington news conference the same day, Civil Service Commission Vice Chairman Jayne Baker Spain, who helped direct the Administration's recruitment effort among women, said progress had been hindered by the science or mathematics training requirements for 60% of middle and high level federal jobs.

The Organization for Women of the Social Security Administration had filed suit March 14 in U.S. District Court in Baltimore charging that "highly qualified women" were "ignored and discounted" by the agency, and that the agency's promotional plan was not being carried out.

Organizations representing women scientists filed suit in U.S. District Court in Washington March 28 against Robert Marston, director of the National Institutes of Health (NIH), and Elliot Richardson, secretary of Health, Education & Welfare (HEW), charging discrimination against women in appointments to NIH advisory panels that controlled $2 billion annually in research and training funds.

Richardson had ordered in September 1971 that one third of all such posts be filled by women. However, according to Sylvia Roberts, attorney for the plaintiffs, the order exempted "technical panels" from the requirement. Roberts said March 28 that the proportion of women on all advisory panels had dropped from 5.4% to 4.2% between 1968 and 1971.

The plaintiffs included the Association for Women in Science, The Association of Women in Psychology, Caucus of Women Biophysicists, Sociologists for Women in Society, Association for Women in Mathematics, National Organization for Women and Women's Equity Action League.

Richardson Jan. 14 had issued a report prepared by HEW's Women's Action Program. He pledged to enforce over 100 recommendations for reform of HEW's employment practices and its social programs affecting the role of women.

Richardson ordered top assistants to establish timetables for implementation. Upgrading and counseling services would be provided for female HEW employes, while part time jobs and day care arrangements would be provided for working HEW mothers.

Legislation was recommended to bar sex discrimination in vocational education supported by HEW. Currently, men were given preference in some state-run programs.

Wilma Scott Heide, president of the National Organization for Women, said Jan. 13 she doubted Richardson's commitment to enforce the report, and charged collusion between HEW and universities to delay enforcement of women's job rights.

NASA bias charged. Ruth Bates Harris, deputy assistant director for equal employment in the National Aeronautics & Space Administration (NASA), was dismissed effective Oct. 26, 1973 after meetings with NASA Administrator James C. Fletcher, during which Mrs. Harris—a black—had reportedly relayed complaints that the agency had been lagging in hiring women and minorities.

Mrs. Harris' office had submitted a report to Fletcher Sept. 20 charging that minority and female employment at NASA had increased only from 4.1% in 1966 to 5.1% in June 1973, the lowest percentage among federal agencies. NASA had never given priority to equal employment, the report said, adding that the agency's middle management was "insensitive" to the problem.

Dudley G. McConnell, Mrs. Harris' immediate superior (whose replacement had been called for in the report), said Oct. 28 that Mrs. Harris had been dismissed not because of the critical report but because of "differences of opinion" on NASA programs.

Fletcher told the Senate Aeronautical and Space Sciences Committee Oct. 30 that Mrs. Harris had been fired because of "discord" in the equal employment office.

Mrs. Harris was reported Aug. 18, 1974 to have been rehired by NASA to a different position at a higher salary.

Mrs. Harris' new post was deputy assistant administrator for community and human relations; the position from which she had been dismissed carried the same rank in NASA's equal employment programs. The complaint she had filed with the Civil Service Commission had not yet been ruled on.

Sen. William Proxmire (D, Wis.), chairman of the Appropriations subcommittee for NASA funds, had ordered NASA Jan. 11 to double the 1975 budget of its equal employment office and to report to the subcommittee every three months on progress in hiring minorities and women.

NASA documents revealed that the agency had also failed to act against project contractors which had not met minority hiring goals.

U.S. sues 2 cities. The Justice Department, citing provisions of the 1972 Equal Employment Opportunity Act, filed civil suits Aug. 7, 1972 against government agencies in Montgomery, Ala. and Los Angeles charging them with racial discrimination in hiring for public jobs.

(A consent decree was filed in the Montgomery case Oct. 3, and the department reported Jan. 24, 1973 that the suit had thus been resolved. The Los Angeles case brought a consent decree June 27, 1974.)

The suits marked the first time the department had initiated action against state or local government agencies under the 1972 employment act.

In the Montgomery suit, filed in U.S. district court in Montgomery, the Justice Department accused the city, its water department, sanitary sewer board and the city-county personnel board of giving some black workers lower-paying job classifications even though they performed the same work as higher-paid whites.

The Los Angeles Fire Department was accused of pursuing "policies and practices that discriminate against black, Mexican-American and Oriental applicants for employment."

Policemen & firemen: *Alabama*—U.S. District Court Judge Frank M. Johnson Jr. Feb. 7, 1972 ordered Alabama's Department of Public Safety to hire an equal number of whites and blacks until 25% of personnel were black, roughly the proportion of blacks in the state population.

None of the 644 state policemen were black. Johnson charged that discrimination had been practiced, but left it up to the state to find the qualified blacks.

The suit had been brought by the National Association for the Advancement of Colored People.

(An Associated Press survey reported Feb. 1 found only 27 blacks among 5,000 state police personnel in eight Southeastern states. Alabama and Mississippi had none, Georgia and Florida two each, South Carolina and Louisiana four each, Tennessee six and North Carolina nine.)

Johnson's ruling was upheld April 19, 1974 by the U.S. 5th Circuit Court of Appeals.

Department Director C. E. Dothard said that within the next month 25 blacks will have joined the 625-man force, bringing black representation to 4%. Blacks already made up 23% of the department's support personnel, Dothard said.

The Supreme Court June 27, 1977 invalidated, by 8 to 1, an Alabama law setting minimum height and weight standards for the state's corrections officers (5 feet, 2 inches and 120 pounds). These standards were found in violation of Title VII of the 1964 Civil Rights Act because they automatically disqualified 40% of the state's women and only 1% of its men. Justice Byron R. White dissented.

Pennsylvania—A federal district court judge in Philadelphia May 26, 1972 ordered the city's police department to hire at least one black policeman for each two whites added to the force during the next five weeks.

The order by Judge John P. Fullam applied until July 1, pending further orders in a suit charging the city with racial bias in hiring and promoting black policemen. The suit before Fullam's court was filed in December 1970 by the state of Pennsylvania and several individual blacks as a class action against the city, the mayor, the police chief and other officials.

In his pretrial directive, Fullam instructed Philadelphia police officials to fill only police vacancies that existed before March 1, 1972.

Fullman continued his order July 8 and extended it to include promotions.

Ohio—A U.S. district court judge ruled that Cleveland could hire 188 policemen to replace transferred personnel, but must reserve 18% of the places for blacks or individuals with Spanish surnames, it was reported Dec. 23, 1972.

Connecticut—Federal District Court Judge Jon O. Newman Jan. 29, 1973 ordered Bridgeport, Conn. to hire blacks and Puerto Ricans to fill half the vacancies in the police force until they constituted 15% of the force.

Newman said the city's Civil Service Examination denied equal protection of the law to minority groups. Only 14 blacks and three Peurto Ricans were on the 485-member force, though the groups constituted 25% of the city's population. All future job tests would be submitted to the court for approval.

Newman also set minority hiring quotas for detective, sergeant, lieutenant and captain positions over the next two years.

California—Four civil rights organizations March 13, 1973 filed a complaint with California's state Fair Employment Practices Commission against the state's 28 largest cities, charging job bias against blacks and Spanish-surnamed people in police and fire departments.

The organizations said the two groups constituted 27% of the cities' population, but only 9% of the police and 5% of the firemen. They asked the commission to order population parity in the positions by 1977, to open up about 8,000 jobs.

Complainants were the National Association for the Advancement of Colored People, the League of United Latin-American Citizens, the American GI Forum and the Mexican-American Political Association.

In two rulings reported Dec. 2, federal district judges in San Francisco ordered quota systems for the employment of minorities in the city's police and fire departments.

Concerning the police department, Judge Robert F. Peckham ordered that three minority persons (defined by Peckham as "blacks, Latinos and Asians") be hired for every two whites at the level of patrolman until minority representation reached 30%. A one-to-one ratio in appointments to the rank of sergeant was to be in effect until 30% of that rank were from minorities.

Peckham also enjoined the city's Civil Service Commission from using a hiring and promotion test which he said was discriminatory. He ordered future tests submitted to him for approval.

The city's fire department was ordered by Judge William T. Sweigert to fill half of more than 200 vacancies with members of racial minorities.

The U.S. Department of Justice June 27, 1974 obtained a consent decree requiring percentage quotas for minority hiring in the Los Angeles fire department and requiring a recruiting program which would emphasize that women would be eligible for employment. The city also agreed to replace the term "fireman" with "firefighter."

The agreement provided a long-range goal of hiring racial minorities in proportion to their representation in the city's civilian labor force. To meet the goal, the city agreed that, beginning July 1, 50% of appointments as firefighters would be from black, Mexican-American and Asian-American applicants. The agreement also included a court injunction forbidding discrimination against employees already hired.

The department noted that when a suit was filed against the city in 1972, 1.5% of 3,150 firefighters were black, 3% were Mexican-American, and none were Asian-American.

The department June 2, 1977 charged the Los Angeles Police Department with discriminating against women, blacks and Spanish-surnamed Americans in its hiring practices. The civil rights suit followed 18 months of unsuccessful negotiations between the police and the Law Enforcement Assistance Administration, whose annual $4.8-million subsidy to the Los Angeles department was threatened by the legal action.

The Justice Department reported that as of December 31, 1976, the 7,383-member force was 2.2% female, 5.9% black and 8.8% Hispanic.

The U.S. Supreme Court ruled, 5 to 4, March 27, 1979, that a race discrimination suit against the Los Angeles Fire Department had become moot due to changes in the situation that had led to the suit. At the same time, the justices threw out a hiring quota imposed by a lower federal court without deciding the question of whether the court had the power to impose the quota.

Chief Justice Warren E. Burger and Justice Lewis F. Powell Jr. dissented, calling the majority's finding of mootness "a questionable means of avoiding" the issues of the case. Justice Potter Stewart and William H. Rehnquist argued in a separate dissent that the case should have been sent back to the lower court "with directions to narrow the scope of the remedy substantially." The case was *Los Angeles v. Davis.*

Illinois—The U.S. Department of Justice March 15, 1973 filed a civil suit in federal district court in Chicago, charging that the city had discriminated against blacks and Spanish surnamed persons in hiring and promoting firemen.

The department noted that only 4% of Chicago's 5,000 firemen were black and only .5% Puerto Rican or Mexican-American, although 32% of the city's people were black and 11% had Spanish surnames. The suit sought a change in hiring practices, including elimination of allegedly unnecessary and discriminatory hiring and promotion tests, a recruitment program and compensation for past discrimination.

In suits filed Aug. 14, the department accused the police departments of both Chicago and Buffalo, N.Y. of bias against blacks, women and Spanish-surnamed persons in employment opportunities and conditions of employment.

The Chicago suit was the fist brought by the Justice Department under the antibias regulations of the department's Law Enforcement Assistance Administration, which had made fund grants to the Chicago police.

Both suits charged that the proportion of minorities employed by the police was far below the minority percentages of the cities' population. The suits sought recruitment programs for minorities and women, hiring of applicants in sufficient numbers to offset past discrimination and compensation for those who had been unlawfully denied employment.

U.S. District Judge John Lewis Smith Jr. Dec. 18, 1974 ordered the Treasury Department's Revenue Sharing Office to halt its revenue sharing payments to Chicago until the city took affirmative action to end racial discrimination in its police department. The action followed a finding Nov. 7 by Federal Judge Prentice Marshall that the Chicago police department's hiring, promotion and personnel practices discriminated against blacks and women.

Judge Smith, who issued his decision in Washington, was acting on a suit by two civil rights groups, the Chicago branch of the National Association for the Advancement of Colored People (NAACP) and the Afro-American Patrolmen's League of Chicago. The plaintiffs charged the police department with discriminatory hiring practices and asserted that the city violated the law by using revenue-sharing funds for the department.

Meanwhile, Judge Marshall Dec. 16 accepted an interim hiring plan for the police department calling for 600 new employes. Of the 600 hired, 400 were to be from minority groups or women.

Marshall Jan. 5, 1976 ordered the Chicago Police Department to establish racial quotas for police hiring. He enjoined the Treasury Department from paying revenue-sharing funds to the city until this order was obeyed.

The quotas specified by the judge were: 42% black and hispanic males, 16% women, and 42% white males. At the time of the ruling, blacks and hispanics made up 17% of the police force (in contrast to a 40% share of the general city population).

Judge Marshall also reaffirmed a previous ruling of his, made in December 1974. In that ruling, the city was required to admit groups of 200 for police training, the groups to be composed of 100 black or hispanic males, 33 women, and 67 white males.

Marshall March 25, 1977 authorized the release of the revenue-sharing funds because Chicago's police department was in compliance with his hiring guidelines. The U.S. 7th Circuit Court of Appeals Jan. 11 had upheld Marshall's impounding of the funds to enforce compliance.

Teachers: New York—Albert Shanker, who headed New York City's United Federation of Teachers, said July 19, 1972 that he supported "recruitment and training programs" to increase the number of minority teachers, but the union would fight any "quota system."

Shanker's warning against quotas was in answer to an announcement that day that

the U.S. Department of Health, Education & Welfare (HEW) had scheduled a probe of the New York City school system to uncover any discrimination against minority children, especially Spanish-speaking groups.

J. Stanley Pottinger, director of HEW's Office for Civil Rights, said the study would consider "the language and cultural characteristics of the children to be served as compared to the linguistic abilities of their teachers and the relevance of instructional approaches and materials." He released figures showing that only 1.3% of New York teachers had Spanish surnames and 7.8% were black, though 25.7% of the students had Spanish surnames and 34.5% were black.

Pottinger said "Asian and native American children, and children of Italian, Greek, Haitian and Eastern European ancestry" would also be studied. The probe had been requested by Sen. Jacob Javits (R, N.Y.) and Rep. Herman Badillo (D, N.Y.).

California—Federal District Court Judge Samuel B. Conti ruled Nov. 4, 1972 in favor of 4,000 white teachers and administrators in the San Francisco school system and ordered the Board of Education to abandon a minority hiring plan as discriminatory.

The board had planned to appoint four minority group members for every five new administrators appointed for five years, to increase the minority share of the total number of administrators from 20% to 37.5%. Conti said "no one race or ethnic group should ever be accorded preferential treatment over another."

Michigan—Federal Judge Albert J. Engel July 18, 1973 ordered integration of teachers and administrators in the Grand Rapids, Mich. school system but rejected a contention by the National Association for the Advancement of Colored People (NAACP) that segregation existed among the system's 70,000 students.

Ruling in a suit filed by the NAACP in 1970, Engel also dismissed from the suit the 11 suburban districts which the NAACP had sought to have included in a metropolitan area integration plan. Grand Rapids school officials had also wanted the suburbs included in any plan to prevent the flight of city whites to the suburbs.

According to testimony, enrollment in eight inner-city schools was at least 90% black, although blacks made up only 20% of the city's population.

Other Developments

Women's job status changed little. The Women's Bureau of the Labor Department reported that while the proportion of women in professional, managerial and other high status jobs had increased slightly between 1968 and 1971, average salaries for women had declined as a percentage of men's salaries over a longer period, between 1955 and 1970, it was disclosed Aug. 26, 1972.

Women, who constituted 38% of the work force, increased their share of professional-technical and managerial jobs by about 1.5% over the period, rising to 39% in the first category and 17% in the second.

But in 1970, the bureau reported, the average woman earned only 59% as much as a man in the same job, down from 64% in 1955. The gap was narrowest in professional jobs, where women earned 67%, but greatest in sales jobs, where they were paid only 43% of male salaries. Only 1% of female managers on salary were paid $25,000 or more in 1970, compared with about 10% of male managers.

Fresh data on the status of working women were made public five months later. In an unprecedented special section on the economic role of women, the President's Economic Report to Congress, released Jan. 30, 1973, said women had not made much progress in achieving job equality or equal pay since 1956.

Although 43.8% of women of working age were in the work force, constituting 37.4% of the total work force, there had been only a "very small change" in "the extent of occupational segregation by sex" since 1950, perpetuating the concentration of women in lower paying jobs, the report noted. However, women had made gains in recent years in some job categories, including accountants, radio operators and editors and reporters. The report listed the proportion of women in over 250 job classifications.

Within the various job classifications, the report said, "the low representation of women in positions of responsibility is striking."

Among women who worked at all during 1971, average earnings were about 40% as large as those of men, in part a reflection of the larger number of part-time women workers. With adjustments made for the varying work hours, women still averaged only 66% of male earnings.

Part of the difference was attributed to lower experience levels of women, which in turn was said to be caused largely by the fact that women did not remain in the work force as continuously as men. But even taking these factors into account, the report claimed, the average rose to only 80%. Among men and women holding the same type of job at the same company, however, earnings were found to be equal.

Black women heads of households who worked all year had average earnings of $5,227, the report said, compared with $6,527 for white women. But the gap disappeared among women with higher education.

The report did not attempt to determine to what extent the inequality resulted from direct discrimination or cultural factors, including the choice of many women of "a life divided between home responsibilities and work." But it claimed "some of the hesitancy of women to enter or to stay in the labor force is undoubtedly the result of societally determined factors that restrict the possibilities open to them," including different career orientations beginning in the first years of school.

The report was prepared by the Council of Economic Advisers, including Marina Von Neumann Whitman, appointed in 1972.

In a series of reports made public later, the Census Bureau said that while some U.S. women had made gains in getting jobs and more wives outearned their husbands than in the past, average earnings for working women with either a college or high school education were still scarcely more than half the earnings of similarly educated males.

The Census Bureau said March 9 that full-time women workers 25-64 years old with a high school diploma earned $5,067 in 1969, 56% of the $9,067 earned by males, while full-time women workers with four years of college earned $7,238 that year, or 55% of the $13,103 male figure. Among blacks, the discrepancy was somewhat less.

The differential varied widely in different professions. Women domestics with four years of high school earned only 37% of their male counterparts, while women computer specialists earned 75% of males' salaries in similar jobs.

A Census Bureau analysis reported Feb. 11 that women accounted for 65.3% of the increase in jobs between 1960 and 1970, when they held 37.8% of the 76.6 million jobs. The largest gains by women were in the clerical, service, sales and operatives categories, while only 43.7% of new professional and technical workers and 28.6% of new managers were women.

The bureau reported March 18 that 3.2 million wives had incomes greater than their husbands in 1970, or 7.4% of the 44 million husband-wife households, up from 5.7% in 1960.

GM in sex job accord—General Motors Corp. (GM) and the Equal Employment Opportunities Commission (EEOC) filed a consent decree in U.S. district court in St. Louis under which GM agreed to try to fill at least 20% of all new hourly rate production and assembly jobs with women at its St. Louis assembly plant, it was reported Jan. 17, 1973.

The settlement was the first reached under new EEOC court case initiation powers. GM agreed to make affirmative recruitment efforts to place women in the jobs, after laid-off employes were rehired. After a two-year period, the utilization of women would be reevaluated.

College & university jobs. The Health, Education & Welfare (HEW) Department Oct. 4, 1972 issued a 17-page set of minority employment guidelines for about 2,-500 colleges and universities holding federal contracts. The guidelines were drawn up at the request of educators faced with the loss of federal contracts for inadequate affirmative action plans.

The guidelines ruled out quotas for women or minority groups, but said that numerical "goals and timetables" would be required. The goals would be determined by "an analysis by the contractor of its deficiencies and of what

it can reasonably do to remedy them, given the availability of qualified minorities and women and the expected turnover in its work force." If "changed employment conditions" or other factors prevented the school from reaching the goal despite "good-faith effort," as determined by an investigative team, the school will be considered to have "complied with the letter and the spirit" of the executive order requiring affirmative action.

J. Stanley Pottinger, director of the HEW Office for Civil Rights, said a total of $23 million in federal contracts had been withheld in the previous two years from noncomplying schools, but all the funds were eventually released after new plans were drawn up.

Before the guidelines were officially released, civil rights groups said the rules would make the executive order "virtually meaningless." In a letter to Pottinger reported Sept. 8, Marian Edelman, writing for the Washington Research Project and also in behalf of the National Urban League, the National Association for the Advancement of Colored People, the National Urban Coalition and the National Council of Negro Women, said the guidelines would replace a "result-oriented compliance system" with a "vague process." Edelman also said the rules would place university faculties in a privileged status, strengthening "a sentiment among many blacks and whites that the poor and less well educated are left to bear the brunt of civil rights compliance."

Pottinger replied, in a Washington Post interview reported Sept. 8 that the guidelines were merely a clarification of existing policy.

Columbia contract ban lifted—HEW's Office for Civil Rights agreed Feb. 29, 1972 to accept Columbia University's interim report on its plan to comply with sexual and minority job rights requirements. The office then provisionally lifted its freeze on $13.8 million in federal contract funds.

Director J. Stanley Pottinger gave Columbia President William J. McGill until April 6 to present a full affirmative action plan, including data on the name, race, sex, position, salary, experience and promotions of all 10,000 faculty and service employes.

Although Columbia had been the only university currently under suspension, it was reported Feb. 10 that seven other schools had been threatened with similar action, and that college and university affirmative action plans occupied half the staff of the Office for Civil Rights. In particular, over 400 individual and class action charges had been brought by women concerning hiring, promotion or pay.

The American Council on Education had reported that women held only 22% of campus faculty posts in 1964, compared with 28% in 1940, and that their salaries averaged $1,500 less than those of their male counterparts.

But McGill warned Feb. 25 that "if we take one more step into the centralization of the hiring process, and we tell the faculty that they must consider race and sex as criteria, this place will blow sky high."

The HEW announced Sept. 1 that it had agreed to accept a "final affirmative action" plan submitted by Columbia University, ending a three-year dispute that had temporarily held up several million dollars in federal contracts.

Growing Conflict & Uncertainty

DeFunis Case & Confused College-University Policies

Conflict and confusion over the controversial issue of quotas and affirmative action in education and employment continued to grow during the mid-1970s. In the DeFunis case, the Supreme Court decided to forgo an opportunity to provide guidance on an increasingly troublesome issue—a complaint that white applicants were denied admission to law, medical (or other professional) schools in order to admit allegedly less qualified minority applicants.

High Court ducks DeFunis case. The Supreme Court April 23, 1974 declined to rule on the constitutionality of law school admissions policies giving preference to members of minority groups at the expense of white applicants. In an unsigned opinion, the court majority of five justices held that the case was moot because the student who originally brought the suit to gain admission to the University of Washington Law School was to graduate from the school in June 1974.

Marco DeFunis Jr., a white Phi Beta Kappa graduate of the University of Washington, sued in 1971 after being rejected for admission by the law school and subsequently learning that 36 minority ap-

plicants—with lower predicted first year averages than his—had been admitted. A trial court, agreeing that the admissions policies violated DeFunis' right to equal protection under the law, ordered the law school to admit the defendant. The Washington State Supreme Court later reversed the order, but Justice William O. Douglas interceded, granting a stay pending U.S. Supreme Court resolution of the case.

Justices voting to hear the case were William J. Brennan Jr., Thurgood Marshall, Byron R. White and Douglas. They said the majority action "clearly disserves the public interest." In a separate dissent, Douglas said the admissions policies at issue were unconstitutional because they were based on race. Preferences for students from deprived backgrounds were valid, he said, if they were granted without reference to race.

The court majority did not preclude a decision at a later date: "If the admissions procedures of the law school remain unchanged, there is no reason to suppose that a subsequent case . . . will not come with relative speed to this court, now that the Supreme Court of Washington has spoken."

Princeton ends quota. Princeton University trustees voted Jan. 19, 1974 to admit women on an equal basis with men, abolishing a quota system which had limited women to about 300 per undergrad-

117

uate class, compared with approximately 800 men.

U.S. sues Louisiana. The Justice Department filed suit against the state of Louisiana March 14, 1974 to force desegregation of the state-supported university system. The suit was filed at the request of the Department of Health, Education and Welfare, which had found Louisiana in violation of civil rights laws governing institutions receiving federal aid.

The Justice Department said the suit was its first against an entire state college system.

The suit charged that even after technical integration of the system in 1953, the state had perpetuated and expanded a dual network of campuses by locating separate branches of traditionally white and black schools in the same cities. Cited as examples were Southern University and Louisiana State University (LSU), both with campuses in Baton Rouge, New Orleans and Shreveport; Southern was more than 99% black, as was Grambling College, while other schools in the system, including LSU, were 89%–97% white.

Mississippi segregation suit. The Justice Department charged Jan. 20, 1975 that the student bodies and faculties of Mississippi's 25 state colleges and universities were illegally racially segregated. Contained in a proposed supplemental complaint, the charge was submitted to the U.S. District Court in Aberdeen, Miss. Having already intervened in 1971 in a private suit to desegregate the state's two land-grant colleges, the Justice Department sought to broaden its attack on Mississippi's alleged dual system of higher learning by combining the new complaint and the existing suit.

The proposed complaint, which named Gov. William L. Waller and key state higher education officials as defendants, asked the court to prohibit them from continuing to operate a racially dual system and to order them to develop and implement a desegregation plan.

According to the complaint, student admission policies, faculty hiring and assignment practices, resources, programs and activities of the institutions were largely segregated by race. Such acts and practices, the complaint charged, perpetuated an unlawful, dual system and deprived black students of equal protection under the law.

More than 72,000 students were enrolled in the state's eight four-year colleges and universities, its medical center and 16 two-year junior colleges.

The private suit, filed in 1970, charged that the state's two land-grant colleges—predominately black Alcorn A & M and predominately white Mississippi State University—were "integral parts of a dual, segregated system of higher education."

Antibias plans for colleges criticized. A report by the Carnegie Council on Policy Studies in Higher Education, released Aug. 10, 1975, said federal affirmative action programs to end discrimination in college and university faculties were confused and sometimes in conflict with each other. "Seldom has a good cause spawned such a badly developed series of federal mechanisms," the report said.

The report proposed the creation of a federal panel to revise and coordinate regulations and guidelines currently imposed by the Labor Department, the Department of Health, Education and Welfare and the Equal Employment Opportunity Commission. The HEW secretary should be given sole authority to approve affirmative action plans and impose sanctions, it said. Moreover, graduated penalties should replace the single penalty of cancellation of all federal contracts with a school judged to be failing in affirmative action, the report recommended.

Virginia preference plan invalid. U.S. District Court Judge D. Dortch Warriner voided an affirmative action program of Virginia Commonwealth University, on the ground that it gave unfair preference to female job applicants. The May 28, 1976 ruling involved a suit by Dr. James A. Cramer, who said that VCU's department of sociology had considered only female applicants for two job vacancies. Cramer said that he had presented qualifications "equal or better than" those of female applicants.

Warriner's ruling barred the school from implementing an affirmative action program that would discriminate against either sex, and from setting employment quotas based on sex. Warriner said that the "cosmetic remedies" embodied in VCU's hiring plan did not get at the "root cause" of the disparity in numbers of male and female employes. He identified this as "a paucity of available females and minority applicants whose credentials are superior to those of the male applicants for similar employment."

Busing Conflict Persists

School aid legislation limits busing. A conference committee version of a bill authorizing $25.2 billion over four years in aid to elementary and secondary schools and containing restrictions on busing of students was passed by the Senate on a vote of 81–15 July 24, 1974 and by 323–83 House vote July 31. The bill was signed Aug. 21 by Gerald R. Ford, who had succeeded Richard N. Nixon as President.

Busing provisions accepted by the conferees were generally closer to the more lenient Senate bill. The final version prohibited busing for desegregation beyond the school next closest to a student's home, except—as in the Senate bill—when courts determined that more extensive busing was necessary to protect students' constitutional rights.

The final bill did not include a House provision that would have required the courts to reopen consideration of previous integration orders to bring them into compliance with the bill's restrictions. Under the compromise, parents or school districts could seek reopening of cases only if time or distance traveled would be harmful to students' health or would impair the educational process. A court, however, could terminate existing busing orders if it determined that a district was no longer violating students' rights and was not likely to do so in the future.

The conferees also accepted Senate amendments prohibiting busing across district lines unless boundaries were found to have been deliberately drawn to foster segregation and prohibiting implementation of integration orders after the beginning of a school year.

The overwhelming vote in the House— where busing opponents had been insisting that the House's stronger restrictions pre-

vail in conference—was attributed to the defusing effect of the Supreme Court's July 25 decision against cross-district busing.

In the Senate July 24, a last-minute attempt by busing opponents to send the measure back to conference had been narrowly defeated, 55-42.

The original House bill had been approved by 380–26 vote March 27 after the primary busing restriction had been adopted by 293–117 vote March 26 as an amendment almost identical to a House-passed proposal that had been killed by a Senate filibuster in 1972. The amendment would permit busing only after other anti-bias methods had proved ineffective. Even under such circumstances, a student could be bused only to a school "closest or next closest" to his home.

The measure would also permit communities currently under court-ordered busing plans to reopen their court cases if the orders did not conform with the new legislation.

By a vote of 239-168 March 27, the House added a second amendment, by Rep. John M. Ashbrook (R, Ohio), prohibiting the use of federal funds for any form of busing designed to correct racial imbalance.

President Nixon had supported the House bill in a radio address March 23 as "a step in the right direction toward more community and state control" and threatened to veto a bill such as the measure pending in the Senate.

Nixon stated his opposition to "excessive forced busing" and stressed the importance of "neighborhood schools." Parents were "naturally concerned," he said, when courts imposed busing orders based on "complicated plans drawn up by far-away officials in Washington . . ." In the areas of desegregation and aid funds, Nixon added, federal employes must not be placed "in the role of master social planners."

The Democratic Party's Congressional spokesmen on education March 30 criticized the views Nixon had presented. The remarks by Sen. Claiborne Pell (R.I.) and Rep. John Brademas (Ind.) were the Democrats' "equal time" reply to Nixon's March 23 radio address.

Pell accused Nixon of "reopening a painful wound" in calling for strong legis-tive curbs on busing. He said existing busing restrictions had "worked for the past two years" and should be "left alone."

The original Senate version of the bill was adopted by 81–5 vote May 20. Its busing provisions would have allowed pupils to attend the school "closest or next closest" to their homes with the added specification that the proviso was "not intended to modify or diminish" the authority of the courts "to enforce fully" the Constitution. The amendment, proposed by majority and minority leaders Mike Mansfield (D, Mont.) and Hugh Scott (R, Pa.), was adopted May 16 by a vote of 47–46.

The key vote followed a 47–46 rejection May 15 of an amendment identical to the anti-busing amendment approved by the House.

Democrats kill antibusing amendment. Members of the House Democratic caucus, meeting in public for the first time Nov. 19, 1975, voted 172–96 to table (thus kill) a resolution that would have directed Democratic members of the Judiciary Committee to report to the full House a proposed constitutional amendment prohibiting school busing for purposes of racial desegregation.

The vote represented a victory for Speaker Carl Albert (D, Okla.) and Rep. Peter W. Rodino Jr. (D, N.J.), chairman of the Judiciary Committee. Albert said that since the Supreme Court had already upheld several busing orders, the amendment would "usurp" the court's powers. He also argued that the issue was "so explosive and so controversial" that it would do harm to the Democratic Party. Rodino said he rejected the idea that the caucus could direct a member to vote on a constitutional issue against his or her conscience.

Rep. Dale Milford (D, Tex.), one of the resolution's sponsors, countered that "individual rights have a place in the Constitution, and the right to attend the school within the neighborhood is an individual right that our citizens are demanding and that is well worth protecting."

Sen. John G. Tower (R, Tex.), sponsor of a similar proposal, had met President Ford Oct. 27 to seek Ford's support for the amendment. Ford, Tower said, declined "at this time" to give his support but was ordering studies of alternative methods of achieving equal access for all to quality education.

Coleman scores busing amendment—Sociologist James S. Coleman told the Senate Judiciary Committee Oct. 28 that although he no longer considered busing a valid means of desegregating schools, he could not support a constitutional amendment that would ban busing. "If a democratic government can't resolve issues of this nature without resorting to the Constitution," he said, "then we are in a bad way."

In order for a desegregation effort to be effective, Coleman said, it had to expand the educational rights of blacks and other minorities instead of seeming to restrict those of whites. One way to do this, he suggested, was to allow black children to attend suburban schools of their choice.

Gov. Julian M. Carroll of Kentucky supported the proposed amendment, telling the Judiciary Committee Oct. 28 that "forced busing is damaging educational quality, contributing to white flight, disrupting community and family life, wasting important state and local resources and creating special problems of law enforcement." He urged a moratorium on future court-ordered busing and a rescinding of existing busing orders.

Mathews opposes busing. Dr. F. David Mathews was confirmed by Senate voice vote July 22, 1975 to the post of secretary of health, education and welfare.

At a hearing on his nomination by the Senate Finance Committee July 15, Mathews questioned the value of school busing. Busing to achieve racial balance in public schools "has not produced good results," he said, and "has left many people feeling their rights have been violated." He supported "equal educational opportunity for all children," he said, "but any policy of the United States should be judged in terms of its effectiveness." "If it is ineffective, surely we are an inventive enough people to produce something else," he said.

Sen. Jacob K. Javits (R, N.Y.) took issue with these remarks when Mathews appeared July 17 before the Senate Labor and Public Welfare Committee, which was not processing the nomination but had jurisdiction over many HEW programs. "There is no such thing in the federal law as 'forced busing' to achieve racial balance," Javits said, "and I submit to you not to accept the term." The only busing for racial balance, Javits continued, had been ordered by the courts or by state education departments.

Mathews replied that he had looked further into the matter since the earlier hearing and found that the busing plans were "lawful court orders." "They are to be respected," he said, "to be respected by the secretary of HEW." He pledged in this and all other issues "to uphold the law of this land as written."

When he defended his earlier stand that busing had proven ineffective and "a practical measure should be judged by its effectiveness," Javits asked him if he could suggest an alternative. "No, I have no substitute," Mathews answered.

The Finance Committee's recommendation for confirmation was unanimous July 21.

Ford pushes for busing review. Ron Nessen, White House press secretary, said May 18, 1976 that President Ford had told Attorney General Edward H. Levi to "look for an appropriate case" in which to ask the Supreme Court to reconsider the use of court-ordered busing to desegregate schools. The announcement came during mounting controversy over the disclosure May 14 that the Justice Department tentatively had decided to file a brief in support of a suit opposing court-ordered busing in Boston.

Ford long had been on record as opposed to forced busing. White House aides said May 18 that Ford's previously undisclosed order to Levi to seek high court review had been given Nov. 20, 1975. Since the Supreme Court's 1971 unanimous ruling that allowed courts to require busing, the Justice Department generally had supported desegregation efforts.

The report of a White House push for review was criticized by civil rights leaders. They argued that government support for a review would heighten racial tensions and possibly encourage busing opponents to commit violence.

Busing supporters also held that the White House order to Levi could be viewed as a Ford political move to satisfy conservative voters who otherwise might support Ronald Reagan in his bid to get the Republican presidential nomination.

Ford denied May 19 that the planned request for review was political. He noted that the White House had not publicized the move in time for it to play a role in the Michigan primary. Ford stressed that the decision on which case to seek Supreme Court review was in Levi's hands.

The White House and the Justice Department were known to differ in their objections to busing. Ford had said that he was "totally" opposed to forced busing, but the Justice Department said May 20 that the brief it had prepared for the Boston case accepted the essential legitimacy of busing as a judicial remedy for discrimination. However, the department proposed to ask the Supreme Court to place some curbs on the scope of court-ordered busing plans. Solicitor General Robert H. Bork wrote the brief.

Earlier drafts of the brief had been firmly against busing. Bork modified the drafts. The Justice Department delayed the filing in response to opposition from Transportation Secretary William T. Coleman (the only black member of the Cabinet), J. Stanley Pottinger, head of the Justice Department's civil rights division, Sen. Edward W. Brooke (R, Mass.), and officials of the National Association for the Advancement of Colored People.

Busing cases: _Alabama_—U.S. District Court Judge Frank M. Johnson Jr. May 22, 1974 accepted an integration plan offered by the Montgomery County, Ala. school board that would, in general, allow elementary school pupils to attend neighborhood schools. Johnson rejected plans involving cross-city busing submitted by black groups and the federal government, ruling that while some schools would have high percentages of black students under the school board plan, all students would attend a "substantially desegregated school for a majority of their school careers."

Kentucky—A U.S. judge in Louisville July 30, 1975 ordered desegregation of the city's schools. The program would call for busing of 22,600 pupils, "a little less than half" of whom would be black. Judge James F. Gordon said protests against his decision would be tolerated as

long as they "are not violent, are not pro-
fane and are not threatening in nature"
but he warned those "who would resort to
public disorder" to "think twice."

Missouri—Health, Education & Welfare Department officials notified Kansas
City July 15, 1975 that the second
fall desegregation program submitted by
its school district since March had been
rejected. The department had objected to
plans calling for the busing of only black
students.

In St. Louis, the city's Board of Education and an organization representing
black parents agreed on a plan to integrate the school system without busing,
it was reported in the New York Times
Dec. 27. The plan, contained in a consent
order settling a suit brought against the
board by the parents in 1972, provided for
the transfer of teachers to integrate the
faculty of each school. It also required the
school board, which admitted in the
decree that the system was segregated, to
report to a federal district court on
whether integration could be achieved
through the creation of magnet schools—
high schools with specialized curricula
which drew their students from the entire
city.

Early opposition to the plan came only
from the St. Louis Teachers Association,
whose president said the group would oppose arbitrary transfers of teachers.

Delaware—In a 5–3 decision Nov. 17,
1975, the Supreme Court upheld a lower
federal court ruling that Delaware's
school districting law was unconstitutional because it prevented the busing of
children between Wilmington and its
suburbs. Without comment, the court
majority upheld an April 15 decision by a
three-judge panel in Wilmington calling
for redistricting proposals involving city-
suburban busing.

At issue in the case was a 1968 state law
that in effect called for the reorganization
of all Delaware school districts, except the
predominantly black district of Wilmington. The three-judge panel, upholding
claims of minority students in Wilmington
that the law was racially discriminatory,
concluded that the statute's "unconstitutional exclusion of Wilmington" was the
kind of evidence the Supreme Court had
had in mind when it ruled in 1974 that
busing across city-suburban lines was acceptable only when deliberate, illegal

segregation affecting city and suburbs had
occurred.

The lower court panel also had cited
state public housing policies and transportation subsidies for white children attending private schools as evidence that
segregation had been deliberately promoted by officials. Wilmington's schools
were 83% black, and surrounding suburban schools were 94% white.

Justice Rehnquist, joined by Burger and
Justice Lewis F. Powell Jr., dissented.
Calling the decision "extraordinarily slip-
shod judicial procedure," Rehnquist
argued that it left all parties uncertain as
to what had actually been decided.

In a ruling based on the Supreme Court
decision, the three-judge federal court in
Wilmington May 19, 1976 ordered the
state Department of Public Instruction
to begin formulating a desegregation plan
to amalgamate the center city's largely
black schools and the predominantly white
suburban schools.

The Justice Department, in a brief
filed with the U.S. 3rd Circuit Court of
Appeals in Philadelphia March 18, 1977,
endorsed city-suburban cross-busing to
desegregate schools in the Wilmington
Del. area. However, the department said
the busing should be limited to that
necessary to rectify constitutional
abuses—it should not be conducted with
the goal of achieving "a desirable racial
mix."

The brief argued that interdistrict busing was justified because there was
substantial evidence of continuing racial
discrimination affecting both the city and
the suburbs. However, the brief took exception to the extensive busing ordered by
the three-judge trial court in the Wilmington case. "The existence of schools
predominantly attended by members of
one race," the brief said, "does not in itself amount to racial discrimination."

Furthermore, the brief argued, "a court
is not at liberty to produce a result merely
because it may find the result desirable.
The existence of a violation of the Constitution does not authorize a court to bring
about conditions that never would have
existed in the absence of official racial discrimination."

The Justice Department was not
directly a party to the case, and its position was expressed in a friend-of-the-court
brief. The department asked the appeals
court to uphold the lower court plan in-

sofar as it remedied previous official discrimination, but to strike down those parts of it that were based "on a goal of achieving racial balance."

The cross-district busing order was upheld by a 4–3 decision of the 3rd Circuit Court of Appeals May 18. The court objected, however, to "language in the District Court's opinion which can be interpreted as requiring an enrollment of 10% to 35% black students in each grade." Rejecting the idea of quotas to achieve a racially desirable mix, the appeals court held that the desegregation plan should aim simply to have the schools in the Wilmington area "returned to the position they would have been in but for the constitutional violations that have been found."

The Supreme Court Oct. 3 decided, 4–3, not to review the Wilmington decision.

Chief Justice Warren E. Burger, joined by Justices Lewis F. Powell Jr. and William H. Rehnquist, said he would have sent the case back to the lower court for reconsideration.

Texas—The Supreme Court, in a 7–2 decision entered Dec. 6, 1976, vacated an appellate-court ruling that had ordered extensive busing of students in Austin, Tex. to end discrimination against blacks and Mexican-Americans. The high court ordered the U.S. Court of Appeals, Fifth Circuit, to reconsider the case in light of a June Supreme Court ruling that discriminatory intent—not merely discriminatory effect—had to be proved if a government action were to be ruled unconstitutional.

Thus the appeals court, in reconsidering the case, could still hold that a broad desegregation plan was justified if it first found that there had been discriminatory intent on the part of Austin officials.

The Justice Department had argued in a brief to the high court that there was evidence of such discriminatory intent. At the same time, the department said that it was concerned that the appeals court's decision, if it were upheld, could have penalized neighborhood schools that had become racially segregated through no fault of the school system or no intent on the part of its officials.

The high court order vacating the plan was issued without an opinion subscribed to by the full majority. Powell, in an opinion joined by Rehnquist and Chief Justice Burger, said that, whether evidence of

discriminatory intent were found, the cross-town busing ordered by the appeals court "appears to exceed that necessary to eliminate the effect of any official acts or omissions."

Powell said that "large-scale busing" was permissible only when it was ordered to achieve a degree of integration that "would have existed had the school authorities fulfilled their constitutional obligations in the past." Powell said that the standard he had indicated "would rarely result in the widespread busing of elementary-age children." The other four justices in the majority offered no opinion.

Brennan and Marshall dissented. They held that the appeals court ruling had been based on a correct understanding of prior Supreme Court rulings. The case was Austin Independent School Dist. v. U.S. (76-200).

The Austin busing plan had been proposed by the Nixon Administration May 14, 1971 under a Supreme Court mandate.

Officials in the Department of Health, Education and Welfare (HEW) submitted the plan to Judge Jack Roberts of the U.S. district court in Austin. It called for the crosstown busing of an undetermined number of students to achieve a mix among the black and Mexican-American minorities and the white majority. The plan would leave all but one school in the city with a white or "Anglo" majority.

Austin, the sixth largest city in Texas, had about 56,000 students in 56 elementary schools, 19 junior high schools and eight high schools. About 15% of the students were black and about 20% Mexican-American. Austin had two secondary schools and seven elementary schools that had virtually all-black enrollments, all in all-black neighborhoods.

J. Stanley Pottinger, director of HEW's Office of Civil Rights, said the Austin plan was "the first indication" of the government's interpretation of the Supreme Court's busing decision.

Attorney General John N. Mitchell said May 13 that HEW's proposal for Austin "will be broad enough to satisfy the [Supreme Court] mandate and, hopefully, to meet the educational needs of the community."

Roberts June 28 and July 18, 1971 rejected the crosstown busing plan, and President Nixon disavowed it Aug. 3.

School Problem Continues

Schools still segregated. In a report marking the 20th anniversary of the Supreme Court decision ordering an end to public school segregation, the Department of Health, Education and Welfare said May 17, 1974 that based on data compiled in a late 1972 survey, 11.2% of black students attended schools where there were no white children. The report noted that segregation was clearly an urban problem: in 20 large Northern and Southern cities, 25% of the black pupils attended all-black schools.

The survey also found that more than 71% of the public schools in the North had enrollments of more than half black. Comparable figures for other areas were 68% in border states and 53.7% in the South.

The Health, Education & Welfare Department had said Jan. 17 that discrimination still existed in the Topeka, Kan. school system, a defendant in the landmark 1954 Supreme Court decision outlawing segregation.

HEW had begun an investigation in December 1973 after being named a party in a new suit against the city. The department's latest action included an order for the city to submit corrective plans.

HEW said it had found that a "substantial number" of schools had disproportionate minority enrollments and that attendance zone transfers had impeded integration. Most minority junior high and elementary pupils, HEW said, attended schools with facilities generally inferior to those in the predominantly white schools.

Rights efforts in North, West assailed. A private civil rights study group charged Sept. 9, 1974 that the government had failed to desegregate schools in Northern and Western states despite legal requirements that it do so.

In its report, the Center for National Policy Review said government efforts had been characterized by "bureaucratic

caution, needless delays, administrative inefficiency and sloppy investigation."

The report said the Department of Health, Education & Welfare (HEW) had not made sufficient use of a weapon that had proved effective in integrating schools in Southern and Border states—the cutoff of federal funds to segregated districts.

In preparing the report, the center reviewed HEW files on 84 cases involving Northern and Western schools undertaken since 1964. Of these, the report said, 52 were still "open" as of July 1, 1973, and no enforcement of any kind had been undertaken in 37 of the 52 cases. The report noted that the average case remained unresolved for more than three years before the district involved was informed that it was violating the law.

According to the report, only four of the 84 districts investigated had been forced to undergo formal enforcement proceedings in which a fund cutoff was threatened.

The report included statistics which, while not perfectly analogous, showed the differences among regions in the progress of integration. In 1964, the report said, 98% of black students in 11 Southern states were in all-black schools; the figure had fallen to 9% by 1972. The latest figures for the North and West, however, showed 1.6 million of 2.8 million black students (57%) were in schools that were at least 80% black.

Responding to the report Sept. 6, HEW Secretary Caspar W. Weinberger said the cutoff of federal school funds was an extreme weapon which in some cases should be supplanted by "persuasion and discussion." He said there were instances in which fund cutoffs had increased the degree of segregation.

Weinberger denied that HEW was lax in enforcing the law, contending that delays were caused by the "very fierce" public opposition in many Northern cities. He said the public in the South had been "much more willing to accept desegregation."

U.S. agencies scored on rights effort. A report by the U.S. Commission on Civil Rights, released Jan. 22, 1975, accused the federal government of laxity in enforcement of civil rights laws in education. The 400-page document singled out for criticism the Department of Health, Education and Welfare (HEW), the Internal Revenue Service (IRS) and the Veterans Administration (VA).

In its recommendations to President Ford, the report warned, "We are at a dangerous crossroad in connection with school desegregation.... We cannot afford—because of organized resistance in Boston or any other community—to turn back. Extraordinary action is called for...." To insure effective civil rights compliance, the commission said, the President should appoint a White House coordinator of enforcement to bring about "vigorous and effective enforcement of the constitutional mandate to desegregate...."

The commission found that HEW had failed to issue comprehensive guidelines on such matters as busing and city-suburb desegregation because of pending court or Congressional action. "Administrators are entitled to guidelines based on today's law. If the law changes, changes can be made in the guidelines," the report said.

To a large extent, the report contended, HEW had depended too heavily and too long on voluntary compliance "to the virtual exclusion" of the ultimate sanction of cutting off funds. As a result many educational institutions stopped taking government enforcement efforts seriously, the report asserted.

The report suggested HEW monitor at least 25% of the colleges receiving federal funds each year and take prompt action to assure minorities and women equal job opportunities.

The commission accused the IRS of negligence because it was not fully using its power to withhold or withdraw tax-exempt status from nonprofit and private schools, many of which were created by communities to avoid sending children to integrated schools. The IRS had sent a questionnaire to church-sponsored schools in 1971 but had yet to finish reviewing the responses, the report noted.

The commission said the VA had failed to fulfill its responsibility of insuring equal educational opportunities in the trade schools and in apprenticeship and on-the-job training programs it supervised.

Anti-bias use of U.S. aid inadequate— Charging that federal enforcement of regulations prohibiting discrimination in

the spending of revenue-sharing funds had been "fundamentally inadequate," the U.S. Commission on Civil Rights Feb. 14 urged Congress to appropriate $7.5 million to ensure proper monitoring of the program.

In the fourth of its series of reports on federal civil rights enforcement, the commission said it found "abundant evidence ... that discrimination in the employment practices and delivery of benefits of state and local governments is far-reaching, often extending to programs funded by general revenue sharing." (The report noted that it was sometimes difficult to trace the uses of revenue sharing funds, as some recipients used the funds to free money that was in turn used for discriminatory purposes.)

To bring about effective enforcement of antidiscrimination regulations, the commission report said, the revenue-sharing office of the Treasury Department should delegate compliance work to other, presumably more experienced federal agencies working under standards developed by the Justice Department. The report also urged that statistical data on public employment by states and localities be reviewed regularly for evidence of discrimination and that Office of Revenue Sharing cut off or defer quarterly payments to recipients failing to correct discriminatory practices.

In a March 11 report, the commission urged the federal agencies to bar aid to schools that failed to desegregate voluntarily. Such schools, the report said, should be given 90 days to initiate integration plans before the Department of Health, Education and Welfare began proceedings to end federal financial assistance.

The recommendation was contained in the commission's report, "Twenty Years after Brown: Equality of Educational Opportunity."

The report said that the percentage of black students attending integrated schools in the South had increased but had remained unchanged in the North. Between 1968 and 1972 the proportion of blacks attending predominantly white schools in the South rose from 19% to 46%. In the North in 1972, 71% of blacks continued to attend predominately black schools. "There appear to be legitimate fears," the report noted, "that the South is in a transitional stage and is moving toward duplication of Northern residential segregation as desegregated schools are undercut by increasingly separated neighborhoods."

Among the report's other recommendations:

■ The Internal Revenue Service should revoke tax exemptions held by private, segregated schools, and the U.S. government should withdraw aid from them.

■ Federal funds should be withheld from school districts failing to meet special needs of non-English-speaking pupils.

■ A national standard, adaptable to local situations, should be formulated to insure that school districts were in compliance with federal desegregation laws. Busing should be a valid instrument of desegregation.

■ As an integration incentive, federal funding for new school construction projects should be made available to districts meeting federal desegregation rules.

Judge orders HEW to enforce integration. U.S. District Court Judge John H. Pratt ordered the Department of Health, Education & Welfare March 14, 1975 to act swiftly to enforce desegregation guidelines in 125 school districts in 16 Southern and Border states. Ruling on a suit by the NAACP Legal Defense and Educational Fund, Inc., Pratt also ordered HEW to move firmly in another 39 school districts whose voluntary desegregation efforts had been unsuccessful.

"There appears to be an overreliance by HEW on the use of voluntary negotiations over protracted time periods and a reluctance in recent years to use the administrative sanction process where school districts are known to be in noncompliance," Pratt said in his ruling.

Pratt's ruling gave HEW 60 days in which to notify each of the 125 districts that it would have to answer the charge that a "substantial" racial disproportion existed in one or more of its schools. The point at which racial imbalance occurred, Pratt's ruling said, was when there was a 20% disproportion between local minority pupils and their percentage for the entire district.

The court also set up a procedure for handling future complaints of noncompliance: HEW would have 90 days to determine if a district was in compliance with the law. When a district was found to be in

noncompliance, it would be given an additional 90 days to take voluntary corrective action. If, after 180 days, the district was still in noncompliance, HEW would commence within 30 days enforcement proceedings "through administrative notice of hearing or any other means authorized by law." (Knowledgeable observers noted, however, that a school district could lengthen the enforcement process with court appeals.)

The 125 districts were in Arkansas, Delaware, Florida, Georgia, Kentucky, Louisiana, Maryland, Mississippi, Missouri, North Carolina, Oklahoma, South Carolina, Tennessee, Texas, Virginia and West Virginia.

HEW sued on enforcement failure. In a suit filed by three civil rights organizations in Federal District Court in Washington July 3, 1975, the Health, Education & Welfare Department was assailed for failure to end school segregation in Northern and Western states.

A class action entered on behalf of 18 families and of the interests of minority children in 33 states, the suit charged that HEW Secretary Caspar W. Weinberger and Peter E. Holmes, director of the department's office of civil rights, had "deliberately renounced and abandoned their Title 6 [of the Civil Rights Act of 1964] duty to assure that no student or faculty segregation on the basis of race or national origin is practiced in the northern-western public school systems receiving HEW assistance."

The National Association for the Advancement of Colored People (NAACP), the Center for National Policy Review and the NAACP Legal Defense and Educational Fund, Inc. joined in bringing the suit, which also alleged that HEW had not investigated complaints of school segregation or imposed requirements for speedy adherence to civil rights legislation. The suit would oblige HEW either to force the schools to end segregation or to terminate their federal assistance funds. The families represented by the suit were from Ohio, California, Wisconsin and Indiana.

Coleman dubious about integration. James S. Coleman, sociologist and the principal author of a 1966 study often cited to justify school desegregation, said that the flight of whites from desegregating city school systems threatened to defeat the purpose of integration, it was reported April 6, 1975.

Addressing the American Educational Research Association in Washington, Coleman offered a somber assessment of the impact of desegregation during the past few years. More attention should have been paid to how middle-class whites would react to rapid racial mixing of their schools, he suggested. Given the premise that culturally disadvantaged children tended to learn better when their classmates came from culturally advantaged homes, Coleman said, the flight of the middle class from the cities dimmed the prospect of black children being more successful in school through desegregation.

Careful analysis of whites' reactions and the other indirect effects of desegregation might yield results advocates and opponents of desegregation would find preferable to what was currently happening, Coleman contended. Federal, state and local officials were fearful of political consequences, Coleman said, and left desegregation almost entirely to the courts. As the courts were necessarily "blind" to such factors as white flight, they turned out to be "probably the worst instrument of social policy," he said. "Desegregation through the courts probably will have served in the long run to separate whites and blacks more severely than before," Coleman stated.

Further opinions on the subject, expressed by Coleman in a June 3 interview in his office at the University of Chicago and in a preliminary draft of a study of the effects of integration during 1968–72, were reported by the New York Times June 7.

In the interview at his office, Coleman declared: "Integration isn't losing any support, but as I see it, the strategies are basically producing resegregation, unfortunate strategies that are the outgrowth of court cases. We need an approach that is more stable, because if integration is going to come to exist in this country, we have to devise ways where after two or three years of integration we won't end up with resegregation."

In his draft report of the study, undertaken for the Urban Institute in Washington, D.C., Coleman compared desegregation data taken from the 20 largest school districts in the country, including New York and Chicago, with data taken from the next 50 largest districts. His main finding was that in the largest districts "induced integration" brought about by court order, especially that which required busing, had caused the rapid movement of whites from the cities and a subsequent resegregation. Coleman found that integration in the smaller districts was more stable. He criticized the courts because they "attempted to eliminate all facets of segregation, not only that arising from state action, but that which arose from individual action." The judiciary, Coleman said, "doesn't have the means" to combat segregation caused by individual action. "It doesn't have the funds and resources to provide holding power to make the schools stable." Also, if "there had not been an attempt to carry out widespread class integration, then the fear of incidents would have been much less, and the experience with integration would have been much more positive." In his study, Coleman noted that he was more optimistic about the future of integration than his findings indicated and that this was especially so in the area of interracial dating and marriage. "No society is going to be completely integrated until there is widespread interracial marriage."

Coleman's views were criticized June 13 by two leading sociologists in the field of race relations at a news conference called in New York by the NAACP. Dr. Robert L. Green of Michigan State University and Dr. Thomas F. Pettigrew of Harvard University described Coleman's findings as "premature" and said their "major fault" lay in his failure to explore other possible reasons for the large-scale movement of whites from the cities to the suburbs. They noted that Coleman "has not actually asked individual white parents who have moved to the suburbs why they did so." Green and Pettigrew attempted to separate the issue of busing from that of white migration to the suburbs by pointing out that in Detroit in 1965–70, when schools were highly segregated and there was no court-ordered busing, a total of 30,240 white students moved to the suburbs. They also pointed out a "contradiction" in Coleman's assertion that busing did not affect integration in smaller districts but caused a flight to the suburbs in larger ones.

Michigan educator pessimistic. The 1975 annual National Urban League conference, held in Atlanta, was told by a state education leader that he was finding some school integration "impractical."

John W. Porter, superintendent of public instruction for Michigan, said July 29 school integration was "still laudable, and I continue to support it," but was "becoming increasingly impractical" in large cities "not only because of logistics but more importantly because of changing attitudes, competing forces and a rapidly changing class structure." He said he felt "some of us are better off" because of "the country's equal educational experience" but that "the masses are worse off now in many respects than in 1954."

School desegregation lag persists. Federal statistics, released June 19, 1976 by Sens. Jacob K. Javits (R, N.Y.) and Edward W. Brooke (R, Mass.), showed that there had been a slight decline in the segregation of black children in the 1970s, balanced by a slight increase in the segregation of Spanish-surnamed children.

The figures also showed Southern and border states to be far in advance of states in the Northeast and Middle West in integration efforts. The information, which had been gathered by the Civil Rights Office of the Department of Health, Education and Welfare, covered the period from the fall of 1970 through the 1974–75 school year.

Nationally, the percentage of black children attending predominantly minority public schools dropped from 71% in 1970 to 67% for the 1974–75 school year. In the South, more than 44% of black children in 1974 were in schools with less than half minority enrollment; for the Northeast and Middle West, the corresponding figure was about 19%.

The proportion of Spanish-surnamed children attending minority schools rose from 64% in 1970 to 71% for the 1974–75 school year. The Civil Rights Office figures were the first published that documented a national pattern of Hispanic segregation.

The data were drawn from 31,800 schools that enrolled 90% of the nation's black students and 75% of the students with Spanish surnames.

Private-school bias illegal. The Supreme Court June 25, 1976 invalidated discrimination by private nonsectarian schools. It held, 7–2, that denial of entry to black children by such schools was not protected by the constitutional guarantee of free association.

"It may be assumed," Justice Potter Stewart wrote for the majority, "that parents have a First Amendment right to send their children to educational institutions that promote the belief that racial segregation is desirable, and that the children have an equal right to attend such institutions.

"But it does not follow that the practice of excluding racial minorities from such institutions is also protected by the same principle."

The Constitution, Stewart noted, "places no value on discrimination." The court found that the exclusion of blacks by the schools violated a law, known as Section 1981, of the 1866 Civil Rights Act. That measure was enacted to implement the ban on slavery. The section guaranteed blacks the same rights as whites to "make and enforce contracts."

Stewart delimited the decision to commercially operated nonsectarian private schools. It did not concern, he said, the right of "a private social organization to limit its membership on racial or any other grounds." Nor did it involve "any question of the right of a private school to limit its student body to boys, to girls, or to adherents of a particular religious faith," he said.

Stewart said also that the case did not bear on the question of "private sectarian schools that practice racial exclusion on religious grounds."

Justices Byron R. White and William H. Rehnquist dissented.

The action was brought by two black families against two schools in northern Virginia. The Justice Department had intervened as a friend of the court in support of the plaintiffs.

The cases were Runyon v. McCrary (75–62); Fairfax-Brewster School Inc. v. Gonzales (75–66); Southern Independent School Assn. v. McCrary (75–278); McCrary v. Runyon (75–306).

School sex bias rules proposed. The Department of Health, Education and Welfare June 18, 1974 proposed regulations against sex discrimination in educational institutions receiving federal aid. The regulations were designed to cover schools from pre-elementary through graduate levels, but allow numerous exemptions, particularly in the area of admissions.

A prohibition against discrimination in recruiting and admissions would apply to high school-level vocational schools, co-educational public colleges and all graduate and professional schools. Pre-elementary, elementary, non-vocational secondary schools, private undergraduate colleges and the few traditionally one-sex public colleges would be exempt from the prohibition.

Regarding treatment of students, the regulations would ban sex discrimination in such benefits as insurance, employment assistance and counseling, as well as in scholarships and other financial aid. Sex-segregated classes would be prohibited in all subjects except hygiene and sex-education classes, if parents objected to integrated classes on sex.

In the controversial area of athletics, the rules would permit, but not require, teams of mixed sexes. If a school chose to establish separate teams, "comparable" types and levels of competition would have to be provided for women, and discrimination in the provision of equipment and supplies would be banned. The HEW statement noted, however, that "equal aggregate expenditures" were not required.

The regulations would permit single-sex housing, but would require that facilities be comparable and ban discrimination on availability, curfews, fees and rules regarding off-campus housing.

Regarding employment, the regulations would ban sex bias in recruiting, pay and fringe benefits for teachers and other staff, and would require that pregnant teachers receive that same benefits as other "temporarily disabled employes."

Rules against sex bias issued—HEW rules against sex discrimination banned by Title IX of the 1972 Higher Education Act were issued June 3, 1975.

The new rules, which were approved by President Ford May 27, required educational institutions to end discriminatory practices against women in school admissions, employment, financial aid, vocational and academic counseling and athletics.

At the same time HEW made public its proposed anti-discrimination regulations, the department released another proposal calling for a change in its overall enforcement policies. Under the proposal, HEW would no longer investigate all individual complaints of discrimination, racial or otherwise, and would instead concentrate on bringing broad cases against selected targets. When priorities were "dictated by the morning mail" and every incoming complaint required full investigation, HEW Secretary Caspar W. Weinberger said June 3, "the limited sources of the department may be diluted by the need to investigate unsupported complaints, leaving really major forms of discrimination virtually unexamined." The proposal would allow HEW's Office of Civil Rights to focus on the "main, systematic forms of discrimination" and would "assure a more balanced and comprehensive effort," Weinberger said.

The rules against sex discrimination in education were to affect 16,000 public school districts and 2,700 colleges and universities, Weinberger said. Elementary schools would have one year to comply, while secondary schools and colleges would be allowed up to three years. Failure to comply would mean loss of federal aid.

Weinberger said HEW would approach Title IX enforcement "in a constructive spirit. We want to achieve the goals of the title as soon as possible, rather than undergo a series of futile confrontations and endless lawsuits." He urged good-faith compliance by all schools.

The most controversial aspect of the anti-discrimination rules concerned athletics. They said that elementary and secondary school physical education classes would have to be coeducational, with the exceptions that schools could separate students for contact sports and also group them according to ability.

Colleges would not be obligated to spend equal amounts of money on men's and women's sports, but would be expected to provide "necessary funds" to insure equal athletic opportunities for women. In contact sports, such as football and basketball, separate teams for both sexes could be provided if a significant segment of female students so desired. If separate teams were fielded, discrimination in supplies, travel and per diem allowances and quality of coaching would be prohibited. When athletic scholarships were offered to men, scholarships for women, based on the number of participants, would also have to be offered.

Opposition to the regulations on athletics was immediately heard from the National Collegiate Athletic Association, which had sought to gain exemptions for revenue-producing intercollegiate sports, such as basketball and football, on the grounds that these sports often provided money for the remainder of a college's athletic program. HEW was "throwing out the baby with the bathwater," said an NCAA spokesman.

Women's groups had complained, however, that ticket sales revenues frequently were only spent on men's sports, leaving women to find their own ways of supporting women's athletics. Weinberger, meanwhile, explained that HEW had based its decisions against exempting revenue-producing sports on a number of legal rulings. He added that he failed to find anything in the proposals that would put intercollegiate athletics out of business.

Other provisions of the proposed antidiscrimination rules:

Shop and other vocational courses would have to be made available equally to boys and girls. Guidance counselors could not deter women from entering male-identified occupations. Preference in admissions could not be given on the basis of sex. Pregnant girls could not be barred from school or involuntarily placed in separate classes because of their condition.

Integration of NYC school ordered. In what was said to be the first decision of its kind, a federal district court judge in New York Jan. 28, 1974 ordered federal, state and city housing authorities, along with city departments of education, police, parks and transportation, to cooperate in formulating plans to integrate a junior high school in the borough of Brooklyn. As of 1973, 43% of the school's pupils were black, 39% hispanic and 18% white.

Ruling in a suit filed by the National Association for the Advancement of Colored People, Judge Jack B. Weinstein ordered housing officials to provide a joint plan "to undo the racial imbalance" in publicly-supported housing in the area served by the school. Weinstein said all levels of government had failed to take "available steps" to reverse trends toward segregation in both housing and education, and concluded that "federal complicity in encouraging segregated

schooling through its housing programs" was unconstitutional.

Noting that entrenched segregation at the school had discouraged white families from moving into the area's public housing, Weinstein said the plans should include "advertisements and inducements" directed at the white middle class to "stabilize" the district's population.

Weinstein ordered the city's transportation department to provide busing plans for short-term balancing of the school's enrollment; the police department was to submit plans for adequate protection of children in the area; and the parks department—whose facilities were heavily used by the school—was ordered to provide a separate plan.

Judge retreats on order—Judge Weinstein issued a final ruling July 26 which considerably softened his earlier landmark decision that city, state and federal agencies must cooperate to alter housing and social patterns in order to integrate a junior high school in the Borough of Brooklyn.

Weinstein gave the city's central school board and the district board until the beginning of the 1977 school year to raise the number of white students in the school to 70%, the overall percentage of white junior high pupils in the district.

To attain this proportion, Weinstein ordered that feeder patterns within the district be redrawn to reflect the racial make-up of the district as a whole. The junior high school would also be made a special "school for gifted children" to attract students from throughout the district. Weinstein noted that such plans would conform with the recent Supreme Court decision against cross-district busing.

Weinstein retained the right to order an extensive intra-district busing program if it appeared within the first year that the softer plans were failing to attract sufficient numbers of white students.

Federal Regulation & Affirmative Job Action

Rights unit criticizes U.S. agencies. A report by the U.S. Commission on Civil

Rights, released Nov. 12, 1974, charged 5 federal regulatory agencies with failure to combat job discrimination in the industries they regulated. The study cited four agencies—the Interstate Commerce Commission (ICC), the Civil Aeronautics Board (CAB), the Federal Power Commission (FPC) and the Securities and Exchange Commission (SEC)—for not having issued rules forbidding job discrimination. The report called anti-discrimination rules issued by the Federal Communications Commission (FCC) "highly inadequate."

The agencies "appear to assume that their independent regulatory status allows them to stand above the national commitment to equal employment opportunity," the commission said in a cover letter to Congress and the President. "This commission finds," the letter said, "their position neither legally nor morally justifiable."

The study found heavy underutilization of minorities and women in the industries regulated by the ICC, CAB and FPC, except in lowest job classifications. Although petitions on equal opportunity employment regulations had been before the ICC and CAB since 1972, neither agency had yet acted, the report said. Moreover, the FPC had not accepted a Justice Department opinion affirming its authority to combat industry discrimination, the report added. The SEC had a poor record of employment of minorities in general and of women above the clerical level, the study commented, "but the SEC has refused to adopt mandatory equal employment guidelines for its regulatees."

The SEC Jan. 14 had refused to fulfill a request from women's rights and church groups that the agency require "affirmative action" programs against race and sex discrimination in the securities industry.

The SEC said the groups' contention that women and nonwhites were often confined to low-level jobs might be historically accurate. But the commission cited recent changes in employment patterns as indications of improvement. Acknowledging that it had the authority to impose antidiscrimination rules, the SEC suggested that the Equal Employment Opportunity Commission would be the appropriate agency to handle such complaints.

The General Accounting Office charged in a report made public by Sen. William Proxmire (D, Wis.) July 1, 1976 that the Treasury Department had been lax in enforcing federal anti-bias laws and regulations at the nation's financial institutions. Proxmire cited figures showing that women represented 65% of all bank employes, but held only 21% of the higher-ranked jobs. Minority workers, Proxmire said, accounted for 16% of bank workers, but held only 5.5% of the higher positions.

New national job board urged. The U.S. Civil Rights Commission July 15, 1975 proposed the creation of a national employment rights board because of what it called "fundamentally inadequate" efforts by the federal government to end job discrimination.

The commission said in a 673-page report: "Not only does the federal government suffer from unmistakable underutilization of minorities and women in its middle and higher ranks, but it also has a record of overt discrimination against these groups in the past, which has resulted historically in preference being given to nonminority [white] males." It also charged that there was "no one person, agency or institution which could speak for the federal government" on this matter and that, as a result, "employers, employes and aggrieved citizens are left to their own devices in trying to understand and react to a complex administrative structure."

The proposed board would have "cease and desist" authority and would be able to initiate procedures against any employer, private or government, if it believed Title VII of the Civil Rights Act had been abridged. It could bar federal contractors from doing business with government agencies it found in violation of antidiscrimination laws.

Although the report also criticized the Labor Department's Office of Federal Contract Compliance and the Equal Employment Opportunity Coordinating Council, it had especially strong words for the Civil Service Commission and the Equal Employment Opportunity Commission.

It recommended that the civil service agency adopt procedures making employers set goals and timetables for increasing female and minority employment. The civil service should abolish the "rule of three," requiring a government employer to hire from a list of three top candidates, because "current ranking and testing procedures are unreliable and unjustifiably screen qualified minorities and women." Until minority persons in a ratio equal "to the numbers in the available work force" were hired, the service should allow agencies to make sex and ethnic background criteria for employment, it proposed.

The report advised the Equal Employment Opportunity Commission to focus on systematic discrimination by moving against large employers. Each of its commissioners except the chairman should be given a specific area of responsibility. Persons whose grievances had been on record more than 180 days should be told they could bring private suit.

In related developments, the Wall Street Journal July 21 reported that the Federal Communications Commission (FCC) had proposed revisions of its equal opportunity guidelines that would compel radio and television stations to set up "employment goals and timetables" where "an extremely low rate of minority or female employment persists in a station's work force." Stations with 50 or more fulltime employes would be obliged to report periodically how women and minorities were doing in terms of job titles. The new guidelines were to be made final when the commission had received public comments on them in September.

The National Association for the Advancement of Colored People, at its 1975 convention in Washington, adopted July 4 a resolution calling on the government "to assure that blacks and other minorities and women who have secured employment or promotion as the result of affirmative action or other equal employment programs not be deprived of the benefits of that employment under the last-hired, first-fired theory." The federal agencies named in the resolution were "the Equal Employment Opportunity Commission, the Civil Service Commission, the [Labor Department's] Office of Federal Contract Compliance and other administrative agencies, federal and state." Although the statement in its final form passed quickly, it had gone through several changes of wording in order to avoid

antagonizing NAACP members whose connections with organized labor made them reluctant to tamper with the principle of job seniority. William F. Pollard, director of civil rights for the American Federation of Labor and Congress of Industrial Organizations (AFL-CIO), remarked June 30: "Seniority did not create this recession, and the abolition of it won't cure it." He pointed out the following day that seniority "is color-blind. We have over two million blacks in the AFL-CIO, and seniority protects them too."

(A judge in the U.S. Court of Appeals for the Fifth Circuit ruled July 16 that the last-hired, first-fired provisions of the seniority system were constitutional. Black workers laid off by the Continental Can Co., Inc. had tried to show that hiring discrimination in effect before the passage of civil rights laws had put them at the bottom of the seniority system. The judge called the argument "historical, not personal" and declared that plaintiffs who "have never suffered discrimination at the hands of the company are in no better position to complain of the recall system than are the white workers who were hired contemporaneously with them." The verdict overturned a decision by Federal District Court Judge Fred J. Cassibry of New Orleans, who had ordered Continental Can to recall enough black workers to restore the ratio of black/white employes that had obtained in 1971.)

EEOC inquiry scope broadened. A Jan. 23, 1976 ruling by the U.S. Fourth Circuit Court of Appeals in Richmond, Va. extended the powers of the Equal Employment Opportunity Commission (EEOC) to investigate charges of discrimination. EEOC investigations, the court said, could not be restricted to only those cases of discrimination which affected the party that originally filed a complaint.

The decision came on a case in which the EEOC had filed a suit charging racial and sex discrimination against the General Electric Co. The suit was the result of investigations begun after a complaint was filed in 1969 by two black male employes of a General Electric plant in Lynchburg, Va. General Electric had contended that the sex discrimination charge was improper because the EEOC investigation should have been limited to types of discrimination which could affect the original complainants.

The appellate court ruling, on a 2–1 vote, was set forth in a decision written by Judge Donald S. Russell. The decision stated that the EEOC, provided it followed proper administrative procedures, could prosecute "any discrimination stated in the (initial) charge itself or developed in the course of a reasonable investigation of that charge." Such a policy was necessary to prevent an "inexcusable waste of valuable administrative resources," the decision held.

In a dissent, Judge H. Emory Widener argued that the ruling was "irreconcilable with the long line of cases requiring strict compliance" by government agencies with their administrative procedures.

New exam-bias rules signed. Three federal agencies—the Civil Service Commission, the Justice Department and the Labor Department—Nov. 17, 1976 signed new guidelines for determining bias in job tests given by employers. The Equal Employment Opportunity Commission, which in 1970 issued its own guidelines on the matter, called the new ones too lenient.

The agencies that adopted the new guidelines defended them as "more practical and realistic than existing guidelines." A Labor Department official said that the new rules would actually be more effective because "the old guidelines were so stringent that they were unusable." A Treasury Department official said Nov. 17 that the Treasury Department would "most likely" use the new guidelines.

A story in the Nov. 5 Washington Post said that the main difference between the new and the old guidelines centered on how far an employer would have to go to prove that a test was job-related. (A 1971 Supreme Court ruling had barred tests that tended to exclude minorities unless it could be shown that the tests were job-related.) The new guidelines required "validation" of job-relatedness only if it were "feasible." The guidelines allowed use of tests that had not been validated even if the rate of failure for blacks taking the tests was as much as 25% above that for whites.

The guidelines were for judging job tests used by private employers doing business with the agencies, as well as tests used by the agencies themselves.

An official of the National Association for the Advancement of Colored People's Legal Defense and Education Fund assailed the new guidelines as "a parting shot" of the Ford Administration "at a time when they are not politically responsible," the Nov. 5 Washington Post reported. The guidelines "seek to undo gains won in hard fought litigation over many years," the official said.

Critics of the guidelines noted that they might be susceptible to legal challenges, since they conflicted with those issued by the EEOC, the governmental agency with broadest authority over discrimination in employment.

U.S. contractors ignore rules. The General Accounting Office May 4, 1975 reported substantial noncompliance with a 1965 executive order prohibiting federal contractors from discriminating on the basis of race, sex, creed or national origin. The GAO said it found a pattern of "almost non-existence of enforcement actions."

The report had been requested by the Congressional Joint Economic Committee panel studying the economic status of women. But Rep. Richard Bolling (D, Mo.), in releasing the report, said the GAO had "found so many problems in the over-all [antidiscrimination] program that it was meaningless to assess the program against sex discrimination alone."

Construction job goals—The Labor Department July 2, 1974 had imposed minority hiring goals on building contractors and 101 construction union locals in 21 areas. The department said the unions had failed to meet employment obligations under earlier voluntary plans.

Under the new orders, contractors bidding on projects receiving federal funds would be required to see that unions met percentage goals, which were based on population composition of individual cities and regions. Failure to make "good-faith" efforts could result in loss of contracts or suspension.

(The Equal Employment Opportunity Commission had reported June 29 that in the 1969–72 period, minority membership in construction unions had increased from 13.2% to 15.6% [an increase of 52,000 workers], but mostly in lower-paying job categories. The report said that in 1972, 6.9% of the higher-paying unions [such as iron workers, plumbers and sheetmetal workers] were from minorities, while minorities represented 37.6% of the laborers' union.)

Labor Department cases—Among Labor Department cases (in 1976):

■ The Labor Department announced July 16 that Gulf Oil Corp. had agreed to pay $935,000 compensation to 640 minority and women employes who had been discriminated against in hiring or promotion. The settlement—involving Gulf's refinery at Port Arthur, Tex.—also included a commitment by Gulf to increase the hiring and promotion of minority individuals and women.

■ The Wall Street Journal reported Aug. 6 that the Labor Department had begun moves to bar Uniroyal Inc. from holding any federal contracts because of alleged discrimination against female and minority workers. The Journal cited charges of pay inequity, bias in promotions and discriminatory treatment in layoffs and recalls at the company's Mishawaka, Ind. plant. Uniroyal labeled the charges "baseless."

Merrill Lynch charged with job bias. A confidential report filed by the Equal Employment Opportunity Commission concluded that Merrill Lynch, Pierce, Fenner & Smith Inc., the nation's largest brokerage house, "had violated and continues to violate" civil rights laws "by discriminating against blacks, women, Spanish-surnamed Americans and other national minorities on the basis of race, sex and national origin" (reported Sept. 8, 1975). It said violations in "recruiting hiring, assignment, training and promotion and other terms and conditions of employment" had occurred.

Merrill Lynch responded that it felt the commission's findings were unjustified, but the firm indicated it and the EEOC would attempt to "conciliate" the charges, as required by law.

Merrill Lynch June 4, 1976 filed consent decrees under which the firm agreed to pay about $1.9 million to victims of past discrimination and to set targets for minority and female job recruitment. The settlements, filed in U.S. District Court in Pittsburgh, involved two anti-discrimina-

tion suits. One had been filed by the Equal Employment Opportunity Commission, the other by Helen O'Bannon, a woman whose application for a job as an account executive had been rejected by Merrill Lynch. (O'Bannon's suit was joined by the EEOC.)

Merrill Lynch promised to spend $1.3 million on advertising over a five-year period in an effort to attract minority and female applicants. The agreement specified the following hiring quotas for female and minority account executives: For women, 10% in 1976, increasing by 2% each year to 18% in 1980; for blacks, 3.5% each year during the five-years and for persons with Spanish surnames, 2.6% annually during the same period. Merrill Lynch agreed to pay O'Bannon $10,000 plus $182,000 in legal fees.

Puerto Rican bias. A study for the U.S. Equal Employment Opportunity Commission by the Center for Environmental and Consumer Justice found that Puerto Rican businesses discriminated against Puerto Ricans, it was reported May 28, 1974.

The study—a survey of 45 local businesses, including major companies in manufacturing, banking, retail sales, service industries, construction and transportation—found that firms gave hiring and promotion preference to U.S. continentals and Cuban immigrants over Puerto Ricans. There was also extensive discrimination against blacks and women, the study reported.

Working for the Government

Federal agencies accused. Rep. John E. Moss (D, Calif.) May 6, 1975 made public seven hitherto secret Civil Service Commission studies showing that certain federal agencies hired and promoted employes without adequate regard for civil service and equal employment rules designed to protect women and minorities from discriminatory job practices.

Moss, who suggested that the commission had not been "vigorous" in pressing for internal change in these agencies," said that the reluctance of the commission to make the studies public raised questions about its commitment to enforcement of anti-discrimination rules. However, a commission spokesman called the reports "problem oriented and negative, and ... done for internal use. They contain names of people and could be an invasion of privacy and so we do not make them public."

The agencies cited in the studies were: the Equal Employment Opportunity Commission, the National Science Foundation, the Small Business Administration, the Merchant Marine Academy, the Smithsonian Institution, the Department of Transportation, the Social Security Administration and the Atomic Energy Commission, which was divided into two separate agencies Jan. 1.

■ The Senate Government Operations Committee's subcommittee on reports said Sept. 17, 1976 that in 1975 women held 11%, and blacks 4%, of the more than 22,000 positions on federal advisory commissions and committees. Sen. Lee Metcalf, subcommittee chairman, called the finding evidence of a "gross imbalance, which discriminates against both women and blacks."

White wins reverse bias complaint. Robert J. Neyhart, a white employe of the Labor Department's Office of Equal Employment Opportunity, was awarded a delayed promotion and back pay after a Civil Service Commission examiner upheld his complaint that he had been discriminated against because he was not Spanish-surnamed, it was reported March 11, 1975. Neyhart had complained that Velma M. Strode, the office's director, told him he would be named to the $28,000-a-year deputy directorship. Subsequently, Neyhart asserted, Strode changed her mind because of instructions from the White House to place more Spanish-surnamed persons in top positions.

Black employes accuse Labor Department. Twenty-six black employes in the Atlanta office of the Labor Department filed a class action complaint charging the department with racial discrimination in its employment practices, it was reported Sept. 9, 1975.

The complaint, filed on behalf of all black employes in the department's eight-state southeast region, alleged that fewer blacks were employed in high-paying jobs in 1975 than in 1971. During the same 1971–75 period, the complaint said, the concentration of blacks in low-paying positions became more pronounced.

According to the complaint, blacks made up 8.2% of the regional work force in 1971, including 7.2% of the employes in the highest civil service grades and 22% of the employes in the lowest four grades. By January 1975, blacks constituted 15.7% of the work force, but only 5.4% were in high grades, while 32.7% were in the lowest grades, the complaint said.

This disparity between high-level black and white employes arose largely because of discrimination, the complaint said. Most of those hired in the region, the complaint claimed, had come from other agencies that had traditionally excluded blacks. It said whites were hired into high grades despite the availability of blacks with equivalent or better educational and job experience qualifications. In addition, the department tended not to advertise to blacks the availability of promotional opportunities, the complaint said.

State Department accused. Secretary of State Henry A. Kissinger was booed by a largely black audience in Boston Aug. 2, 1976 when he addressed the convention of the National Urban League. The booing erupted when Kissinger, in reply to a question about the scarcity of blacks in the State Department, said, "It serves nobody's purpose to appoint black personnel unless they meet all qualifications." A statement by Kissinger that assignment of an ambassador was not related to the race of the ambassador was also jeered.

The State Department the next day produced figures showing that 1,585 of the departments 12,247 employes were black. Of the 5,799 foreign-service and professional-rank employes in the agency, 262 were black. Five ambassadors (out of 140) were black and four of the five were assigned to African countries. Department officials said that they were trying to increase the proportion of blacks in professional levels through recruitment at black universities and through a special program whereby every year 20 persons—10 women and 10 minority individuals—were brought directly into the middle grades of the foreign service, rather than working their way up to those grades through normal channels.

Bias in Congressional jobs. The Congressional agency responsible for referring and placing applicants for staff jobs acknowledged Aug. 19, 1974 that the offices of some congressmen had filed job requests specifying discriminatory criteria, including race ("white only"), religion ("no Catholics") and astrology ("no water signs"). The agency said the requests were usually honored.

The accusations of discrimination had been published Aug. 18 by the Fort Worth (Tex.) Star-Telegram, which said it had obtained documents showing that at least 20 Congressional offices (19 representatives and one senator) had placed such requests.

The Office of Placement and Office Management, a unit of the Joint Committee on Congressional Operations, said it had found no evidence that the congressmen had personally made the requests. By Aug. 19, 15 of the 20 cited by the Star-Telegram had issued either outright denials of discriminatory practices or statements that the requests had been made without their knowledge.

Sen. Lee Metcalf (D, Mont.), chairman of the joint committee, said Aug. 19 that he had ordered the placement unit to cease accepting discriminatory requests. (The Justice Department, Equal Employment Opportunity Commission and Civil Service Commission said Aug. 20 that because of language in job discrimination laws, they were powerless to act against alleged bias in Congressional hiring.)

Because Congress had exempted itself from civil rights laws, its employes had no legal recourse if they believed they were victims of race or sex discrimination.

Statistics in a study made public June 16, 1975 by the Capitol Hill chapter of the National Women's Political Caucus showed that members of the Senate paid women less than men for doing the same type of work.

Put together by a group of female Congressional employes, the study revealed that 30 of the 100 senators employed no woman making more than $18,000 a year, while every senator employed men earning this amount or more. The median salary for persons being paid more than this amount was $22,627 for women and $28,091 for men.

The report analyzed the January–July 1974 payroll data for 2,300 persons in senatorial employ and found no significant differences in pay practices between Democrats and Republicans. Because payroll data by itself did not show whether variations of experience and length of service were responsible for pay differentials, the report did not ask that Congress amend laws exempting itself from the authority of the Equal Pay Act of 1963 and Title 7 of the Civil Rights Act of 1964.

Data July 31, 1977 from the House Commission on Administrative Review showed that congressmen paid their high-ranking male employes 18%-129% more than they paid women with the same job titles. The latest Capitol Hill Women's Political Caucus survey issued Aug. 4 indicated that U.S. senators paid women 56% of the median wages paid to men, a wider pay gap than in 1974.

A newly formed coalition of Congressional workers, organized in response to disclosures of discrimination in Congressional jobs, urged Aug. 31, 1977 an end to "the ultimate hypocrisy where employes working for the nation's lawmakers lack the simple protections granted by those lawmakers to others."

Anti-bias board for Senate blocked—A measure that would have created a six-member board to review Senate employment practices and pass judgment on discrimination complaints was blocked Sept. 20, 1978 when the Democratic Senate leadership decided not to schedule it for a floor vote in the current session.

Sen. John Glenn (D, Ohio) said he had presented the proposal for scheduling at a meeting of the Democratic Policy Committee and chairmen of the major Senate committees, the Washington Post reported Sept. 22.

The decision against a floor vote was arrived at by consensus rather than "by a hard vote," Glenn said, adding that he "still would like to see it brought up [for a floor vote] because it is needed."

Civil rights and labor lawyer Joseph Rauh said at a news conference Sept. 21 that the decision was a "monumental cover-up by senators who know they'd have to vote for it" if it came up for a floor vote.

Rep. Patricia Schroeder (D, Colo.), who was at the news conference with Rauh, said that she and Rep. Morris Udall (D, Ariz.) had proposed similar protections against discrimination for the House of Representatives.

(The House currently had a committee of representatives and staff to investigate charges of bias, but there was no obligation for House members to submit to the panel's inquiries. Only 108 representatives had volunteered to cooperate with the committee, the Post reported.)

U.S. funds aid bias? Four national organizations Aug. 19, 1975 made public a report charging the $30.2-billion federal revenue sharing program with "financing widespread discrimination in public employment and local services."

The report, entitled "Equal Opportunity under Revenue Sharing," cited what it said were the most recent figures available on public employes as evidence of the existence of "a nationwide pattern of underrepresentation of minorities and women." State and local government spent federal funds on contracts to discriminatory private employers and on inadequate municipal services for the poor and minority neighborhoods, the report said.

The report was also critical of the Treasury Department's Office of Revenue Sharing, which distributed revenue-sharing funds and was responsible for seeing they were not spent in a discriminatory way. The office "delays unconscionably in dealing with complaints" and "has done almost nothing" to remedy such inadequacies in the communities it funded, the report said.

The organizations involved in the study were the Center for National Policy Review, the National Urban Coalition, the League of Women Voters and the Center for Community Change.

In a separate development, Elmer Staats, U.S. controller general and chief administrator of the General Accounting Office, told a Senate subcommittee July 23 that a GAO study of federal revenue sharing had determined that state and local recipients were able to evade federal antidiscrimination regulations by using their own money in areas where civil rights compliance problems might be encountered. Summarizing the GAO study

before the Government Operation Subcommittee on Intergovernmental Relations July 23, Staats urged that the revenue sharing act be broadened to provide that "a government receiving revenue sharing could not discriminate in any of its programs or activities regardless of the source of funding, and revenue-sharing funds would be withheld, after due process, pending acceptable actions to correct discriminatory practices."

Bias in police & fireman jobs. A study by the Police Foundation, a unit of the Ford Foundation, showed that about 6% of the nation's police officers were from racial minorities and less than 2% were women, it was reported April 21, 1974.

The survey found that hiring standards varied widely between men and women, with stricter educational requirements but more relaxed physical and background-check requirements for women.

The study also noted that the 6% figure was inflated by the high minority representation on the forces in Washington, D.C. (37% black) and Hawaii (more than 95% minority).

The states of Alabama and Maryland, under federal court orders imposing hiring quotas, had larger percentages of black uniformed state police officers than all other states, the Race Relations Information Center reported in December 1974 in the final issue of its bi-monthly magazine, the Race Relations Reporter.

Directed by a federal court judge in 1971 to recruit one black for every white hired until its state police force was 25% black, Alabama currently had 28 blacks on a total force of 623 troopers, (4.5%), the center reported. Maryland, under a similar court order to make its state police force at least 16% black, had 58 blacks on a force of 1,440 officers (4%).

Nationally, the center said, blacks constituted 1.5% of the state police forces. American Indians and Hispanics made up about an equal percentage. The figures contrasted with employment data for the nation's 50 largest urban police forces. Of the 86,065 persons employed on these forces, 9% were black, the center said.

The American Civil Liberties Union Sept. 3, 1975 filed a suit in U.S. District Court in Washington asking the court to enjoin the Law Enforcement Assistance Administration from disbursing funds to police departments that discriminated against blacks and women. The suit brought by the ACLU on behalf of a national black police officers association, a national woman police officers organization and several individual plaintiffs, charged that the LEAA had illegally given millions of dollars in federal money to departments that regularly violated federal laws against discrimination in hiring and promotion practices.

An LEAA spokesman responded that the agency had already cut off funds to 20 departments, pending their compliance with LEAA equal employment guidelines. In 17 additional cases, the LEAA threatened funding cutoffs, the spokesman said.

The LEAA March 9, 1973 had issued a guideline to police departments, correctional and court facilities which receive LEAA funds to eliminate minimum height requirements for employment, unless an agency could "convincingly demonstrate that such requirements are necessary for certain job categories."

LEAA said the height requirements had sometimes tended "to disproportionately disqualify persons of certain national origins and races and women." According to the Leadership Conference on Civil Rights, which had advised LEAA on minority employment, Puerto Ricans, Mexican-Americans and Japanese-Americans had been among the affected groups.

LEAA also issued a proposed guideline requiring all law enforcement agencies receiving funds, and operating in an area whose work force was more than 3% composed of minority groups, to implement affirmative action programs to obtain "full and equal opportunity for women and minorities." Correctional facilities would have to increase recruitment among minority groups even if located in suburban or rural areas with few minority individuals.

The U.S. 5th Circuit Court of Appeals ruled March 31, 1974 that the Mississippi highway patrol discriminated against blacks, but stopped short of ordering quota hiring. The court said, however, that a lower court could, "within the bounds of discretion," set temporary hiring quotas, a freeze on hiring of whites "or any other affirmative hiring relief until the patrol is effectively integrated."

According to the court, five of Mississippi's 548 patrolmen were black.

The decision was upheld by the Supreme Court Oct. 21.

The Justice Department Oct. 17, 1974 filed a civil suit charging the Milwaukee police and fire departments with bias in hiring women and minorities. At the same time, a consent order was filed resolving the suit against the fire department and setting hiring goals for minorities.

Under the consent order, the fire department—which had six black men and no women among its 1,120 firefighters—agreed to recruit and hire blacks, persons with Spanish surnames and American Indians until the three groups made up 14% of the department's uniformed personnel. The department agreed to adopt a goal of making at least 40% of its appointments from among qualified applicants from the three minority groups.

The fire department also had to recruit and hire women in numbers reflecting their interest and ability to qualify.

The suit against the police department said that of Milwaukee's 2,200 police officers, only 58 were black and 16 were women.

The Supreme Court April 14, 1975 upheld a ruling requiring Massachusetts cities to give preference in hiring to blacks and Spanish-surnamed individuals to alleviate past racial discrimination in fire departments.

Teachers & principals. A U.S. Court of Appeals ruling in Washington, D.C. May 14, 1974 held that the Department of Health, Education and Welfare (HEW) could not disburse funds to school systems with racially discriminatory teacher assignment policies. The ruling, which reversed a lower court decision, came in a suit to prevent grants totaling $20 million to systems in Baltimore, Detroit, Rochester, N.Y., Los Angeles and Richmond, Calif.

Citing Supreme Court rulings, the court said that faculties in schools receiving federal funds could not be "racially identifiable," and that the effects of racial discrimination must be removed immediately if federal funds were involved. HEW had decided the grants could be made if the school districts promised to end discriminatory practices in the future.

U.S. District Judge William E. Doyle Aug. 15, 1975 ordered the Denver Board of Education to hire more teachers, staff and administrators from minority groups until they reflected the ratio of black and Hispanic students in the school system. "I have to find and determine an almost total noncompliance" with an earlier order mandating increased efforts to hire minorities, Doyle said.

The National Education Association, which had filed numerous actions in Alabama to eliminate discrimination against black teachers, filed suit to force the Lowndes County Board of Education to reopen nine staff positions that had been filled by blacks on a noncompetitive basis, it was reported Nov. 26, 1975. It maintained that by failing to notify qualified whites within the system of the job openings, the board violated a 1973 federal court order barring racial discrimination in faculty hiring. Among the positions so filled were superintendent of schools and two other top administrative posts.

The court order had been issued at a time when a white minority controlled the system. Since 1973, however, political control of the county had passed to blacks.

The Department of Health Education & Welfare March 31, 1976 rejected a teacher-integration plan submitted by the Chicago Board of Education. The board plan, which HEW found to be inadequate, would have embraced about four-fifths of Chicago's public schools by the start of the 1977–78 academic year. It would have assigned 1,500 new teachers and relocated 2,200 full-time substitute teachers to limit the racial makeup of an individual school staff. The plan had set 70% as the maximum representation of any one race.

HEW, however, called for an upper limit of 60% for teachers of one race in any Chicago public school and said this should be achieved by the start of the 1977–78 school year.

At stake in the controversy were federal revenue-sharing funds for Chicago schools.

Chicago school authorities and HEW reached agreement in October 1977. The agreement, signed in Washington Oct. 11, was announced Oct. 12 by HEW Secretary Joseph A. Califano Jr., who called it "a model for the nation."

The goal was to bring the racial composition of the faculty in each school more in line with the racial composition of the system's faculty as a whole. The agreement limited the variation in the current school year to no more than 12.5%. Beyond that, the range of variation was to be reduced as soon as possible to no more than 10%.

A start had already been made to desegregate the system's faculty, which was 53% white, 47% non-white. To attain better balance in racial composition, almost 4,000 of the system's 26,000 teachers had been transferred since June 1976. Before that, almost half the schools had had faculties where the whites were either in the majority by more than 75% or in the minority by less than 25%.

A U.S. Appeals Court in New York ruled Jan. 19, 1976 that a ruling ordering race quotas for principals in the New York City school system was "constitutionally forbidden reverse discrimination."

The overturned decision—a federal district court ruling of Feb. 1975—was designed to protect members of minorities who lacked seniority in their jobs as school principals. Prior to the February ruling, if a school district had to eliminate a position, it would do so by transferring, demoting or dismissing "the least senior person in the job classification." This procedure was called "excessing." The February ruling, however, ordered that the percentage of minority members on an "excessing list" for a school district could not exceed the percentage of the group in the district.

As a result, non-minority members with greater seniority were sometimes excessed instead of minority members with less seniority.

The appellate court, on a 2–1 vote, voided the quota system and restored seniority as the basis for "excessing."

Judge Ellsworth Van Graafeiland, in the decision, said that racial quotas in hiring, to provide "remedial relief" of past discrimination, might receive "limited approval," but there was no justification for extending the quotas to "excessing practices" which were not in themselves discriminatory.

In a dissent, Judge James L. Oakes argued that the quotas were a legitimate means of remedying past discrimination.

U.S. District Court Judge W. Arthur Garrity Jr. Feb. 24, 1976 mandated a 20% quota for employment of black administrators in Boston's public schools and ruled that blacks had to be hired in equal numbers with whites until the quota was reached. The upgrading of acting principals or headmasters to permanent rank would be exempted from the judge's order. Also, the quota could be suspended if there were no qualified black candidate for a position. Garrity observed that such a situation was unlikely to arise.

Garrity's plan barred use of the national Educational Testing Service examination; only tests approved by the U.S. Equal Opportunity Commission could be employed.

The New York Times reported May 22 that the Professional Educators of Los Angeles, a teacher organization, had filed suit to block implementation of a faculty desegregation plan that involved mandatory reassignments of Los Angeles teachers to achieve racial quotas in the city's public schools. The plan, adopted by the school board under threat of a federal-aid cutoff, called for transfers of 1,000 permanent teachers.

The plan's goal was to ensure that minority teachers, who accounted for about 30% of the district's 25,000 teachers, made up not less than 15%, and not more than 50%, of the faculty in each school.

The suit filed by the 11,000-member teachers group called for assignments based solely on experience, education and merit, rather than on race or ethnicity.

The Supreme Court Nov. 29, 1976 declined to hear an appeal filed by a white Louisiana high school coach who had challenged a school board's promotion practices that had been aimed at implementing a court-ordered desegration plan. (The plan had set a goal of obtaining a 50–50 ratio of blacks and whites in certain school jobs.) The white man had been promoted to head coach of a high school. Shortly thereafter the promotion had been revoked so that a black could be given the head coach job. The case was Adcox v. Caddo Parish School Bd. (76-296).

Other government bias items. The city of Jackson, Miss. and the U.S. Justice Department reached an agreement providing quotas for the increased placement of blacks on the municipal payroll and back pay up to $1,000 for currently-employed blacks who had been denied promotion opportunities, it was reported March 31, 1974.

Quotas in the plan set a five-year goal of a 40% black work force, approximately the same percentage as in the city's population. Currently, about 800 of the 3,000 workers were black, most in low-paying job classifications. The 40% figure would apply to both police and fire departments.

The accord also provided that at least one-third of city jobs would be filled by women.

The Department of Justice April 11, 1975 obtained a consent decree requiring the city of Tallahassee, Fla. to hire qualified black persons for every type of city job in proportion to the number of blacks in the city's civilian labor force. The city was ordered to establish a biracial selection committee to identify blacks rejected because of race and notify them of their right to apply for listing on a priority register.

The U.S. Supreme Court Oct. 12, 1976 declined to review and so, in effect, upheld a decision by the Washington-state supreme court that rejected a discrimination suit brought by a white Seattle city worker who contended that the city's affirmative action plan was unconstitutional. The white worker alleged that he had been passed over in promotion in favor of a minority employe, even though he (the white) had scored higher on an exam. The case was Brabant v. City of Seattle (76-196).

The U.S. Supreme Court Dec. 13, 1976 also declined to review an appeal by the state of New Hampshire of an Equal Employment Opportunity Commission requirement that employers (including states) record and annually report to the EEOC the racial and ethnic identity of employes. The case was New Hampshire v. U.S. (76-453).

Among other developments in 1976:

The New Jersey Supreme Court ruled Nov. 30 that the state could not set hiring quotas for blacks to rectify the effects of past discrimination. The ruling struck down a quota, set by the State Division of Civil Rights, for the city of Montclair. The New Jersey high court said that quotas often constituted reverse discrimination, that they had a divisive effect upon society and that they violated "the fundamental precept in a democratic society that merit, not skin color, should determine an individual's place in society."

The Justice Department Nov. 26 filed suit against the city of Boston, charging that the job tests and hiring standards used by the city's Department of Public Works discriminated against blacks and Hispanics. A disproportionate number of minority applicants were disqualified by the tests and standards, the suit said.

Status of Women

Statistical view. The Census Bureau April 27, 1976 issued a compilation of data gathered by various government agencies to provide a composite picture of women in America. Containing statistics on population trends, health, family status, crime, education levels, employment and voting and political activity, the report furnished a quantitative basis for studies of women's progress.

Among the subjects covered by the report:

Education—In 1950, for every 100 men aged 25 to 29 who had finished four years of college, there were 66 women in the same age group with the same amount of education; by 1975, the figure was 77 women. Among women in the 25–29 age bracket, the proportion completing four years of college jumped from 6% in 1950 to 19% in 1975. Women comprised 44% of the 1975 college enrollment.

About 10% of the doctoral degrees awarded in 1950 went to women; this figure had risen to about 16% by 1972. The report cited the growth in the number of women majoring in engineering—from 2% of all such majors in 1966 to 7% in 1974—as an example of women entering fields formerly considered to be the exclusive province of men.

Black female college enrollment increased sharply from the mid-1960s, rising from a little over 100,000 in 1964 to 392,-000 in 1974.

Employment—The number of women working almost doubled from 1950 to 1974; the male labor force increased by only one-fourth in the same period. In 1950, for every 100 men working full time all year, there were 29 women similarly employed; in 1974, the ratio was 47 women to 100 men.

However, the median income of women working full time was only 57% of that for men similarly employed—$6,722 a year for women, $11,835 for men. Paula J. Schneider, the report's chief author, attributed this to the fact that women remained concentrated in a few occupational categories. More than half of all working women were employed in clerical, operative or service positions.

The report also documented a "profound change" in the "traditional relationship between labor force participation and such variables as marital status and the presence and age of children." In 1975, 37% of married women with preschool children were employed; in 1950, the figure was 12%.

The proportion of working women who had white collar jobs increased among both blacks and whites. The increase was greater for blacks, but had not brought them to parity with whites. The figures were: for black women, 42% in 1974, up from 24% in 1964; for white women, 64.4% in 1974, up from 61.8% in 1965.

■ The recent "dynamic rise" in the number of women seeking employment, which had resulted in a "larger proportion of women who are in or near the entry level" of the job market.

■ The shorter average lifetime work experience of women.

The report concluded, however, that even after allowing for these differences, "much of the male-female [pay] differential remains unexplained." The remaining differential, the report said, was presumably the result of discrimination.

The report also found that women constituted 31.8% of the full-time work force, but accounted for only 5.3% of those earning $15,000 or more a year.

It said that the percentage of men working overtime was more than twice that of women—28% vs. 13% (the figures were for May 1975). Those women who did work overtime earned substantially less than men with overtime. The average weekly pay for women who worked overtime was $138; for men it was $215.

The Labor Department Nov. 28 disclosed that the gap in average incomes between men and women had widened over the 20 years from 1955 to 1974. Department statistics, based on Census Bureau data, showed that in 1974 the average earnings of men who worked full time year-round were 74.8% higher than for women who worked similar schedules. In 1955 the difference was 56.4%.

The report listed, by sex and race, these average 1974 annual earnings of full-time year-round workers: White men, $12,343; black men, $9,082; white women, $7,025; black women, $6,611.

It cited factors that could partially explain the earnings gap. Among them:

■ The concentration of women in "lower-status ... traditional" jobs with "limited opportunity for advancement."

Sex bias settlement at Bank of America. The U.S. district court in San Francisco gave approval July 24, 1974 to a settlement of class action sex discrimination suits brought against the Bank of America, the world's largest private bank.

The consent decree, which the bank accepted without admitting guilt, was praised by both the bank and plaintiffs as a breakthrough in women's rights.

Rather than the back-pay provisions of the sort that had become usual in settlements reached with other companies, the agreement provided that the bank would pay $3.75 million over five years into trust funds which would give incentives for female employes to undertake management training, educational and other "self-development" programs leading to management-level promotions.

The agreement set hiring and promotion goals under which the proportion of women officers would be increased from the current 31% to 40% by December 1978, with the sharpest percentage increases to occur in the higher management levels. (About 73% of the bank's 54,000 employes were women.)

Before approving the agreement, the court inserted language to insure that reverse discrimination would not be practiced and that promotion policies would be based on ability as well as percentage guidelines.

Other Developments

Economist says income gap widens. Despite advances made by blacks toward economic parity with whites in the 1960s, later trends indicated that the income gap was once again widening, economist Lester S. Thurow said Nov. 27, 1975.

Thurow, professor of economics at the Massachusetts Institute of Technology, said the increasing disparity in earnings was to be expected, as the essential problem was a "long-run, deeply-embedded relationship in the economy."

Good times or bad, he stated, "black unemployment rates are twice as high as white." The ratio was larger during a recession, he said, because the proportion of black families with two workers declined, while that of white families increased. Also, due to considerations of seniority in hiring and layoffs, young blacks were among those most likely to be out of work when jobs were scarce, increasing the statistical weight of older workers, among whom the disparity in earnings between blacks and whites was greater than among young workers.

Thurow attributed the gain in relative earnings by blacks in the 1960s to the absorption of young blacks into an expanding post-World War II labor force.

Looking to the future, he rejected the U.S. Equal Employment Opportunity Commission as the vehicle for effecting major changes in the distribution of earnings in the U.S. Instead, he urged that an "all-out effort" be made to create a comprehensive government job or permanent "right to work" program.

Jackson for quotas. The Rev. Jesse L. Jackson, president of People United to Save Humanity (PUSH), proposed Sept. 25, 1975 that workers in U.S. industry be hired and laid off on the basis of a "quota principle" in order to minimize the impact of the recession on members of groups which in the past had been discriminated against by employers. He described his proposal as a serious effort to correct the problem of disproportionate unemployment among minority groups.

Retroactive seniority awarded in discrimination cases. The Supreme Court

March 24, 1976 ruled, 5–3, that individuals denied employment because of race, and then later hired by the same organization, should be awarded the seniority and benefits they would have accumulated if hired in the first instance.

The ruling, based on the Civil Rights Act of 1964, would apparently extend to cases involving discrimination based on sex, national origin, or religion, as well as race. It applied to cases where individuals had been refused jobs after the Civil Rights Act went into effect. The ruling did not consider the issue of retroactive seniority for persons who claimed they had not originally applied for a job because they knew that a discriminatory hiring policy had existed.

The ruling was greeted as a major victory by civil rights groups, who had maintained that recent advances in minority employment were being destroyed by recession layoffs made under the "last-hired, first-fired" policy.

Recognizing that the ruling could result in the relative loss of seniority standing by some whites, Justice William J. Brennan Jr. in the opinion wrote that "the burden of the past discrimination" must be shared by whites with blacks. Joining Brennan in the majority were Justices Potter Stewart, Byron R. White, Thurgood Marshall and Harry A. Blackmun.

Chief Justice Warren E. Burger, dissenting, said: "I cannot join in judicial approval of 'robbing Peter to pay Paul'." Justices Lewis F. Powell Jr. and William H. Rehnquist also dissented; Justice John Paul Stevens did not participate in the decision.

The ruling came on a suit brought by two black former employes against Bowman Transportation Co., a trucking firm located in Atlanta.

Whites win rights-law benefits. The Supreme Court June 25, 1976 held that two rights laws protected whites as well as nonwhites.

One law was the 1964 Civil Rights Act, Title VII, which prohibited discrimination by employers. Its applicability to whites as well as nonwhites was by unanimous agreement of the court.

The other law was part of the 1866 Civil Rights Act known as Section 1981, which affirmed that "all persons" shall have the "same right" to "make and enforce con-

tracts, to sue, be parties, give evidence."

In continuing its guarantee of "the full and equal benefit of all laws and proceedings for the security of persons and property," Section 1981 added, "as is enjoyed by white citizens."

The court stressed the application of the provision to "all persons." In going back to the Senate discussion of the legislation before passage, the court found remarks that the law would apply to all persons including whites. The phrase "as is enjoyed by white citizens" was added in the House, the court said, but further debate on the bill reinforced the intent to have coverage for whites as well as nonwhites.

"The statutory structure and legislative history," the court said, "persuades us that the 39th Congress was intent upon establishing in the federal law a broader principle than would have been necessary simply to meet the particular and immediate plight of the Negro slave."

The extension of protection to whites under this provision was voted 7-2 by the court. Justices Byron White and William Rehnquist dissented. The majority opinion was written by Justice Thurgood Marshall, the court's only black member.

The case concerned two white men who claimed discrimination on the basis of race after they were fired for allegedly misappropriating company property. A third man, a black, also implicated in the matter, was not dismissed.

The case was McDonald v. Sante Fe Trail Transp. Co. (75–260).

Damage pay for bias victims. U.S. District Judge Albert V. Bryan Jr. Oct. 22, 1976 ordered Western Electric Co. to pay damages to blacks and women who were victims of bias in hiring and promotion at the company's plant in Arlington, Va. The Alexandria, Va. U.S. District Court ruling applied to about 3,500 past and present employes and job applicants. Paul Reichler, attorney for six blacks who had filed the suit on which the ruling was based, said Oct. 22 that payments to the 3,500 might reach $1.5 million.

Bryan also ruled that two-thirds of those hired or promoted in the future must be black and three-fifths must be women. Bryan cited statistics showing that, between 1970 and 1974, 29.8% of white job applicants at the plant had been hired, compared with 12.7% of black applicants. Over the same period, 26.8% of male applicants were hired, compared with 16.9% of the females, the judge said.

■ U.S. District Judge D. W. Suttle Nov. 23 approved an out-of-court settlement in which Braniff Airways agreed to pay about $1.1 million to 586 black and Spanish-surnamed employes. The agreement gave the employes $900,000 in direct payments and also covered their legal fees. The settlement also specified minority hiring and promotion goals. The agreement brought to an end a suit filed in 1973. The suit also had cited the International Association of Machinists and Aerospace Workers and the International Brotherhood of Teamsters.

Quota ordered in construction union. U.S. District Judge Charles H. Henney, in a 1976 order that became effective Sept. 1, barred discrimination in the International Union of Operating Engineers, one of New York City's largest construction unions. He also ordered the union to achieve 36% minority membership by Sept. 1, 1981. The EEOC had brought the bias charge against three of the union's locals. Blacks and Hispanics accounted for 2.8% of the membership of two of those locals and 6.5% in the third, government lawyers said.

J. P. Stevens decision. U.S. District Judge Franklin T. Dupree June 25, 1976 issued an order to J. P. Stevens & Co. to end discrimination against blacks at its plants in Roanoke Rapids, N.C. Dupree ordered the firm—one of the largest textile companies in the South—to institute compensatory hiring and training plaintiffs said that an analysis of the company's employment and pay practices showed that "black males with 12th-grade education were making less than white males with third-grade educations" and "blacks with 10 years' seniority were making less than whites with two years."

Reagan on 'reverse discrimination.' Ronald Reagan, in a paid ABC telecast July 6, 1976, assailed "reverse discrimination" in what was seen as an appeal to white ethnic voters for support in his unsuccessful campaign for the GOP presidential nomination.

"If you happen to belong to an ethnic group not .recognized by the federal government as entitled to special treatment," Reagan said, "you are a victim of reverse discrimination." He said that this was due to government-ordered "affirmative-action" programs that promote employment of blacks and other minorities.

"I'd like an opportunity to put an end to this federal distortion of the principle of equal rights," Reagan said.

Confusion as 1980s Approach

The Bakke Case

Confusion over the legality of quotas and other forms of affirmative action remained widespread as the decade of the 1970s approached its end. This confusion might be considered exemplified by the Bakke case, the most publicized of the legal proceedings on the issue. In the Bakke case, the Supreme Court held in 1978, in 5–4 rulings, that (a) the minority-admissions program of the University of California Medical School in Davis had discriminated illegally against a white male applicant, but (b) that universities could legally consider race as a factor in admissions.

Medical School Ordered to Admit Bakke, But Race-Related Admissions Upheld. The U.S. Supreme Court, in a 5–4 decision June 28, 1978, affirmed a lower court order requiring the University of California Medical School in Davis to admit Allan P. Bakke. Bakke, a 38-year-old white engineer, claimed that the school's minority-admissions plan had made him a victim of "reverse discrimination."

However, while the first alignment of justices ruled that the medical school's special-admissions program was illegal, another 5–4 alignment held that universities could consider race as one factor in choosing among applicants for admission.

Justice Lewis F. Powell Jr. cast the deciding vote in each aspect of the case, *University of California Regents v. Bakke.*

Powell, in announcing the judgment of the court, said that "preferring members of any one group for no reason other than race or ethnic origin is discrimination for its own sake." Other justices who issued opinions were John Paul Stevens, William J. Brennan Jr., Thurgood Marshall, Harry A. Blackmun and Byron R. White.

Title VI vs. 14th Amendment—The University of California's medical school at Davis, near Sacramento, reserved 16 of 100 places in each year's class for minority students. Bakke, twice rejected by the school, had charged in state court that his civil rights had been violated under both the 14th Amendment and Title VI of the 1964 Civil Rights Act.

A California Superior Court had ruled in Bakke's favor on both grounds. The California Supreme Court also supported Bakke's right to be admitted, but solely on the basis of the 14th Amendment.

(The 14th Amendment guaranteed equal protection of the laws to all citizens. Title VI held that no person could be discriminated against because of his or her "race, color or national origin" under any federally funded program or institution.)

Four of the five Supreme Court justices who voted to abolish the Davis admissions program, and admit Bakke, did so on the more narrow ground of Title VI.

Justice Stevens, in an opinion endorsed by Justices Potter Stewart, William H. Rehnquist and Chief Justice Warren E. Burger, contended that the question of whether "race can ever be used in an admissions decision" was not an issue in the Bakke case and called discussion of the subject "inappropriate."

Stevens said that the "settled practice" of the high court was to "avoid the decision of a constitutional issue if a case can be fairly decided on statutory ground [Title VI]."

The controlling factor, according to the Stevens bloc, was that Davis, a federally funded school, had rejected Bakke because of his race. The group dismissed the argument advanced by the University of California that the only issue was whether the school's minority-admissions plan was constitutional under the 14th Amendment.

The 14th Amendment argument was backed by Justices Brennan, Marshall, Blackmun and Byron R. White. Led by Brennan, the group implied that Title VI was merely a restatement of the 14th Amendment.

The civil rights statute, Brennan said, did not "bar the preferential treatment of racial minorities as a means of remedying past societal discrimination to the extent that such action is consistent" with the 14th Amendment.

The pivotal vote was cast by Justice Powell, who joined the Stevens bloc on the basis of the 14th Amendment, rather than Title VI. Powell held that the Davis program contained a "fatal flaw" in its denial of equal protection of the laws to white applicants.

Bakke's Right to Sue—The right of Bakke, a private citizen, to sue under Title VI was questioned by several justices. Stevens, Burger, Rehnquist and Stewart concluded that he did have the right. Their view was backed by the Justice Department.

Justices Brennan, Powell, Blackmun and Marshall held that, since Bakke's legal standing was not an issue in the lower courts, the high court was required to assume he had the right to sue.

Justice White maintained that had Congress intended Title VI to be invoked in private suits, lawmakers would have written such a provision into the civil rights statute.

White asserted that the Supreme Court, as well as the lower courts, were "without jurisdiction" to consider Bakke's claim under Title VI.

The Race Factor in Admissions—Although the Davis plan was struck down by the high court, the justices ruled, 5-4, that schools could take race or ethnic background into account when they admitted students.

Once again, Justice Powell cast the deciding vote. He was joined in this majority by Justices Brennan, Marshall, Blackmun and White.

Powell stated that the attainment of a diverse student body was a "constitutionally permissible goal for an institution of higher learning." This goal was improper, he indicated, if it was attained through a system of quotas based on race or ethnicity. An applicant's origin, he said, was "but a single though important element."

Universities could attain "beneficial educational pluralism," Powell said, by considering, in addition to race, an applicant's "exceptional personal talents, unique work or service experience, maturity" or "history of overcoming disadvantage." Powell urged schools to adopt programs that treated "each applicant as an individual in the admissions process."

Powell cited Harvard as a school that employed a special-admissions plan to expand "the concept of diversity" to include students from all types of racial and economic backgrounds.

Other Affirmative Action—The Supreme Court's Bakke decision appeared to be a blanket rejection of the use of racial or ethnic quotas in affirmative action plans. However, it left open to question the legality of such programs that were outside the area of college admissions and not based on quotas.

The University of California claimed, and the Supreme Court rejected, the contention that the high court in the past had handed down broad rulings in support of the preferential treatment of minorities.

Justice Powell warned that in such areas as school desegregation, employment discrimination and sex discrimination, the court had "never approved a classification that aids persons perceived as members of relatively victimized groups at the expense of other innocent individuals in the absence of judicial, legislative or administrative findings of constitutional or statutory violations."

Powell cited a 1977 case concerning a Supreme Court award of retroactive seniority to black truck drivers as an example of this doctrine. He said that the scope of judicial remedies to discrimination had not exceeded "the extent of the violations."

Facts on Bakke. Allan Paul Bakke, 38, was an engineer who first applied to medical school in 1972, when he was 32. He filed suit against the University of California at Davis after being rejected on a second application in 1973.

Bakke was born in Minneapolis to parents of Norwegian extraction. His father was a mailman and his mother a teacher.

He graduated from the University of Minnesota, where he was an engineering major and maintained a 3.51 grade-point average (on a 4.0 scale).

Bakke had enrolled in the Naval Reserve Officer Training Corps to help meet educational expenses. He fulfilled his military obligation by serving four years in the Marines, including seven months in Vietnam. He left the Marines in 1967, with the rank of captain.

After the Marines, Bakke took an engineering job with National Aeronautics and Space Administration's Ames Research Center, south of San Francisco.

While he worked at the NASA lab, Bakke took night classes at local colleges to complete premed requirements. He said his experience in Vietnam had interested him deeply in the work of doctors, leading him to decide that he wanted to become a doctor.

He also worked as a volunteer in a hospital while holding the job at the Ames Research Center.

His application to the Davis medical school in 1972 was one of 11 applications he submitted. He was rejected by all the schools. His age—32—was a factor weighing against him.

In a letter he wrote to Davis after his first rejection, Bakke complained that the Davis admissions program, which set aside 16 places for minority members, was discriminatory. He attacked "quotas, open or covert, for racial minorities."

An admissions officer at Davis responded to Bakke, sympathizing with him and tacitly urging him to bring suit against the school's admissions system.

When he applied to Davis for a second time in 1973, he was again rejected. The files of the university suggested that his earlier complaints had weighed in the decision to reject him. (He might have been accepted on his first application except that it was submitted late, because of illness in his family. Most of the places in the class were already taken when his application was considered.)

Although his suit against Davis put him in the center of a national controversy, Bakke led a retiring life, refusing to discuss his case with reporters.

High Court Hears Case. Arguments in the Bakke case had been heard by the Supreme Court Oct. 12, 1977.

The 1977 hearing, which lasted two hours, attracted hundreds of spectators and news reporters and a small number of protesters who demonstrated peacefully against Bakke outside the courthouse.

Fifty-eight *amicus curiae* (friend of the court) briefs, believed to be a record number, were filed with the Supreme Court reflecting deep divisions over the Bakke case. Groups supporting the university's position included black and Hispanic civil rights organizations, the AFL-CIO, the U.S. Commission on Civil Rights and the Congressional Black Caucus. They feared that a pro-Bakke decision might be a major setback, not only for minority school-admissions programs, but also for affirmative-action employment programs.

The pro-Bakke side included the Italian-American Foundation, such conservative organizations as the Young Americans for Freedom and Jewish groups, which had traditionally allied themselves with blacks on civil rights issues.

The Justice Department Sept. 19 had filed an 88-page brief in support of special programs to aid minorities in overcoming the effects of past discrimination. The document declined to endorse the use of quotas to achieve equality and asked the court to decide all such cases on a case-by-case basis.

The Supreme Court Oct. 12 heard arguments by the three principal attorneys in the Bakke case: Archibald Cox, who represented the university; Solicitor General Wade H. McCree Jr. of the Justice Department, and Reynold H. Colvin, Bakke's lawyer.

Cox, who had served as the first Watergate special prosecutor, was a professor of law at Harvard University. In answer to questions by Justices Potter Stewart and John Paul Stevens, he said that neither the Davis special admissions program nor its regular admissions program could be considered a quota. A quota, he said, was something that pointed "the finger at a group which had been marked as inferior. . . . It [the special admissions system] was not stigmatizing in the sense of the old quota against Jews."

Cox argued that special admissions programs that did not use race as one of its criteria "simply won't work."

McCree, a black former federal judge, took the Justice Department position that the case should be sent back to the California courts for reconsideration.

Colvin, a San Francisco attorney arguing his first case before the high court, emphasized that his primary purpose was to have Bakke admitted to the medical school. He had spent 20 minutes restating the facts surrounding the case, when Justice Lewis F. Powell Jr. interrupted to remind him that the court was there "to hear a constitutional argument."

In reply to questions from Justice Byron R. White, Colvin admitted that California officials might have had "compelling interests" in maintaining the special admissions program, but he contended that such interests were not being served in the Bakke case. (The Supreme Court in past decisions had ruled that minority groups might be entitled to preferential treatment, but only if the lack of such treatment would violate the equal protection clause.)

Justice Thurgood Marshall, the only black on the court, asked Colvin if his argument would "be the same if one, instead of 16 seats, were left open."

Colvin answered "yes," and said it was the "principle of keeping a man out because of his race" that was at issue.

Excerpts from Opinions by Six Supreme Court Justices on the Bakke Case

Following are excerpts from the opinions of six Supreme Court justices in the case of the University of California Regents v. Bakke.

The central opinion was written by Justice Lewis F. Powell Jr. Separate opinions, expressing partial dissent or concurrence with the key opinion, were written by Justices William J. Brennan Jr., Byron R. White, Harry A. Blackmun, John Paul Stevens and Thurgood Marshall.

Justice Powell

For the reasons stated in the following opinion, I believe that so much of the judgment of the California court as holds petitioner's special admissions program unlawful and directs that respondent be admitted to the medical school must be affirmed. For the reasons expressed in a separate opinion, my brothers the Chief Justice, Mr. Justice Stewart, Mr. Justice Rehnquist and Mr. Justice Stevens concur in this judgment.

I also conclude for the reasons stated in the following opinion that the portion of the court's judgment enjoining petitioner from according any consideration to race in its admissions process must be reversed. For reasons expressed in separate opinions, my brothers Mr. Justice Brennan, Mr. Justice White, Mr. Justice Marshall and Mr. Justice Blackmun concur in this judgment.

In this court the parties neither briefed nor argued the applicability of Title VI of the Civil Rights of 1964.

Rather, as had the California court, they focused exclusively upon the validity of the special admissions program under the equal protection clause. Because it was possible, however, that a decision on Title VI might obviate resort to constitutional interpretation, we requested supplementary briefing on the statutory issue.

At the outset we face the question whether a right of action for private parties exists under Title VI. Respondent argues that there is a private right of action. He contends that the statute creates a federal right in his favor, that legislative history reveals an intent to permit private actions, that such actions would further the remedial purposes of the statute, and that enforcement of federal rights under the Civil Rights Act generally is not relegated to the states.

In addition, he cites several lower court decisions which have recognized or assumed the existence of a private right of action. Petitioner denies the existence of a private right of action. In its view, administrative curtailment of federal funds under that section was the only sanction to be imposed upon recipients that violated Section 601.

Petitioner also points out that Title VI contains no explicit grant of a private right of action, in contrast to Titles II, III, IV and VII of the same statute.

We find it unnecessary to resolve this question in the instant case. The question of respondent's right to bring an action under Title VI was neither argued nor decided in either of the courts below, and this court has been hesitant to review questions not addressed below. We therefore do not address this difficult issue. Similarly, we need not pass upon petitioner's claim that private plaintiffs under Title VI must exhaust administrative remedies. We assume only for the purposes of this case that respondent has a right of action under Title VI.

The language of Section 601, like that of the equal protection clause, is majestic in its sweep:

"No person in the United States shall, on the ground of race, color or national origin be excluded from participation in, be denied the benefits of or be subjected to discrimination under any program or activity receiving federal financial assistance."

The concept of "discrimination," like the phrase "equal protection of the laws," is susceptable to varying interpretations. We must, therefore, seek whatever aid is available in determining the precise meaning of the statute before us.

Intent of Congress

Examination of the voluminous legislative history of Title VI reveals a congressional intent to halt federal funding of entities that violate a prohibition of racial discrimination similar to that of the Constitution. Although isolated statements of various legislators, taken out of context, can be marshaled in support of the proposition that Section 601 enacted a purely color-blind scheme, without regard to the reach of the equal protection clause, these comments must be read against the background of both the problem that Congress was addressing and the broader view of the statute that emerges from a full examination of the legislative debates.

The problem confronting Congress was discrimination against Negro citizens at the hands of recipients of federal moneys.

Over and over again, proponents of the bill detailed the plight of Negroes seeking equal treatment in such programs.

In view of the clear legislative intent, Title VI must be held to proscribe only those racial classifications that would violate the equal protection clause of the Fifth Amendment.

The parties fight a sharp preliminary action over the proper characterization of the special admissions program. Petitioner prefers to view it as establishing a "goal" of minority representation in the medical school. Respondent, echoing the courts below, labels it a racial quota.

This semantic distinction is beside the point: the special admissions program is undeniably a classification based on race and ethnic background.

The guarantees of the 14th Amendment extend to persons. Its language is explicit: "No state shall deny to any person within its jurisdiction the equal protection of the laws."

The guarantee of equal protection cannot mean one thing when applied to one individual and something else when applied to a person of another color. If both are not accorded the same protection, then it is not equal. Racial and ethnic distinctions of any sort are inherently suspect and thus call for the most exacting judicial examination.

The white "majority" itself is composed of various minority groups, most of which can lay claim to a history of prior discrimination at the hands of the state and private individuals. Not all of these groups can receive preferential treatment and corresponding judicial tolerance of distinctions drawn in terms of race and nationality, for then the only "majority" left would be a new minority of white Anglo-Saxon Protestants.

If it is the individual who is entitled to judicial protection against classifications based upon his racial or ethnic background because such distinctions impinge upon personal rights, rather than the individual only because of his membership in a particular group, then constitutional standards may be applied consistently.

Political Judgments

Political judgments regarding the necessity for the particular classification may be weighed in the constitutional balance, but the standard of justification will remain constant. This is as it should be, since those political judgments are the product of rough compromise struck by contending groups within the democratic process.

When they touch upon an individual's race or ethnic background, he is entitled to a judicial determination that the burden he is asked to bear on that basis is precisely tailored to serve a compelling governmental interest. The Constitution guarantees that right to every person regardless of his background.

Petitioner contends that on several occasions this court has approved preferential classifications without applying the most exacting scrutiny. Most of the cases upon which petitioner relies are drawn from three areas: school desegregation, employment discrimination and sex discrimination. Each of the cases cited presented a situation materially different from the facts of this case.

The school desegregation cases are inapposite. Each involved remedies for clearly determined constitutional violations. Racial classifications thus were designed as remedies for the vindication of constitutional entitlement. Moreover, the scope of the remedies was not permitted to exceed the extent of the violations. Here, there was no judicial determination of constitutional violation as a predicate for the formulation of a remedial classification.

The employment discrimination cases also do not advance petitioner's cause. For example, we approved a retroactive award of seniority to a class of Negro truck drivers who had been the victims of discrimination —not just by society at large, but by the respondent in that case. Such preferences also have been upheld where the legislative or administrative body charged with the responsibility made determinations of past discrimination by the industries affected, and fashioned remedies deemed appropriate to rectify the discrimination.

But we have never approved preferential classifications in the absence of proven constitutional or statutory violations.

Classification by Gender

Nor is the petitioner's view as to the applicable standard supported by the fact that gender-based classifications are not subjected to this level of scrutiny. Gender-based distinctions are less likely to create the analytical and practical problems present in preferential programs premised on racial or ethnic criteria.

With respect to gender there are only two possible classifications. The incidence of the burdens imposed by preferential classifications is clear. There are no rival groups who can claim that they, too, are entitled to preferential treatment.

The resolution of these same questions in the context of racial and ethnic preferences presents far more complex and intractable problems than gender-based classifications. More importantly, the perception of racial classifications as inherently odious stems from a lengthy and tragic history that gender-based classifications do not share. In sum, the court has never viewed such classification as inherently suspect or as comparable to racial or ethnic classifications for the purpose of equal-protection analysis.

We have held that in "order to justify the use of a suspect classification, a state must show that its purpose or interest is both constitutionally permissible and substantial and that its use of the classification is 'necessary to the accomplishment' of its purpose or the safeguarding of its interest."

The special admissions program purports to serve the purposes of: (i) "reducing the historic deficit of traditionally disfavored minorities in medical schools and the medical profession; (ii) countering the effects ol societal discrimination; (iii) increasing the number of physicians who will practice in communities currently underserved; and (iv) obtaining the educational benefits that flow from an ethnically diverse student body. It is necessary to decide which, if any, of these purposes is substantial enough to support the use of a suspect classification.

If petitioner's purpose is to assure within its student body some specified percentage of a particular group merely because of its race or ethnic origin, such a preferential purpose must be rejected not as insubstantial but as facially invalid. Preferring members of any one group for no reason other than race or ethnic origin is discrimination for its own sake. This the Constitution forbids.

The state certainly has a legitimate and substantial interest in ameliorating, or eliminating where feasible, the disabling effects of identified discrimination.

We have never approved a classification that aids persons perceived as members of relatively victimized groups at the expense of other innocent individuals in the absence of judicial, legislative or administrative findings of constitutional or statutory violations.

Petitioner does not purport to have made, and is in no position to make, such findings.

Hence, the purpose of helping certain groups whom the faculty of the Davis medical school perceived as victims of "societal discrimination" does not justify a classification that imposes disadvantages upon persons like respondent, who bear no responsibility for whatever harm the beneficiaries of the special admissions program are thought to have suffered.

Petitioner identifies, as another purpose of its program, improving the delivery of health care services to communities currently underserved. It may be assumed that in some situations a state's interest in facilitating the health care of its citizens is sufficiently compelling to support the use of a suspect classification. But there is virtually no evidence in the record indicating that petitioner's special admissions program is either needed or geared to promote that goal.

The fourth goal asserted by petitioner is the attainment of a diverse student body. This clearly is a constitutionally permissible goal for an institution of higher education. Academic freedom, though not a specifically enumerated constitutional right, long has been viewed as a special concern of the First Amendment. The freedom of a university to make its own judgments as to education includes the selection of its student body.

It may be argued that there is greater force to these views at the undergraduate level than in a medical school where the training is centered primarily on professional competency. But even at the graduate level, our tradition and experience lend support to the view that the contribution of diversity is substantial.

Ethnic Diversity

Ethnic diversity, however, is only one element in a range of factors a university properly may consider in attaining the goal of a heterogeneous student body. Although a university must have wide discretion in making the sensitive judgments as to who should be admitted, constitutional limitations protecting individual rights may not be disregarded.

Respondent urges—and the courts below have held—that petitioner's dual admissions program is a racial classification that impermissibly infringes his rights under the 14th Amendment. As the interest of diversity is compelling in the context of a university's admissions program, the question remains whether the program's racial classification is necessary to promote this interest.

Petitioner's argument that this is the only effective means of serving the interest of diversity is seriously flawed. The diversity that furthers a compelling state interest encompasses a far broader array of qualifications and characteristics of which racial or ethnic origin is but a single though important element. Petitioner's special admissions program, focused solely on ethnic diversity, would hinder rather than further attainment of genuine diversity.

The experience of other university admissions programs, which take race into account in achieving the educational diversity valued by the First Amendment, demonstrates that the assignment of a fixed number of places to a minority group is not a necessary means toward that end. An illuminating example is found in the Harvard College program:

Harvard Program

"In recent years Harvard College has expanded the concept of diversity to include students from disadvantaged economic, racial and ethnic groups. Harvard College now recruits not only Californians or Louisianans but also blacks and Chicanos and other minority students.

"In practice, this new definition of diversity has meant that race has been a factor in some admission decisions. When the committee on admissions reviews the large middle group of applicants who are 'admissible' and deemed capable of doing good work in their courses, the race of an applicant may tip the balance in his favor just as geographic origin or a life spent on a farm may tip the balance in other candidates' cases. A farm boy from Idaho can bring something to Harvard College that a Bostonian cannot offer. Similarly, a black student can usually bring something that a white person cannot offer."

"In Harvard College admissions the committee has not set target quotas for the number of blacks, or of musicians, football players, physicists or Californians to be admitted in a given year. . . . But that awareness . . . does not mean that the committee sets the minimum number of blacks or of people from west of the Mississippi who are to be admitted. It means only that in choosing among thousands of applicants who are not only 'admissable' academically but have other strong qualities, the committee, with a number of criteria in mind, pays some attention to distribution among many types and categories of students."

In such an admissions program, race or ethnic background may be deemed a "plus" in a particular applicant's file, yet it does not insulate the individual from comparison with all other candidates for the available seats.

The file of a particular black applicant may be examined for his potential contribution to diversity without the factor of race being decisive when compared, for example, with that of an applicant identified as an Italian-American if the latter is thought to exhibit qualities more likely to promote beneficial educational pluralism.

Such qualities could include exceptional personal talents, unique work or service experience, leadership potential, maturity, demonstrated compassion, a history of overcoming disadvantage, ability to communicate with the poor, or other qualifications deemed important.

In short, an admissions program operated this way is flexible enough to consider all pertinent elements of diversity in light of the particular qualifications of each applicant and to place them on the same footing for consideration, although not necessarily according them the same weight. Indeed, the weight attributed to a particular quality may vary from year to year depending upon the "mix" both of the student body and the applicants for the incoming class.

This kind of program treats each applicant as an individual in the admissions process. The applicant who loses out on the last available seat to another candidate receiving a "plus" on the basis of ethnic background will not have been foreclosed from all consideration for that seat simply because he was not the right color or had the wrong surname.

It would mean only that his combined qualifications, which may have included similar nonobjective factors, did not outweigh those of the other applicant. His qualifications would have been weighed fairly and competitively and he would have no basis to complain of unequal treatment under the 14th Amendment.

It has been suggested that an admissions program which considers race only as one factor is simply a subtle and more sophisticated—but no less effective—means of according racial preference than the Davis program. A facial intent to discriminate, however, is evident in petitioner's preference program and not denied in this case.

No such facial infirmity exists in an admissions program where race or ethnic background is simply one element—to be weighed fairly against other elements—in the selection process.

Summary

In summary, it is evident that the Davis special admission program involves the use of an explicit racial classification never before countenanced by this Court. It tells applicants who are not Negro, Asian or "Chicano" that they are totally excluded from a specific percentage of the seats in an entering class.

No matter how strong their qualifications, quantitative and extracurricular, including their own potential for contribution to education diversity, they are never afforded the chance to compete with applicants from the preferred groups for the special admission seats. At the same time, the preferred applicants have the opportunity to compete for every seat in the class.

The fatal flaw in petitioner's preferential program is its disregard of individual rights as guaranteed by the 14th Amendment. Such rights are not absolute. But when a state's distribution of benefits or imposition of burdens hinges on the color of a person's skin or ancestry, that individual is entitled to a demonstration that the challenged classification is necessary to promote a substantial state interest.

Petitioner has failed to carry this burden. For this reason, that portion of the California court's judgment holding petitioner's special admissions program invalid under the 14th Amendment must be affirmed.

In enjoining petitioner from ever considering the race of any applicant, however, the courts below failed to recognize that the state has a substantial interest that legitimately may be served by a properly devised admissions program involving the competitive consideration of race and ethnic origin. For this reason, so much of the California court's judgment as enjoins petitioner from any consideration of the race of any applicant must be reversed.

With respect to respondent's entitlement to an injunction directing his admission to the medical school, petitioner has conceded that it could not carry its burden of proving that, but for the existence of its unlawful special admissions program, respondent still would not have been admitted. Hence, respondent is entitled to the injunction, and that portion of the judgment must be affirmed.

Justice Brennan

Opinion of Mr. Justice Brennan, Mr. Justice White, Mr. Justice Marshall and Mr. Justice Blackmun, concurring in the judgment in part and dissenting.

The court today, in reversing in part the judgment of the Supreme Court of California, affirms the constitutional power of federal and state government to act affirmatively to achieve equal opportunity for all. The difficulty of the issue presented—whether government may use race-conscious programs to redress the continuing effects of past discrimination—and the mature consideration which each of our brethren has brought to it have resulted in many opinions, no single one speaking for the court.

But this should not and must not mask the central meaning of today's opinions: government may take race into account when it acts not to demean or insult any racial group, but to remedy disadvantages cast on minorities by past racial prejudice, at least when appropriate findings have been made by judicial, legislative or administrative bodies with competence to act in this area.

The Chief Justice and our brothers Stewart, Rehnquist and Stevens have concluded that Title VI of the Civil Rights Act of 1964 prohibits programs such as that at the Davis Medical School. On this statutory theory alone, they would hold that respondent Allan Bakke's rights have been violated and that he must, therefore, be admitted to the medical school.

Our brother Powell, reaching the Constitution, concludes that although race may be taken into account in university admissions the particular special admissions program used by petitioner, which resulted in the exclusion of respondent Bakke, was not shown to be necessary to achieve petitioner's stated goals.

The Majority Opinion

Accordingly, these members of the court form a majority of five affirming the judgment of the Supreme Court of California insofar as it holds that respondent Bakke "is entitled to an order that he be admitted to the university."

We agree with Mr. Justice Powell that as applied to the case before us Title VI goes no further in prohibiting the use of race than the equal protection clause of the 14th Amendment itself. We also agree that the effect of the California Supreme Court's affirmance of the judgment of the Superior Court of California would be to prohibit the university from establishing in the future affirmative action programs that take race into account.

Since we conclude that the affirmative admissions program at the Davis Medical School is constitutional, we would reverse the judgment below in all respects. Mr. Justice Powell agrees that some uses of race in university admissions are permissible and, therefore, he joins with us to make five votes reversing the judgment below insofar as it prohibits the university from establishing race-conscious programs in the future.

Our nation was founded on the principle that "all men are created equal." Yet candor requires acknowledgment that the framers of our Constitution, to forge the 13 colonies into one nation, openly compromised this principle of equality with its antithesis: slavery.

The consequences of this compromise are well known and have aptly been called our "American dilemma." Still, it is well to recount how recent the time has been, if it has yet come, when the promise of our principles has flowered into the actuality of equal opportunity for all regardless of race or color.

The 14th Amendment, the embodiment in the Constitution of our abiding belief in human equality, has been the law of our land for only slightly more than half its 200 years. And for half of that half, the equal protection clause of the amendment was largely moribund.

'Separate But Equal'

Worse than desuetude, the clause was early turned against those whom it was intended to set free, condemning them to a "separate but equal" status before the law, a status always separate but seldom equal.

Not until 1954—only 24 years ago—was this odious doctrine interred by our decision in *Brown v. Board of Education* and its progeny, which proclaimed that separate schools and public facilities of all sorts were inherently unequal and forbidden under our Constitution.

Even then inequality was not eliminated with "all deliberate speed." In 1968 and again in 1971, for example, we were forced to remind school boards of their obligation to eliminate racial discrimination root and branch. And a glance at our docket and at those of lower courts will show that even today officially sanctioned discrimination is not a thing of the past.

Against this background, claims that law must be "color-blind" or that the datum of race is no longer relevant to public policy must be seen as aspiration rather than as description of reality. This is not to denigrate aspiration; for reality rebukes us that race has too often been used by those who would stigmatize and oppress minorities.

Yet we cannot—and as we shall demonstrate, need not under our Constitution or Title VI, which merely extends the constraints of the 14th Amendment to private parties who receive federal funds—let color blindness become myopia which masks the reality that many "created equal" have been treated within our lifetimes as inferior both by the law and by their fellow citizens.

The threshold question we must decide is whether Title VI of the Civil Rights Act of 1964 bars recipients of federal funds from giving preferential consideration to disadvantaged members of racial minorities as part of a program designed to enable such individuals to surmount the obstacles imposed by racial discrmination.

In our view, Title VI prohibits only those uses of racial criteria that would violate the 14th Amendment if employed by a state or its agencies; it does not bar the preferential treatment of racial minorities as a means of remedying past societal discrimination to the extent that such action is consistent with the 14th Amendment.

Of course it might be argued that the Congress which enacted Title VI understood the Constitution to require strict racial neutrality or color blindness.

First, no decision of this court has ever adopted the proposition that the Constitution must be color blind.

Second, it is inconceivable that Congress intended to encourage voluntary efforts to eliminate the evil of racial discrimination while at the same time forbidding the voluntary use of race-conscious remedies to cure acknowledged or obvious statutory violations.

Third, the legislative history shows that Congress specifically eschewed any static definition of discrimination in favor of broad language that could be shaped by experience, administrative necessity and evolving judicial doctrine.

Thus any claim that the use of racial criteria is barred by the plain language of the statute must fail in light of the remedial purpose of Title VI and its legislative history.

Human Equality

The assertion of human equality is closely associated with the proposition that differences in color or creed, birth or status, are neither significant nor relevant to the way in which persons should be treated. Nonetheless, the position that "our Constitution is color blind" has never been adopted by this court as the proper meaning of the equal protection clause. Indeed, we have expressly rejected this proposition on a number of occasions.

Our cases have always implied that an "overriding statutory purpose" could be found that would justify racial classifications.

We conclude, therefore, that racial classifications are not per se invalid under the 14th Amendment. Accordingly, we turn to the problem of articulating what our role should be in reviewing state action that expressly classifies by race.

Unquestionably we have held that a government practice or statute which restricts "fundamental rights" or which contains "suspect classifications" is to be subjected to "strict scrutiny" and can be justified only if it furthers a compelling government purpose and, even then, only if no less restrictive alternative is available.

But no fundamental right is involved here. Nor do whites as a class have any of the "traditional indicia of suspectness: the class is not saddled with such disabilities, or subjected to such a history of purposeful unequal treatment, or relegated to such a position of political powerlessness as to command extraordinary protection from the majoritarian political process."

On the other hand, the fact that this case does not fit neatly into our prior analytic framework for race cases does not mean that it should be analyzed by applying the very loose rational-basis standard of review that is the very least that is always applied in equal protection cases.

Instead, a number of considerations—developed in gender discrimination cases but which carry even more force when applied to racial classifications—lead us to conclude that racial classifications designed to further remedial purposes "must serve important governmental objectives and must be substantially related to achievement of those objectives."

Gender-Based Classifications

First, race, like "gender-based classifications too often [has] been inexcusably utilized to stereotype and stigmatize politically powerless segments of society."

Second, race, like gender and illegitimacy, is an immutable characteristic which its possessors are powerless to escape or set aside.

In sum, because of the significant risk that racial classifications established for ostensibly benign purposes can be misused, causing effects not unlike those created by invidious classifications, it is inappropriate to inquire only whether there is any conceivable basis that might sustain such a classification.

Instead, to justify such a classification an important and articulated purpose for its use must be shown. In addition, any statute must be stricken that stigmatizes any group or that singles out those least well represented in the political process to bear the brunt of a benign program.

Thus our review under the 14th Amendment should be strict—not "strict in theory and fatal in fact," because it is stigma that causes fatality—but strict and searching nonetheless.

Davis' articulated purpose of remedying the effects of past societal discrimination is, under our cases, sufficiently important to justify the use of race-conscious admissions programs where there is a sound basis for concluding that minority underrepresentation is substantial and chronic, and that the handicap of past discrimination is impeding access of minorities to the medical school.

Such relief does not require as a predicate proof that recipients of preferential advancement have been individually discriminated against; it is enough that each recipient is within a general class of persons likely to have been the victim of discrimination. Nor is it an objection to such relief that preference for minorities will upset the settled expectations of nonminorities.

Moreover, the presence or absence of past discrimination by universities or employers is largely irrelevant to resolving respondent's constitutional claims. The claims of those burdened by the race-conscious actions of a university or employer who has never been adjudged in violation of an anti-discrimination law are not any more or less entitled to deference than the claims of the burdened nonminority workers in *Franks v. Bowman*, in which the employer had violated Title VII, for in each case the employees are innocent of past discrimination.

And, although it might be argued that where an employer has violated an anti-discrimination law the expectations of nonminority workers are themselves products of discrimination and hence "tainted" and therefore more easily upset, the same argument can be made with respect to respondent.

If it was reasonable to conclude—as we hold that it was—that the failure of minorities to qualify for admission at Davis under regular procedures was due principally to the effects of past discrimination, then there is a reasonable likelihood that, but for pervasive racial discrimination, respondent would have failed to qualify for admission even in the absence of Davis' special admissions program.

Preferential Treatment

Thus, our cases under Title VII of the Civil Rights Act have held that, in order to achieve minority participation in previously segregated areas of public life, Congress may require or authorize preferential treatment for those likely disadvantaged by societal racial discrimination.

Such legislation has been sustained even without a requirement of findings of intentional racial discrimination by those required or authorized to accord preferential treatment, or a case-by-case determination that those to be benefitted suffered from racial discrimination. These decisions compel the conclusion that states also may adopt race-conscious programs designed to overcome substantial, chronic minority underrepresentation where there is reason to believe that the evil addressed is a product of past racial discrimination.

Voluntary initiatives by the states to achieve the national goal of equal opportunity have been recognized to be essential to its attainment.

We therefore conclude that Davis' goal of admitting minority students disadvantaged by the effects of past discrimination is sufficiently important to justify use of race-conscious admissions criteria.

Properly construed, therefore, our prior cases unequivocally show that a state government may adopt race-conscious programs if the purpose of such programs is to remove the disparate racial impact its actions might otherwise have and if there is reason to believe that the disparate impact is itself the product of past discrimination, whether its own or that of society at large. There is no question that Davis' program is valid under this test.

Certainly, on the basis of the undisputed factual submissions before this court, Davis had a sound basis for believing that the problem of underrepresentation of minorities was substantial and chronic and that the problem was attributable to handicaps imposed on minority applicants by past and present racial discrimination.

The second prong of our test—whether the Davis program stigmatizes any discrete group or individual and whether race is reasonably used in light of the program's objectives—is clearly satisfied by the Davis program.

Whites Excluded

True, whites are excluded from participation in the special admissions program, but this fact only operates to reduce the number of whites to be admitted in the regular admissions program in order to permit admission of a reasonable percentage—less than their proportion of the California population—of otherwise underrepresented qualified minority applicants.

We disagree with the lower courts' conclusion that the Davis program s use of race was unreasonable in light of its objectives. First, as petitioner argues, there are no practical means by which it could achieve its ends in the foreseeable future without the use of race-conscious measures. With respect to any factor (such as poverty or family educational background) that may be used as a substitute for race as an indicator of past discrimination, whites greatly outnumber racial minorities simply because whites make up a far larger percentage of the total population and therefore far outnumber minorities in absolute terms at every socio-economic level.

It appears that economically disadvantaged whites do not score less well than economically advantaged whites, while economically advantaged blacks score less well than do disadvantaged whites. These statistics graphically illustrate that the University's purpose to integrate its classes by compensating for past discrimination could not be achieved by a general preference for the economically disadvantaged or the children of parents of limited education unless such groups were to make the entire class.

Second, the Davis admissions program does not simply equate minority status with disadvantage. Rather, Davis considers on an individual basis each applicant's personal history to determine whether he or she has likely been disadvantaged by racial discrimination. The record makes clear that only minority applicants likely to have been isolated from the mainstream of American life are considered in the special program; other minority applicants are eligible only through the regular admissions program.

No Difference in Approaches

Finally, Davis' special admissions program cannot be said to violate the Constitution simply because it has set aside a predetermined number of places for qualified minority applicants rather than using minority status as a positive factor to be considered in evaluating the applications of disadvantaged minority applicants. For purposes of constitutional adjudication, there is no difference between the two approaches. In any admissions program which accords special consideration to disadvantaged racial minorities, a determination of the degree of preference to be given is unavoidable, and any given preference that results in the exclusion of a white candidate is no more or less constitutionally acceptable than a program such as that at Davis. Furthermore, the extent of the preference inevitably depends on how many minority applicants the particular school is seeking to admit in any particular year so long as the number of qualified minority applicants exceeds that number. There is no sensible, and certainly no constitutional, distinction between, for example, adding a set number of points to the admissions rating of disadvantaged minority applicants as an expression of the preference with the expectation that this will result in the admission of an approximately determined number of qualified minority applicants and setting a fixed number of places for such applicants as was done here.

The Harvard program as those employing it readily concede, openly and successfully employs a racial criterion for the purpose of ensuring that some of the scarce places in institutions of higher education are allocated to disadvantaged minority students. That the Harvard approach does not also make public the extent of the preference and the precise workings of the system while the Davis program employs a specific, openly stated number, does not condemn the latter plan for purposes of 14th Amendment adjudication. It may be that the Harvard plan is more acceptable to the public than is the Davis "quota." If it is, any state, including California, is free to adopt it in preference to a less acceptable alternative, just as it is generally free, as far as the Constitution is concerned, to abjure granting any racial preferences in its admission program. But there is no basis for preferring a particular preference program simply because in achieving the same goals that the Davis Medical School is pursuing, it proceeds in a manner that is not immediately apparent to the public.

Accordingly, we would reverse the judgment of the Supreme Court of California holding the medical school's special admissions program unconstitutional and directing respondent's admission, as well as that portion of the judgment enjoining the medical school from according any consideration to race in the admissions process.

Justice White

I write separately concerning the question of whether Title VI of the Civil Rights Act of 1964, 42 U.S.C. Section 2000d et seq., provides for a private cause of action. Four Justices are apparently of the view that such a private cause of action exists, and four Justices assume it for purposes of this case. I am unwilling merely to assume an affirmative answer. If in fact no private cause of action exists, this court and the lower courts as well are without jurisdiction to consider respondent's Title VI claim.

A private cause of action under Title VI would, in terms both of the Civil Rights Act as a whole and that title, not be "consistent with the underlying purposes of the legislative scheme" and contrary to the legislative intent.

The role of Title VI was to terminate federal financial support for public and private institutions or programs that discriminated on the basis of race. Section 601, 42 U.S.C. Section 2000d, imposed the proscription that no person, on the grounds of race, color or national origin, was to be excluded from or discriminated against under any program of activity receiving federal financial assistance. But there is no express provision for private actions to enforce Title VI, and it would be quite incredible if Congress, after so carefully attending to the matter of private actions in other titles of the act, intended silently to create a private cause of action to enforce Title VI.

Justice Blackmun

I participate fully, of course, in the opinion that bears the names of my brothers Brennan, White, Marshall and myself. I add only some general observations that hold particular significance for me, and then a few comments on equal protection.

I yield to no one in my earnest hope that the time will come when an "affirmative action" program is unnecessary and is, in truth, only a relic of the past. I would hope that we could reach this stage within a decade at the most. But the story of Brown v. Board of Education, decided almost a quarter of a century ago, suggests that that hope is a slim one. At some time, however, beyond any period of what some would claim is only transitional inequality, the United States must and will reach a stage of maturity where action along this line is no longer necessary. The persons will be regarded as persons, and discrimination of the type we address today will be an ugly feature of history that is instructive but that is behind us.

It is somewhat ironic to have us so deeply disturbed over a program where race is an element of consciousness, and yet to be aware of the fact, as we are, that institutions of higher learning, albeit more on the under-

graduate than the graduate level, have given conceded preferences up to a point to those possessed of athletic skills, to the children of alumni, to the affluent who may bestow their largess on the institutions, and to those having connections with celebrities, the famous and the powerful.

I am not convinced, as Mr. Justice Powell seems to be, that the difference between the Davis program and the one employed by Harvard is very profound or constitutionally significant. The line between the two is a thin and indistinct one. In each, subjective application is at work. Because of my conviction that admission programs are primarily for the educators, I am willing to accept the representation that the Harvard program is one where good faith in its administration is practiced as well as professed. I agree that such a program, where race or ethnic background is only one of many factors, is a program better formulated than Davis' two-track system. The cynical, of course, may say that under a program such as Harvard's one may accomplish covertly what Davis concedes it does openly. I need not go that far, for despite its two-track aspect, the Davis program, for me, is within constitutional bounds, though perhaps barely so.

I suspect that it would be impossible to arrange an affirmative action program in a racially neutral way and have it successful. To ask that this be so is to demand the impossible. In order to get beyond racism, we must first take account of race. There is no other way. And in order to treat some persons equally, we must treat them differently. We cannot—we dare not—let the equal protection clause perpetrate racial supremacy.

Justice Stevens

The Chief Justice, Mr. Justice Stewart, and Mr. Justice Rehnquist join, concurring in the judgment in part and dissenting in part.

This is not a class action. The controversy is between two specific litigants. Allan Bakke challenged petitioner's special admissions program, claiming that it denied him a place in medical school because of his race in violation of the federal and California Constitutions and of Title VI of the Civil Rights Act of 1964. The California Supreme Court upheld his challenge and ordered him admitted. If the state court was correct in its view that the university's special program was illegal, and that Bakke was therefore unlawfully excluded from the medical school because of his race, we should affirm its judgment, regardless of our views about the legality of admissions programs that are not now before the Court. The trial court did not order the university to admit Bakke because it concluded that Bakke had not shown that he would have been admitted if there had been no special program. Instead, it ordered the university to consider Bakke's application for admission without regard to his race or the race of any other applicant. The order did not include any broad prohibition against any use of race in the admissions process; its terms were clearly limited to the university's consideration of Bakke's application.

The California Supreme Court, in a holding that is not challenged, ruled that the trial court incorrectly placed the burden on Bakke of showing that he would have been admitted in the absence of discrimination. The university then conceded "that it [could] not meet the burden of proving that the special admission program did not result in Bakke's exclusion." Accordingly, the California Supreme Court directed the trial court to enter judgment ordering Bakke's admission. Whether the judgment of the state court is affirmed or reversed, in whole or in part, there is no outstanding injunction forbidding any consideration of racial criteria in processing applications.

It is therefore perfectly clear that the question whether race can ever be used as a factor in an admissions decision is not an issue in this case, and that discussion of that issue is inappropriate.

Our settled practice is to avoid the decision of a constitutional issue if a case can be fairly decided on a statutory ground.

In this case, we are presented with a constitutional question of undoubted and unusual importance. Since, however, a dispositive statutory claim was raised at the very inception of this case, and squarely decided in the portion of the trial court judgment affirmed by the California Supreme Court, it is our plain duty to confront it. Only if petitioner should prevail on the statutory issue would it be necessary to decide whether the university's admissions program violated the equal protection clause of the 14th Amendment.

Racial Stigma

Petitioner contends that exclusion of applicants on the basis of race does not violate Title VI if the exclusion carries with it no racial stigma. No such qualification or limitation of section 601's categorical prohibition of "exclusion" is justified by the statute or its history.

It seems clear that the proponents of Title VI assumed that the Constitution itself required a colorblind standard on the part of government.

The act's proponents plainly considered Title VI consistent with their view of the Constitution and they sought to provide an effective weapon to implement that view.

As with other provisions of the Civil Rights Act, Congress' expression of its policy to end racial discrimination may independently proscribe conduct that the Constitution does not. However, we need not decide the congruence or lack of congruence—of the controlling statute and the Constitution since the meaning of the Title VI ban on exclusion is crystal clear: Race cannot be the basis of excluding anyone from participation in a federally funded program.

As succinctly phrased during the Senate debate, under Title VI it is not "permissible to say 'yes' to one person, but to say 'no' to another person, only because of the color of his skin."

The university's special admissions program violated Title VI of the Civil Rights Act of 1964 by excluding Bakke from the medical school because of his race. It is therefore our duty to affirm the judgment ordering Bakke admitted to the university.

Accordingly, I concur in the court's judgment insofar as it affirms the judgment of the Supreme Court

of California. To the extent that it purports to do anything else, I respectfully dissent.

Justice Marshall

I agree with the judgment of the court only insofar as it permits a university to consider the race of an applicant in making admissions decisions. I do not agree that petitioner's admissions program violates the Constitution. For it must be remembered that during most of the past 200 years, the Constitution as interpreted by this court did not prohibit the most ingenious and pervasive forms of discrimination against the Negro. Now, when a state acts to remedy the effects of that legacy of discrimination, I cannot believe that this same Constitution stands as a barrier.

The position of the Negro today in America is the tragic but inevitable consequence of centuries of unequal treatment. Measured by any benchmark of conduct or achievement, meaningful equality remains a distant dream for the Negro.

It is because of a legacy of unequal treatment that we now must permit the institutions of this society to give consideration to race in making decisions about who will hold the positions of influence, affluence and prestige in America. For far too long, the doors to those positions have been shut to Negroes. If we are ever to become a fully integrated society, one in which the color of a person's skin will not determine the opportunities available to him or her, we must be willing to take steps to open those doors. I do not believe that anyone can truly look into America's past and still find that a remedy for the effects of the past is impermissible.

It has been said that this case involves only the individual Bakke and this university. I doubt, however, that there is a computer capable of determining the number of persons and institutions that may be affected by the decision in this case.

I fear that we have come full circle. After the Civil War our government started several "affirmative action" programs. This court in the civil rights cases and *Plessy v. Ferguson* destroyed the movement toward complete equality. For almost a century no action was taken and this nonaction was with the tacit approval of the courts. Then we had *Brown v. Board of Education* and the Civil Rights Acts of Congress followed by numerous affirmative action programs. Now, we have this court again stepping in, this time to stop affirmative action programs of the type used by the University of California.

Reaction to the Bakke Decision. A multitude of groups had taken an interest in the Bakke case, and most of them found something in the decision that they could regard as a vindication of their views. Some groups, however, expressed concern about the ruling and its impact.

Bakke himself was "very pleased, very grateful, very relieved that the thing is over," his attorney said.

But the other party to the case could also see the ruling as a triumph. David Saxon, president of the University of California, said that although the court ruled that the admissions system operated

by the medical school at the Davis campus was unacceptable, "the overwhelming bulk of our admissions program appears [in the light of the Supreme Court decision] to be entirely lawful."

Gary Morison, an assistant counsel for the university in the Bakke case, said that the court "agreed with the core of the university's argument that ethnic minority status may lawfully be taken into account . . . . That was the most important issue, and we have won on that issue."

The Carter Administration praised the decision. Attorney General Griffin Bell said the ruling was a "great gain for affirmative action. It's the first time the Supreme Court ever upheld affirmative action and it did in as strong a way as possible."

Joseph Califano, secretary of the Department of Health, Education and Welfare, said the ruling "strongly supports this nation's continuing effort to live up to its historic promise—to bring minorities and other disadvantaged groups into the mainstream of American society through admissions policies that recognize the importance of diverse, integrated educational institutions."

At a press conference June 28, a group of black leaders expressed mixed feelings about the ruling. Urban League Director Vernon Jordan said that "the most important thing is that a majority of the Supreme Court backed the use of race as a permissible factor in affirmative actions programs."

That had been a key concern of most supporters of affirmative action.

Benjamin Hooks, executive director of the National Association for the Advancement of Colored People, said he was disappointed that Bakke had gained admission to medical school. But, Hooks added, he saw "a strong ray of hope" in the presentation of the Harvard admissions system as an example of a constitutionally acceptable affirmative action program.

The Rev. Jesse Jackson, another prominent civil rights leader, was critical of the ruling, depicting it as part of a national "move to the right." He said that blacks might have to respond to the decision by resorting to the tactics of the civil rights movement: sit-ins or economic boycotts.

Rep. Parren J. Mitchell (D, Md.), chairman of the Congressional Black Caucus, said he was "not pleased" by the ruling but added that it was not "the death knell for affirmative action."

Norman Dorsen, chairman of the American Civil Liberties Union, estimated that 90% of the affirmative action programs currently in existence would not be upset by the ruling.

Dorsen cautioned, however, that the ruling might "sap the will" of officials responsible for affirmative action efforts.

A similar worry was expressed by Julius Edelstein, vice chancellor of City University of New York. Edelstein said

the decision was a "psychological catastrophe" that would be seen by many minorities as a "shutting of the door in their faces."

University officials generally welcomed the ruling, seeing it as a permit to continue current policies. John Peltason, president of the American Council on Education, said the ruling "left the options open. The overwhelming number of affirmative action programs now in place will meet the standards outlined by the court."

The groups that had supported Bakke emphasized the sections of the ruling that they liked. Ron Robinson, executive director of Young Americans for Freedom, said the decision was "an important step in eliminating the practices of reverse discrimination and quotas. It is now up to Congress to pick up where the court has left off."

Arnold Forster, general counsel of the Anti-Defamation League of B'nai B'rith, said the league was "comforted that, once and for all, the United States Supreme Court has held that racial quotas are flatly illegal."

Forster said he had reservations about the ruling, however, because it was not clear how race could be used as only one factor in admissions "without that factor eventually becoming the determining factor."

Many observers maintained that the Bakke decision still left important questions about affirmative action unresolved, and so it would be followed by further litigation. Robert Bork, solicitor general in the Ford Administration and currently a law professor at Yale University, said, "This isn't a landmark decision."

Bork continued, "It doesn't tell us how much race counts. We're told that we can count race somewhat, but not too much. That's going to be difficult to apply."

Harvard's Admissions Plan. The admissions program of Harvard University, cited as a model by Justice Lewis Powell, was described by Harvard officials as unstructured and subjective. Powell praised the Harvard system as an "illuminating example" of "diversity without fixed quotas."

In a brief submitted by Harvard on the Bakke case, the university said that only about 150 persons in each incoming undergraduate class were admitted on the basis of academic preeminence.

The remaining persons accepted were selected out of a large pool of academically qualified candidates with the object of creating a diverse student body. The brief argued that "a farm boy from Idaho can bring something to Harvard College that a Bostonian cannot offer. Similarly, a black student can usually bring something that a white student cannot."

Thus the admissions committee gave some attention to an applicant's race, along with a wide number of other nonacademic criteria, such as geographic origin, socioeconomic class and extracurricular interests.

The committee tried to accept more than just a few blacks, so that they would not feel isolated, but no minimum number was set.

As an example of the admissions process, the brief gave a hypothetical example in which the admissions committee considered three applicants—one, an academically gifted child of a black doctor, the second, a less gifted child of semiliterate black parents and the third, a white child with exceptional artistic ability.

The university, the brief said, might choose the less-gifted black over the more-gifted one, and also might take the white student over both black students.

A spokesman for Harvard said that for the coming academic year, 1,628 men and women had been selected out of 12,710 applicants. Of those accepted, 8.1% were black, 5.7% were Asiatic-Americans, 4.6% were of Hispanic origin and .4% were American Indians.

Higher Education

Medical & Law School Fluctuations. The number of black students who entered U.S. medical and law schools declined slightly for the school year beginning in 1977, according to a Washington Post report Oct. 8, 1978. The proportion of blacks totaled 6.7% of first-year medical students in the fall of 1977, compared with the peak of 7.5% in 1974. Blacks made up 4.9% of fall 1977's entering law school class, compared with the peak of 5.3% in 1976.

In 1968 just before affirmative action programs started, blacks accounted for 2.7% of first-year medical students and 3.1% of first-year legal students. A 1977 study by the Educational Testing Service showed that only one in four blacks would have been accepted by law schools if academic criteria had been the only basis for admission and affirmative action programs had not aided black applicants.

Officials of the medical and law associations attributed the decline to greater opportunities for blacks in other fields, such as business and engineering, and to less willingness by admissions officers to accept students with poor academic records.

Tennessee Merger Ordered. Federal District Judge Frank Gray Jr. Jan. 31, 1977 ordered two of the universities in Tennessee to merge by July 1, 1980 in order to end segregation. The merger, which the judge characterized as a "radical remedy," would affect Tennessee State University and the Nashville campus of the University of Tennessee. According to a lawyer for the Tennessee Code Commission, the ruling represented the first time a judge had ordered institutes of higher education to merge.

HEW issues college desegregation plan. In response to a federal court order, the Health, Education & Welfare Department July 3, 1977 announced a five-year desegregation plan for state-supported colleges in Arkansas, Florida, Georgia, North Carolina, Oklahoma and Virginia. The new guidelines covered 260 Southern schools cited in a 1970 lawsuit brought by the NAACP Legal Defense Fund against HEW. The suit had charged the federal agency with failing to enforce civil rights laws aimed at eliminating the vestiges of the dual school systems established in the South during the days of state-sanctioned segregation.

U.S. District Court Judge John Pratt, who had ordered HEW to issue the guidelines, had cautioned the department "to take into account the unique importance of black colleges" in preparing the desegregation plan, since it would involve 13 traditionally black schools. Accordingly, to help those schools retain their identities, the plan delayed "for two years establishment of numerical goals and timetables" for enrollment of whites.

Other details of the HEW standards included:

Increasing the total number of black students attending public colleges, particularly four-year, predominantly white schools.

Taking action to reduce the black dropout rate, currently 8% to 20% higher than for whites.

Increasing the number of white students enrolled at predominantly black colleges.

Equalizing the proportion of black and white state college graduates who continued on to professional or graduate schools.

Equalizing distribution of state resources to all institutions.

Increasing the number of black faculty and college administrators.

The desegregation plans initially submitted by Georgia, Virginia and North Carolina were rejected by the HEW in February 1978. Those of the other states were accepted. But revised plans were accepted by HEW for Georgia and Virginia in March and for North Carolina May 12.

The accord with Georgia, reached March 8, called for a 16% increase in the number of blacks enrolling in the state-supported college system. The number of black students entering the 13 predominantly white four-year colleges and universities was to be increased by 8%.

In addition, more blacks were to be hired for faculty and staff throughout the college system, black enrollment was to be boosted in the graduate schools of law and medicine and programs were to be strengthened at the three predominantly black colleges in Georgia.

In announcing the agreement with Virginia, HEW Secretary Joseph A. Califano Jr. said March 17 that specific commitments had been made to increase black enrollment in the state supported colleges.

The other parts of the agreement were to increase employment opportunities for qualified blacks at state colleges and universities and to "enhance the two traditionally black universities," Norfolk State and Virginia State.

North Carolina also agreed to increase black enrollment in its 16-college system (11 of them predominantly white, five predominantly black). There would be efforts made to increase black enrollment in graduate schools and to hire more black instructors and administrators.

Califano had cautioned North Carolina March 22 that he was beginning administrative action under the 1964 Civil Rights Act to cut off federal aid to the state universities. The aid totaled $68 million in fiscal 1977.

The first step would be to deprive the state of any new grants that might "contribute to continued segregation," Califano said.

The university, backed by Gov. James B. Hunt Jr., gave notice it would challenge a fund cutoff. University officials stressed their opposition was not based on hostility to desegregation but a disagreement with certain of HEW's original demands, such as a requirement for elimination of duplicate curricula and merger of campuses.

The opposition was not confined to the white community. Administrators at the black colleges were wary at first of any realignment that would cut back their "outlet for minority aspirations," as one put it.

Black College Ruled Discriminatory
Federal District Judge Frank M. Johnson Jr. ruled May 1, 1978 that Alabama State University had engaged in "a pattern and practice of discrimination against whites" in hiring its faculty and staff.

The university, founded in 1875, had a predominantly black enrollment. Only 36 of 196 members of its teaching faculty, and only four of its 56 administrative staff members, were white, Johnson noted.

Johnson found the school in violation of a 10-year-old injunction prohibiting racial discrimination in all state institutions. That ruling had been made in a suit brought by blacks against discriminatory practices at predominantly white schools.

Few Gains in College Jobs for Women.
A survey of U.S. colleges and universities showed that the number of women in full-time faculty positions had not increased since 1972. In that year, the federal government banned sex discrimination in education.

The report, based on data from 600 institutions, was prepared by the American Association of University Women. The study was made public April 7, 1978.

The number of faculty women in full-time positions remained at 25%, and most were concentrated in the lower-ranking jobs, such as lecturers and assistant professorships.

Women held 8% of full professorships, 16.5% of all tenured positions and 18% of all deanships.

The number of women presidents remained at 6%. The number of women business administrators also was unchanged at 5%.

Study finds bias against women Ph.Ds. Women with doctorates were discriminated against in salary and promotion opportunities in favor of men, and this disparity increased with years of experience, according to a study released by the Educational Testing Service Jan. 5, 1978. Using a sample of 3,658 doctorate recipients in 1950, 1960 and 1968, the report said men averaged $18,700 five to six years after receiving degrees and $27,100 after 22 or 23 years, compared with $16,400 and $21,800 for women.

The report noted recent signs of improvement for women Ph.Ds in status and pay, but added, "Whether current changes are the beginning of a trend or tokenism, as some claim, remains to be seen."

Marriage and motherhood were cited as obstacles to professional advancement of the women. More than 25% of women doctorate recipients became divorced or separated, compared with 10% of the men, the report said, indicating that "doctoral work itself or the ensuing professional commitment undoubtedly created conflicts."

Women 'Transform' Legal Profession. Women attorneys made up over 9% of the legal profession, the Wall Street Journal reported May 31, 1978. This percentage compared with the total for the year 1970, when fewer than 3% of practicing lawyers were women.

Women also were gaining as law-firm partners and in all areas of legal work. About 25% of all law school students were women—10 times the number enrolled 10 years before.

Sex-Bias Ruling Voided. The Supreme Court ruled, 5-4, Nov. 13, 1978 that a lower court had erred in a job discrimination case by placing an unnecessary burden of proof on the defendant. The case was *Board of Trustees v. Sweeney.*

The case involved Christine M. Sweeney, a faculty member at Keene State College in New Hampshire. Sweeney was elevated to full professor from associate professor in 1976 after twice being denied a promotion. She filed a civil suit against the college, charging employment discrimination on the basis of sex. Sweeney cited in the suit the denials of promotion and a salary structure for women instructors that was alleged to be lower than that of their male counterparts.

A federal district court ruled in favor of Sweeney and ordered the college to make her promotion retroactive to 1975 with back pay. The U.S. 1st Circuit Court of Appeals upheld the district court. In doing so, the appeals court held that to rebut a job bias charge, an employer had to "prove absence of discriminatory intent."

The Supreme Court, without hearing argument, nullified the decision and sent the case back to the appeals court for reconsideration in light of *Furnco Construction Corp. v. Waters,* a June high court ruling.

In an unsigned opinion, the Supreme Court majority held that the *Furnco* decision had established that an accused employer need only "articulate some legitimate, nondiscriminatory reason" for his conduct, and that it was left to the employee to prove that the given reason was a pretext for discrimination.

Justice John Paul Stevens, in a dissenting opinion, accused the majority of drawing a "novel" and "illusory" distinction between the words "articulate" and "prove." He said that his interpretation of the *Furnco* ruling was that an employer had to "prove" that he had based his conduct on a legitimate consideration.

Stevens was joined by Justices Potter Stewart, Thurgood Marshall and William J. Brennan Jr.

'Italian Bakke Case' Declined. The Supreme Court April 23, 1979 declined to review, thus upheld, a ruling that denied an Italian-American man the right to sue a law school for rejecting his application to a special admissions program.

The case, *DiLeo v. Board of Regents,* had been nicknamed by observers the

"Italian Bakke case" because of its simi-larity to Allan Bakke's case.

The DiLeo case concerned Philip F. DiLeo, a New Yorker and the son of poor Italian immigrants. He was twice turned down for one of 29 slots in the special admissions program of the University of Colorado School of Law on the ground that he did not belong to one of the deprived "identifiable groups" for which the pro-gram was established. The groups were principally blacks, Hispanics and Ameri-can Indians.

DiLeo sued for admission, but lost in the Colorado Supreme Court. The state court held that he would not have qualified for the law school's regular admission's program, even if the 29 slots had not been set aside, and therefore he lacked the legal standing to sue the school.

Federal Views & Actions

Califano backs down on quotas. Joseph Califano Jr., secretary of health, educa-tion and welfare, endorsed quotas for school admissions and job hiring during an interview March 17, 1977. But Califano backed down March 31 and said he had erred in supporting quotas.

In his March 17 interview Califano said he once thought quotas would not work, but his experience providing legal representation for women at Newsweek magazine and for employes of El Paso Natural Gas Company had changed his mind.

Speaking about the Bakke case, then in the courts, Califano told the interviewer that he thought it "important what we not lose the ability to have affirmative action programs which would give minorities and women the opportunity to get into the major graduate schools and universities in the country."

Califano also said that he believed "busing is one of the tools that can and should be used in certain circumstances" to desegregate schools. Califano noted that Congress had passed laws limiting HEW's ability to require busing. He op-posed the congressional restrictions, Cali-fano said, although he did not see much possibility of their being lifted.

Califano endorsed busing across school district lines in order to "crack the white noose around inner cities." However, Califano added that he thought that on the whole "society places too much of the desegregation burden on local educational systems." Greater emphasis, he said, should be given to achieving integration through improving housing and employ-ment opportunities for minorities.

Califano's retreat came two weeks later. In a phone interview published in the April 1 New York Times, Califano ac-knowledged that quotas was "obviously a nerve jangling word." Califano said that what he had really meant to say was that equal opportunity should be available for all and that "affirmative action" was re-quired to rectify the consequences of past or ongoing discrimination.

By affirmative action, Califano said he meant that special training courses should be provided and talent searches should be conducted by employers and schools in order to assure that various fields would be open to minorities and women. However, he added, affirmative action did not mean using quotas to set definite percentages of minorities or women to be hired or admitted to a school.

Califano's earlier statement on quotas had stoked controversy on the already touchy issue. In a letter released March 31, 44 educators from universities across the country had urged President Carter to reject Califano's stance. "In one stroke," the letter said, Califano proposed "to ar-rogate to himself the power to determine who shall and who shall not enjoy equality of opportunity...." The letter argued that "if it [the government] is permitted to dis-criminate against whites and males today, it is permitted to discriminate against anyone else tomorrow." Among those signing the letter were Sidney Hook and Bruno Bettelheim of Stanford University, Nathan Glazer of Harvard University and Eugene Rostow of Yale University.

The letter said that Califano, in suggest-ing quotas, was in "flagrant defiance of law." Califano in the March 31 interview denied that quotas were against the law, noting that courts had ordered the hiring of minority individuals in certain cases where there had been obvious and extreme discrimination.

Califano said in a graduation speech June 5 that the government would rely on "numerical goals" in measuring minority access to higher education.

In his address at New York City's City College, Califano distinguished between goals and "arbitrary quotas," which he said would not be part of the government's enforcement program.

Califano did not say how numerical goals, used as "benchmarks of progress," would differ in practice from quotas. He said the government would not, for the "near term," employ financial pressure to force colleges and universities to meet the goals. (Some college officials had expressed concern that the government might withhold research grants from institutions failing to meet the goals or use federal scholarships to channel students from certain colleges.)

The government, Califano said, "want[ed] to rely on the good faith and special effort of all who join in the final march against discrimination." However, numerical goals were a necessary means of monitoring the efforts of colleges and the progress of minorities, Califano said.

Califano said colleges had to make "more strenuous efforts" to discover talented and motivated minority students. He said "imaginative programs of compensatory training" should be developed, along with new financial-aid programs.

Aid cutoffs considered—Califano had said Feb. 17 that he would halt federal education aid if he determined that recipient school districts were not desegregating in compliance with federal civil rights law. At the same time, Califano ordered reviews of six desegregation cases—involving three districts in Arkansas and three in Texas—left over from the Nixon and Ford Administrations.

The six districts had all been ruled in violation of federal law by an administrative law judge or by HEW's reviewing authority, and fund cutoff orders had been entered in all cases. However, the Nixon and Ford Administrations had not favored cutoffs of funds, and consequently final approval of the cutoffs had not been given. The last school district to suffer a loss of federal aid for noncompliance during the Nixon-Ford years was that of Ferndale, Michigan, which had its funds cut off in June 1972.

Califano said he had ordered the review of the six Arkansas and Texas cases to determine whether the original findings of noncompliance—which had been made from one to nearly four years ago—were still valid. The review would be carried out within 30 days, Califano said, and he would act "swiftly" if it was found that violations still existed.

Califano said HEW had "no desire ever to cut off funds to any school district or other educational institution." "But," he continued, "the way to insure compliance with civil rights laws is to make clear that we will order fund cutoffs if we must."

Califano said that, under his predecessors at HEW, civil rights enforcement policy had been "marked by mismanagement, confusion and uncertain leadership." The actions he was taking, Califano said, were intended to "restore the integrity of HEW's civil rights program" and to help in "rekindling the commitment" of the department to "a forceful and fair enforcement of the civil rights laws passed Congress."

Califano also said he was taking measures to insure that school districts and colleges file forms by May 15 attesting to compliance with sex discrimination law. He said he would order school districts to submit data on the racial, ethnic and sexual composition of elementary and secondary schools. The data had been published for the even years from 1968 through 1972, but it had been omitted in 1974.

Sex bias warning given. Nearly two-thirds of the nation's school districts and colleges had not submitted statements of assurance that they were complying with a 1972 federal sex discrimination law, or had submitted "unacceptable" statements, according to an HEW report March 15. HEW said that those schools and colleges would be informed immediately that they would have 60 days to send in adequate assurances, after which they would face proceedings leading to a cut-off of federal aid.

The 1972 law applied to school systems and colleges receiving federal aid. HEW said that adequate assurances had been received from 6,742 school districts and colleges, while 13,576 had submitted no assurances or inadequate ones.

Education Office reorganized. Commissioner of Education Ernest L. Boyer

April 11, 1977 ordered a reorganization of HEW's Office of Education.

Among the specific organization changes Boyer announced:

An Affirmative Action Office would be set up to take charge of programs currently handled by four separate offices. The Affirmative Action Office would oversee programs dealing with women, minorities and the handicapped.

Busing & Other Education Issues

Commission for busing. The U.S. Commission on Civil Rights said in a Feb. 15, 1977 report that progress in desegregating public schools in many cities could only be achieved if students were bused between cities and suburbs. In the two decades since the Supreme Court had barred school segregation in 1954, segregation had "grown worse, not better" in many cities, according to the rights panel report.

"To a very large extent," the report said, the remaining problems of segregation in public schools were problems that existed in big cities. The five largest school systems in the country—those of New York, Chicago, Los Angeles, Philadelphia and Detroit—had enrollments that were more than half minority students, the report noted. In the suburbs surrounding the cities, the report said, the public schools had predominantly white enrollments. As a consequence, desegregation plans, if they were to achieve "substantial integration," would have to include suburbs along with cities, the report said.

The report conceded that city-suburb busing had evoked strong public opposition. It also noted the Supreme Court's 1974 decision on a Detroit metropolitan busing plan and a similar ruling Jan. 25 on an interdistrict busing plan for Indianapolis had effectively barred judicial recourse to plans involving the crossing of school district lines. However, the report argued that metropolitan busing would generally not involve increased transit times for pupils. The report also noted that metropolitan busing plans for merged city-suburban districts had been successfully implemented in a number of areas, among them Louisville-Jefferson County,

Ky.; Charlotte-Mecklenburg County, N.C., and Nashville-Davidson County, Tenn.

The rights commission urged the Carter Administration and Congress to encourage city-suburb integration plans by providing federal funds to areas that set up such plans. The report observed that a "negative climate . . . fostered by the statements and actions of some of our political leaders" was one of the "principle obstacles to a sensible and effective remedy for public school segregation."

Busing Funds Ban. Compromise legislation cleared by Congress Dec. 7, 1977 and signed by the President Dec. 9 barred the Health, Education & Welfare Department from using federal funds to require, directly or indirectly, the busing of students to schools other than the one to which they were nearest.

The provision was part of the Labor-HEW fiscal 1978 appropriations bill. The two houses of Congess in June had approved different version of the ban.

The vote in the House came June 16. As reported to the House floor, the bill barred HEW from threatening to withhold aid to local districts unless they bused students to achieve integration. Such a restriction—sponsored originally by Sen. Robert Byrd (D, W.Va.)—had been incorporated in HEW-Labor funds bills since 1975. On the floor, Rep. Ronald M. Mottl (D, Ohio) argued that the restriction needed to be strengthened in order to forestall any attempt by HEW to circumvent it through requiring the 'pairing' or 'clustering' of schools.

('Pairing' referred to the merging of two schools, one with a predominantly minority enrollment, for integration purposes. Press reports in early June had indicated that HEW had reached the conclusion that the Byrd restriction did not bar the department from requiring districts to pair schools.)

Mottl described the pairing policy as a "legalistic somersault" devised by "social engineers" at HEW with the aim of frustrating the intent of Congress.

Critics of the Mottl amendment charged it was unconstitutional. They also argued that it would have no impact on court-ordered busing, which accounted for the great majority of busing to achieve integration.

However, the Mottl amendment gave House members the opportunity once again to go on record as opposed to busing, and it was adopted June 16 by a 225–157 vote.

The next day the House by voice vote adopted an amendment proposed by Rep. Robert S. Walker (R, Pa.) barring use of HEW funds to enforce "ratios, quotas or other numerical requirements" to achieve race- or sex-related objectives for hiring or school admissions. However, before it was adopted, the amendment was modified to omit specific reference to "goals and timetables." Most HEW affirmative action efforts centered around getting institutions and firms to adopt such "goals and timetables."

The Senate June 28 rejected, 64–31, an amendment by Sens. Jesse Helms (R, N.C.) and S. I. Hayakawa (R, Calif.) against HEW affirmative action. The amendment would have barred HEW from setting "timetables, goals, ratios, quotas or other numerical requirements" for the admission, hiring or promotion of persons of a particular race or sex by educational institutions.

The vote on the Helms-Hayakawa amendment was a victory for the Carter Administration, which backed affirmative action programs. However, the Senate June 28 rejected an Administration position on school integration. The Senate voted, 47–43, to bar HEW from requiring school districts to pair or cluster schools.

Before the vote on pairing, pro-busing senators had already lost, 51–42, an attempt to delete all anti-busing provisions from the bill.

Dayton Busing Upheld—The Supreme Court Dec. 1, 1975 had upheld a ruling by the U.S. 6th Circuit Court of Appeals that the so-called Esch Amendment (after Rep. Marvin Esch, Republican of Michigan) to the federal education law did not prevent the courts from ordering increased school busing to desegregate the Dayton, Ohio school system. The lower court said that the education law, "read as a whole," did not bar increased busing because other remedies were inadequate to desegregate the Dayton system. The Esch Amendment called on judges to explore other alternatives before ordering busing.

Citywide Busing & Remedial Courses.
The Supreme Court ruled June 27, 1977

in separate cases that federal courts had the power to issue school desegregation orders, including citywide busing, or to order school districts to devise remedial courses for the victims of educational bias.

In *Dayton Board of Education v. Brinkman,* the high court voted, 8–0, to vacate an appeals court ruling upholding a broad school desegregation plan for Dayton, Ohio. Writing for the court, Justice William H. Rehnquist said that the imposition of a "system-wide remedy" was not justified under the circumstances. However, the court reiterated its landmark 1973 position that when school segregation had a citywide impact and was the result of illegal actions by authorities, citywide busing could be ordered.

The Dayton plan, which the court noted had worked well in its first year (1976–77), was left in effect, however, pending reconsideration by lower courts. Justice Thurgood Marshall did not participate.

In the second case, *Millikin v. Bradley,* the high court unanimously upheld a lower court decision ordering Michigan to pay part of the cost of remedial programs for the victims of Detroit school segregation. (The programs had been ordered in addition to the extensive busing plan already underway in the city.) It had been estimated that funding such programs would cost Michigan about $5.8 million.

Chief Justice Warren E. Burger, writing for the court, contended that children who had been "educationally and culturally set apart from the larger community [would] inevitably acquire habits of speech, conduct and attitudes reflecting cultural isolation." He said the need for remedial courses in Detroit "flowed directly from constitutional violations by state and local officials."

Dayton Busing Plan Voided—The plan under which 16,700 Dayton, Ohio school students were bused to achieve racial balance was voided Dec. 15 by the same federal judge who had ordered the plan put into effect in the 1976–77 school year.

Judge Carl B. Rubin acted under the Supreme Court's June 27 order.

In his new ruling, Judge Rubin said that racial imbalance in a school system did not necessarily violate the Constitution if the schools were racially imbalanced for reasons other than discrimination. The plaintiffs in the case, Rubin said, had failed to prove "segregative intent."

While lifting the legal obligation from the board to pursue the desegregation program, Rubin advised the board it had a moral obligation to reduce racial imbalance in the schools.

Ohio Busing Orders Upheld. The Supreme Court July 2, 1979 upheld wide desegregation orders for two large Ohio school systems. The rulings in *Columbus Board of Education v. Penick* and *Dayton Board of Education v. Brinkman* affirmed decisions by the U.S. 6th Circuit Court of Appeals.

The decisions in both cases supported the high court doctrine established in *Keyes v. School District No. 1* (1973) that a federal court could order a remedy to school segregation when that segregation was shown to be the result of intentional actions by a school board or another local government unit. The *Keyes* ruling allowed federal judges to order the district-wide busing of students, even if only a portion of the school system was segregated.

The Supreme Court divided, 7–2, in the Columbus case, which involved a plan to bus 37,000 students to achieve racial balance. The plan, drawn up by U.S. District Judge Robert Duncan, had never been implemented because the school board had appealed to the higher courts.

The high court voted, 5–4, to uphold the validity of an existing program in Dayton that mandated the busing of more than 13,000 students each day in that city. Dayton had been under a federal order to desegregate its schools since 1954, the year of the Supreme Court's historic ruling in *Brown v. Board of Education.*

Justice Byron R. White, writing for the court in both Ohio cases, held in each instance that cities had an ongoing, "affirmative duty" to end racial separation in their schools once it was established that such separation had been intentionally caused by their school boards.

Justices Lewis F. Powell Jr. and William F. Rehnquist dissented in the Columbus case. They were joined by Justice Potter Stewart and Chief Justice Warren E. Burger in the Dayton case.

Basically, the dissenters argued that court-ordered busing was not justified in these cases because there was no clear line between school segregation caused by official policies and that caused by housing patterns. (The Supreme Court had held in the past that federal courts could not order remedies for racially imbalanced schools

that were the result of segregated housing patterns.)

Rehnquist called the Columbus decision "as complete and dramatic a displacement of local authority by the federal judiciary as is possible in our federal system."

Columbus Busing Ordered—U.S. District Judge Robert Duncan Aug. 2 ordered the busing of 50,000 students in Columbus, Ohio to begin Sept. 5.

The Columbus Board of Education had attempted to delay desegregation with a request for busing to be implemented in phases. The school board's phasing-in plan would have permitted the busing of elementary school students in 1979, and postponed the busing of middle and high school students until September 1980. Duncan rejected this plan on the grounds that the plaintiffs would face "an additional year of denial of rights" and that any delay would increase the difficulties already present in the task.

Busing in Cleveland. As the 1979–80 school year opened in Cleveland, a city reported to have Ohio's largest school system with an estimated 88,000 pupils, two-thirds of whom were nonwhite, a desegregation plan went into effect Sept. 10, climaxing a six-year legal battle. In 1976, a federal district court had found the Cleveland school system guilty of intentional segregation of its schools. But desegregation efforts were delayed because of integration law suits involving other Ohio school districts.

Under the plan for the fall term, as many as 9,500 Cleveland pupils, black and white, were to be bused to classes. The court-ordered plan set a deadline of September 1980 for a systemwide integration that could involve busing as many as 52,000 pupils.

The plan provoked considerable controversy in Cleveland. On Sept. 9, some 2,000 advocates and opponents of busing staged rallies simultaneously on a bridge spanning a waterway that separated the city's white and black neighborhoods. The main anti-busing group in Cleveland, Citizens Opposed to Rearranging Kids, called for a school boycott.

Chicago begins limited busing plan. The Chicago public school system opened the

1977 fall term Sept. 7 with only scattered protest against a desegregation plan featuring a small-scale busing operation for minority pupils.

White parents performed picketing duty at several schools, but only one arrest was reported.

White pupils boycotted some schools on the Southwest Side, but participation dwindled drastically Sept. 8. A walk-out by 300 Bogan High School pupils Sept. 13 led to their suspension for three school days.

Police formed a corridor for safe entry of pupils when pickets held up buses going into the Southwest Side Sept. 12.

The police also moved into an antibusing rally of 1,000 persons in Bogan Park Sept. 11; four persons were injured, 11 were arrested. Another 33 arrests were made outside the Bogan High School Sept. 13 when protesters refused orders to disperse.

The disorder lessened after police announced a "get-tough" policy Sept. 14. Picketing was continued at only four of 51 schools involved in the desegregation plan.

The plan itself began with the busing of 496 children, most of them black or Spanish-speaking, from 15 severely overcrowded schools. The 36 receiving schools were in predominantly white neighborhoods on the Southwest and Northwest Sides.

A policeman and a school board official were aboard each of the 24 buses used. Patrol cars followed the buses.

Pupil participation in the plan, which was voluntary, increased gradually after opening day.

The plan was ordered into effect after federal administrative Judge Everett J. Hammarstrom had ruled Feb. 17 that Chicago's public schools were not in compliance with civil rights law and should be deprived of federal aid. Hammarstrom said that the Chicago Board of Education had not provided adequate programs for Spanish-speaking students, and that too high a proportion of black teachers were assigned to predominantly black schools.

HEW's Civil Rights Division in April 1979 found Chicago's public schools still in violation of civil rights laws. HEW proposed Aug. 31 that the city start a desegregation plan that would require the Chicago school system to begin a compulsory busing program by September 1980.

The proposal, labeled a "feasibility" plan, would involve transporting 114,000 students, or 23% of the total enrollment, to schools outside their neighborhoods.

Milwaukee School Desegregation. A 14-year-old Milwaukee school desegregation case was settled out of court May 4, 1979 with the approval of U.S. Judge John Reynolds.

In 1976 Reynolds had ordered the city's schools to desegregate. The city's school board appealed the order, which was returned to Reynolds' court for further proceedings. Finally, the city's school administration and the plaintiffs agreed to suggest a settlement.

The settlement, recommended by lawyers for both sides, was intended to maintain the racial balance of students that had been established since 1976 and to prevent further discrimination in schools for the next five years. The agreement would abolish all-white schools but allow some to remain all-black.

According to the rules of the agreement, 75% of all students would have to attend desegregated schools, when more than 50% of the students in Milwaukee schools were black. (Black students comprised 45% of the city's schools in 1979, and the percentage was expected to rise to 49% in 1980.)

The required black enrollment for desegregated elementary or junior high schools would be 20% to 60%, and 25% to 60% for high schools. The rules further stipulated that there could be no fewer than 250 blacks in each high school.

Panel Finds Desegregation Lagging. The U.S. Civil Rights Commission took Congress to task Feb. 13, 1979 for "harassing amendments" that made it difficult to enforce school desegregation policies.

The commission also urged the Health, Education and Welfare Department "to step up its actions against noncomplying districts and cut off funds where essential to gain compliance."

The findings were in the panel's annual assessment of school desegregation.

Its primary finding, as stated by commission Chairman Arthur S. Flemming, was that, "We should be further down the road than we are at this time."

Although a quarter-century had passed since the Supreme Court's 1954 basic school desegregation decision, the panel said, nearly half—46%—of the country's minority children were still attending segregated facilities.

The panel was especially critical of a congressional amendment that made HEW powerless to require busing to achieve racial balance. The amendment, passed in 1977, forbade HEW from cutting off funds to districts that refused to comply with busing requirements.

Flemming said the commission was in agreement that the integration of suburban communities with inner-city school districts was "absolutely essential" if desegregation goals were to be achieved.

Another finding of the report was that the highest segregation rates were in the northeast (65%) and north central (68%) regions of the country. The percentages were based on the number of minority students who were attending segregated schools.

The lowest average level of segregation, 34%, was found in the southeast.

South Has Most Integrated Schools. The South had made more progress than the urban areas of the North in school integration over the past 10 years, according to a study reported May 9, 1979.

The study, which was conducted by the Institute for Southern Studies at Chapel Hill, N.C., found that the percentage of nonwhite students in the South who attended segregated schools was 12% in 1976. About one in 10 minority students attended schools with nearly 100% minority enrollment.

By contrast, 17% of all nonwhite students in the U.S. as a whole attended segregated schools.

However, the most striking comparison between northern and southern school enrollments was found in the industrial northern states of Illinois, Indiana, Michigan, New York, Ohio and Pennsylvania, where 31% of minority students attended segregated schools in 1976.

Washington Bus Ban Invalid. An anti-busing initiative approved in Washington state was declared unconstitutional June 15, 1979 by U.S. District Judge Donald S. Voorhees. He ruled that racial discrimination had been involved in the overwhelming passage of the ballot proposal in 1978. Voorhees said the initiative was "overly inclusive," because it limited school board assignments of pupils to the closest or next

closest school to their homes with few exceptions and allowed court-ordered busing only.

Anti-Busing Amendment Defeated. The House of Representatives July 24, 1979 defeated a proposed constitutional amendment to ban school busing.

The vote was 216 to 209 against approving an amendment to prohibit busing "on account of race, color or national origin." (A two-thirds majority vote was required for passage of a constitutional amendment.)

Ninety-five Democrats and 114 Republicans supported the amendment, while 176 Democrats and 40 Republicans voted against it.

The key argument in the debate over the amendment was made by congressmen who said that they opposed busing but objected to a constitutional change to "correct" the situation.

Rep. Ron Mottl (D, Ohio), who was the leader of the pro-amendment forces, said after the vote: "It's not only a personal disappointment, but a disappointment for the American people who don't approve of court-ordered busing."

"We had the momentum," said Rep. Don Edwards (D, Calif.), who opposed the amendment. "We had worked awfully hard and had a nationwide campaign going. And when Americans think about it, they hate to monkey with the Constitution."

Mottl's original anti-busing amendment had called for the prohibition of busing beyond the nearest school and for Congress to legislate equal education opportunities.

After it was noted that his amendment would ban busing to alleviate overcrowding and would have allowed Congress to write a federal educational policy, Mottl accepted changes. He backed an amendment offered by Rep. Marjorie S. Holt (R, Md.) that limited the ban to busing for racial purposes and eliminated congressional authority to mandate educational policy.

Bused black children show improved test scores. The New York Times reported Feb. 14, 1977 that a Chicago Board of Education study had shown that black children bused to schools with predominantly white enrollments had done better on reading and mathematics tests than other black children from the same neighborhoods who had attended predominantly black schools. The scores of the white children at the schools to which the black pupils were bused were unaffected.

The study cited as examples the 1976 reading scores of bused and not-bused black students. By age groups, those scores were (the scores of the bused students are given first): eight-year olds: 3.5, 3.3 (i.e., third grade-fifth month, third grade-third month); 11-year olds: 5.1, 4.8, and 13 year olds, 6.7, 5.7. A Chicago school official noted that two considerations had to be taken into account when interpreting the study: the bused students had not been selected at random but came from motivated families who might themselves have helped improve the test scores, and the ratio of white to black children was 9 to 1 in the receiving schools.

Jobs: The Weber Case

Voluntary Quotas Valid. The Supreme Court ruled, 5–2, June 27, 1979 that employers and unions could establish voluntary programs, including the use of quotas, to aid minorities and women in employment. Such programs were legal, the court held, even when there was no evidence of past discrimination by the employers.

The cases, consolidated for judgment, were: *Kaiser Aluminum & Chemical Corp. v. Weber, Weber v. U.S.* and *United Steelworkers of America v. Weber.*

The decision turned back a challenge by a white worker, Brian F. Weber, to a special training program at the Gramercy, La. plant of Kaiser Aluminum & Chemical Corp. Weber had been denied a place in the program, although two black workers with less seniority than he had been admitted.

Two lower federal courts had supported Weber's argument that the program violated Title VII of the 1964 Civil Rights Act. The provision barred discrimination in employment on the basis of race.

The Supreme Court reversed the lower courts. Justice William J. Brennan Jr., writing the majority opinion, maintained that an interpretation of Title VII that "forebade all race-conscious affirmative action would bring about an end com-

pletely at variance with the purpose of the statute and must be rejected. ... It would be ironic indeed if a law triggered by a nation's concern over centuries of racial injustice ... constituted the first legislative prohibition of all voluntary, private race-conscious efforts to abolish traditional segregation and hierarchy."

Brennan stressed the "narrowness" of the majority position. He noted that the Gramercy plant program, which was administered jointly by Kaiser and the United Steelworkers, was intended to be a temporary one. (The program was to expire as soon as the percentage of black skilled craft workers approximated the percentage of blacks in the local labor force.)

It was also noted the program did not "require the discharge of white workers and their replacement with new black workers ... [or] create an absolute bar to the advancement of white employees; half of those trained in the program will be white."

The purpose of the program, Brennan said, was to "eliminate a manifest racial imbalance." Title VII, he suggested, could not be invoked to prevent private parties from voluntarily instituting plans for that purpose.

Justice Harry A. Blackmun issued an opinion concurring with the majority result, but disagreeing with Brennan's "expansive approach" to Title VII. Blackmun, citing the opinion of a lower court judge in the Weber case, said that "employers and unions who had committed 'arguable violations' of Title VII should be free to take reasonable responses without fear of liability to whites."

Justice William H. Rehnquist and Chief Justice Warren E. Burger issued separate dissents. (Burger also endorsed Rehnquist's opinion.)

Rehnquist said the majority holding was a "tour de force reminiscent not of jurists ... but of escape artists, such as Houdini. ... Quite simply, Kaiser's racially discriminatory admission quota is flatly prohibited by the plain language of Title VII."

Burger accused the majority of rewriting Title VII "to achieve what it regards as a desirable result." The statute, he said, "was conceived and enacted to make discrimination against any individual illegal. ... I fail to see how 'voluntary compliance' with the no-discrimination principle that is the heart and soul of Title VII as currently written will be achieved by permitting employers to discriminate against some individuals to give preferential treatment to others."

Justices Lewis F. Powell Jr. and John Paul Stevens did not participate in the ruling. Powell was recovering from surgery during oral arguments on the case and chose not take part in the final decision. Stevens gave no reason for his absence, but it was known that his Chicago law firm had represented Kaiser in the past.

Reaction to the Decision—Brian F. Weber, who lost his case before the Supreme Court June 27, said that he was "really disappointed" by the ruling. He told reporters that he believed the decision would "have a negative effect on people all over the country toward blacks, and it shouldn't. It's not the blacks we were fighting, but the law. It was not a personal thing."

Jewish groups and other white ethnic organizations joined Weber in criticizing the decision. Larry M. Lavinsky, an official of the Anti-Defamation League of the B'nai B'rith, contended that "private employers may read this decision as sanctioning racial quotas." (B'nai B'rith had traditionally been opposed to racial quotas; Jews had often been victimized by such systems in the past.)

An attorney for the Polish-American Congress, Leonard Walentynowicz, suggested that the Weber ruling made legal unfair favoritism. "We believe in affirmative action," he said, "but we believe it should be available to all minorities, not a select group."

On the opposite side, civil rights leaders, the heads of labor groups and Carter Administration officials all praised the Weber decision.

Benjamin L. Hooks, executive director of the National Association for the Advancement of Colored People, called the ruling "the most important civil rights decision in recent history. . . . Had we lost this case, the cause of affirmative action would have been set back 10 years."

George Meany, president of the AFL-CIO, said that the decision was "a victory for all who believe in racial justice and who are committed to private voluntary action to end discrimination."

Labor Secretary Ray Marshall characterized the ruling as a "vindication" of affirmative action as a "major tool for achieving equity in the workplace."

Eleanor Holmes Norton, head of the Equal Employment Opportunity Commission, applauded the Supreme Court action and indicated that it might lead to a relaxation in the EEOC's affirmitive action guidelines, which required proof of past discrimination before corrective programs could be ordered.

Women's rights groups and Hispanic-American organizations also lauded the Weber ruling.

Following are excerpts from the majority opinion of Justice William J. Brennan Jr. in the Weber case, handed down June 27.

We emphasize at the outset the narrowness of our inquiry. Since the Kaiser-USWA plan does not involve state action, this case does not present an alleged violation of the Equal Protection Clause of the Constitution. Further, since the Kaiser-USWA plan was adopted voluntarily, we are not concerned with what Title VII requires or with what a court might order to remedy a past proven violation of the act. The only question before us is the narrow statutory issue of whether Title VII forbids private employers and unions from voluntarily agreeing upon bona fide affirmative action plans that accord racial preferences in the manner and for the purpose provided in the Kaiser-USWA plan. That question was expressly left open in *McDonald v. Santa Fe Trail Trans. Co.*, which held, in a case not involving affirmative action, that Title VII protects whites as well as blacks from certain forms of racial discrimination.

Respondent argues that Congress intended in Title VII to prohibit all race-consious affirmative action plans. Respondent's argument rests upon a literal interpretation of Sec. 703 (a) and (d) of the Act. Those sections make it unlawful to "discriminate . . . Because of . . . race" in hiring and in the selection of apprentices for . . . training programs. Since, the argument runs, *McDonald v. Santa Fe Trans. Co.*, supra, settled that Title VII forbids discrimination against whites as well as blacks, and since the Kaiser-USWA affirmative action plan operates to discriminate against white employees solely because they are white, it follows that the Kaiser-USWA plan violates Title VII.

Respondent's argument is not without force. But it overlooks the significance of the fact that the Kaiser-USWA plan is an affirmative action plan voluntarily adopted by private parties to eliminate traditional patterns of racial segregation.

Reliance on Section 703

In this context respondent's reliance upon a literal construction of Sec. 703 (a) and (d) and upon McDonald is misplaced. The prohibition against racial discrimination in Sec. 703 (a) and (d) of Title VII must therefore be read against the background of the legislative history of Title VII and the historical context from which the Act arose. Examination of those sources makes clear that an interpretation of the sections that forbade all race-conscious affirmative action would "bring about an end completely at variance with the purpose of the statute" and must be rejected.

Congress' primary concern in enacting the prohibition against racial discrimination in Title VII of the Civil Rights Act of 1964 was with "the plight of the Negro in our economy." (remarks of Sen. [Hubert] Humphrey).

Accordingly, it was clear to Congress that "the crux of the problem (was) to open employment opportunities for Negroes in occupations which have been traditionally closed to them," and it was to this problem that Title VII's prohibition against racial discrimination in employment was primarily addressed.

It plainly appears from the House Report accompanying the Civil Rights Act that Congress did not intend wholly to prohibit private and voluntary affirmative action efforts as one method of solving this problem.

Our conclusion is further reinforced by examination of the language and legislative history of Section 703 (j) of Title VII.

Opponents of Title VII

Opponents of Title VII raised two related arguments against the bill. First, they argued that the Act would be interpreted to require employers with racially imbalanced work forces to grant preferential treatment to racial minorities in order to integrate. Second, they argued that employers with racially imbalanced work forces would grant preferential treatment to racial minorities, even if not required to do so by the Act. Had Congress meant to prohibit all race-conscious affirmative action, as respondent urges, it easily could have answered both objections by providing that Title VII would not require or permit racially preferential integration efforts. But Congress did not choose such a course. Rather Congress added Section 703 (j) which addresses only the first objection. The section provides that nothing contained in Title VII "shall be interpreted to require any employer ... to grant preferential treatment ... to any group because of the race ... of such ... group on account of" a de facto racial imbalance in the employer's work force. The section does not state that "nothing in Title VII shall be interpreted to permit" voluntary affirmative efforts to correct racial imbalances. The natural inference is that Congress chose not to forbid all voluntary race-conscious affirmative action.

We therefore hold that Title VII's prohibition in Sec. 703 (a) and (d) against racial discrimination does not condemn all private, voluntary race-conscious affirmative action plans.

Permissible Affirmative Action

We need not today define in detail the line of demarcation between permissible and impermissible affirmative action plans. It suffices to hold that the challenged Kaiser-USWA affirmative action plan falls on the permissible side of the line. The purposes of the plan mirror those of the statute. Both were designed to break down old patterns of racial segregation and hierarchy. Both were structured to "open employment opportunities for Negroes in occupations which have been traditionally closed to them."

At the same time the plan does not unnecessarily trammel the interests of the white employees. The plan does not require the discharge of white workers and their replacement with new black hires. Nor does the plan create an absolute bar to the advancement of white employees; half of those trained in the program will be white. Moreover, the plan is a temporary measure; it is not intended to maintain racial balance, but simply to eliminate a manifest racial imbalance. Preferential selection of craft trainees at the Gramercy plant will end as soon as the percentage of black skilled craft workers in the Gramercy plant approximates the percentage of blacks in the local labor force.

We conclude, therefore, that the adoption of the Kaiser-USWA plan for the Gramercy plant falls within the area of discretion left by Title VII to the private sector voluntarily to adopt affirmative action plans designed to eliminate conspicious racial imbalance in traditionally segregated job categories. Accordingly,

the judgment of the Court of Appeals for the Fifth Circuit is reversed.

Employment

EEOC Guidelines; Bias Suits. The Equal Employment Opportunity Commission announced Dec. 12, 1978 final guidelines that were intended to encourage employers to hire voluntarily more women and minorities by protecting the employers from "reverse-discrimination" charges.

The commission defined affirmative action as "those actions appropriate to overcome the effects of past or present practices, policies or other barriers to equal employment opportunity."

The guidelines rested on a provision of the Civil Rights Act protecting employers for employment practices undertaken "in good faith, in conformity with and in reliance on any written interpretation or opinon" of the EEOC.

The guidelines provided that Title VII of the act wasn't violated if the employer conducted a "self-analysis" of his employment system, determined there was a "reasonable basis" for concluding that affirmative action was appropriate and took affirmative actions "reasonable in relation to the problems disclosed." In determining that there was a reasonable basis for affirmative action, the employer would not have to admit that he had violated the law.

EEOC said it would continue to investigate "reverse-discrimination" charges but would not proceed with a case if it found an employer was conforming to the guidelines. It added that EEOC would issue an opinion protecting the employer in the event of individual, private lawsuits.

EEOC to Monitor Corporations. A campaign to root out "systematic patterns and practices" of discrimination in big business had been announced Jan. 4, 1978 by Equal Employment Opportunity Commission Chairman Eleanor Holmes Norton. Interviewed by the New York Times, Norton said the commission would begin monitoring corporate employment practices and, where necessary, initiate class action suits without waiting for individuals to file complaints.

The EEOC currently had a backlog of more than 130,000 complaints and 160 pending class action suits. Under the Carter Administration, the enforcement of equal employment laws—currently divided among 25 federal agencies—was being consolidated under the EEOC.

Norton's announcement came less than a week after the Department of Health, Education and Welfare, as part of a settlement of three long-standing suits, had agreed to eliminate (by September 1979) its backlog of more than 3,000 discrimination complaints.

The suits, holdovers from the Nixon and Ford Administrations, had charged HEW with failure to enforce civil rights laws barring discrimination on the basis of sex, race and physical handicaps. Other terms of the agreement would allow HEW to devote more time to investigating overall compliance with civil rights laws in institutions rather than concentrating its efforts on individual complaints of discrimination.

Sears 'Conflicts' Suit Loses. U.S. District Judge June L. Green in Washington May 15, 1979 dismissed a suit brought by Sears Roebuck & Co. challenging federal equal-employment laws as contradictory.

The suit had asked the court to order 10 federal agencies to issue uniform guidelines on how to resolve what Sears called "conflicts" between the various anti-bias requirements based on race, sex, veterans' status, age and physical or mental handicaps.

The company pointed out, for example, that it had given preference to veterans, who were mostly men, in the years after World War II and now could be accused of denying equal opportunity to women.

As a class action suit, the challenge sought a ruling that could have been applied to all retail businesses. Sears was the largest retailer in the country.

Judge Green said the alleged conflict was "not sufficiently concrete" to give Sears the legal standing to have its contentions tried on their merits. Federal courts were limited by the Constitution, she said, "to the adjudication of cases or controversies."

This ruled out "advisory opinions" and resolving "hypothetical questions" that were best left to the legislative and executive branches of government, she said.

"Sears must recognize that personnel policies reflecting earlier and more limited national attitudes must be modified to widen employment opportunities for all," Green said.

"To be sure, realization of the national policy of genuine equal opportunity for all citizens is a formidable task, but not one beyond the notable skill and competence of Sears."

A long-standing investigation of Sears by the Equal Employment Opportunity Commission was in the background of the case. No charges against the company had been filed as yet, so the suit was interpreted by some observers as an attempt by the company to take the initiative and gain sympathy with its cause.

Edward R. Telling, Sears's chairman and chief executive officer, referred in a statement May 15 to "the overwhelming response to our suit throughout the nation."

The response, he said, "represents a clear call to the Administration and to the Congress to resolve this question: When the majority of Americans are covered by protective statutes, who gets jobs when not all can?"

Telling claimed that Sears already had an "outstanding" affirmative action program.

Eleanor Holmes Norton, chairman of the Equal Employment Opportunity Commission, in a statement welcoming the court's decision May 15, categorized Sears's suit as "frivolous litigation."

Sears had asked the court to require the U.S. to "coordinate the enforcement of the anti-discrimination statutes and, specifically, to issue uniform guidelines which instruct employers how to resolve existing conflicts between affirmative-action requirements based on race and sex and those based on veterans' status, age and physical or mental handicaps."

Among other things, the suit charged that federal agencies had violated anti-discrimination laws themselves.

It also accused the government of having failed to enforce civil rights laws, including those in education and housing, that would have provided a better qualified and more diverse work force.

Sears, the nation's largest general merchandise retailer, employed about 417,000 persons. It was the second-largest employer of females in the U.S. (American

Telephone & Telegraph Co. was the largest.)

Sears had been in a conciliation process with the Equal Employment Opportunity Commission since 1977 on a federal charge that the company had discriminated against women and minorities in hiring. The action itself dated back to 1973.

Sears Ends Federal Contract Work— Sears announced April 24 that it would no longer bid on nor accept federal contracts, "for an indefinite period, effective immediately."

Chairman Edward R. Telling said Sears had decided to stop doing business with the government because the Office of Federal Contract Compliance had begun a "campaign of harassment, subterfuge or retaliation" against the firm because of its suit challenging federal employment regulations.

Weldon Rougeau, head of the compliance office, said the company's action was "further evidence that Sears does not wish to comply with equal employment opportunity and affirmative action requirements imposed on all government contractors."

Telling said the end to government contract work would cost Sears about $20 million—about .1% of its $18 billion annual sales volume in 1978.

Veterans Preference Law Upheld. The Supreme Court ruled, 7–2, June 5, 1979 that states may give veterans advantage in public service employment without discriminating against women. The case, *Personnel Administrator v. Feeney,* concerned a Massachusetts law that had been struck down by three lower courts.

The law, enacted at the end of the 19th century, gave Massachusetts veterans absolute and lifetime preference in hiring for state civil service jobs. The statute was challenged by Helen B. Feeney, a state employee who three times had been denied promotions because male veterans with lower test scores were given the jobs she sought.

Two federal district courts and a three-judge federal appellate panel had ruled that the law discriminated against women in violation of the equal protection clause of the 14th Amendment.

The Supreme Court reversed the lower courts. Justice Potter Stewart, in his majority opinion, acknowledged that the law operated "overwhelmingly to the advantage of males." (The vast majority of veterans were men.) But, he asserted, that result did not in itself make the statute unconstitutional. Stewart maintained that the 14th Amendment guaranteed "equal laws, not equal results."

The law would be illegal, Stewart concluded, if it "was originally devised or subsequently reenacted because it would accomplish the collateral goal of keeping women in a stereotypic and predefined place in the Massachusetts civil service."

To the contrary, Stewart argued, the history of the statute showed that the "benefit of the preference was consistently offered to 'any person' who was a veteran."

In a dissent endorsed by Justice William J. Brennan Jr., Justice Thurgood Marshall held that the law reflected "purposeful gender-based discrimination" and contended that the statute bore "no substantial relationship to a legitimate governmental objective."

Marshall agreed with the appeals court panel that Massachusetts could aid its veterans with a less sweeping law.

The Massachusetts statute was stronger than similar laws in other states, and therefore the ruling was regarded by knowledgeable observers as a protection against legal challenges to the other laws.

Reaction to the Decision—Veterans' organizations and women's rights groups differed sharply in their reactions June 5 to the job-preference decision.

John M. Carey, national commander of the American Legion, characterized the high court ruling as a "restatement of allegiance to the veteran population by a grateful nation."

Ellie Smeal, president of the National Organization for Women, called the decision "devastating" and suggested that it was a major setback for the women's movement. "We have now been given the double whammy," she explained. "Women have been told they're not wanted in the armed forces and then that, for the rest of their lives, the women who are more qualified will be passed over in favor of men who are less qualified for governmental service."

Changes in Federal Job Procedure. President Jimmy Carter Feb. 23, 1978 sent to

Congress a plan to consolidate efforts against discrimination in federal hiring and promotions.

The brunt of the responsibility to insure equal-employment practices and opportunities would fall to an expanded Equal Employment Opportunity Commission (EEOC).

The President introduced his proposals at a White House ceremony attended by civil rights and congressional leaders. Both groups had worked with the Administration in formulating the plan.

The President told the gathering of several hundred persons that he believed "this is the single most important action to improve civil rights in the past decade."

It was, he said, "an important step toward a more competent government and toward a more just society."

Carter said that the current set-up was "chaotic," that almost 40 statutes and regulations concerning job discrimination were being administered by 18 departments and agencies.

Under the new plan, the EEOC would have responsibility for developing equal-employment standards for the entire federal government and for monitoring compliance.

This function currently fell to the Equal Employment Opportunity Coordinating Council, which would be abolished under Carter's plan.

The council comprised representatives of the EEOC, the Civil Service Commission, the Civil Rights Commission and the Labor and Justice departments.

The EEOC also would assume authority for enforcing equal employment opportunity for federal employees. This authority currently was held by the Civil Service Commission.

From the Labor Department, the EEOC would assume jurisdiction on matters involving equal pay and age discrimination.

Under the government reorganization act, the President's plan would go into effect automatically unless vetoed by either house of Congress within 60 days.

In his message to Congress, Carter pledged to "aggressively enforce our civil rights laws."

As part of the overall effort, Carter announced his intention to issue an executive order to transfer to the Labor Department all authority to have federal contractors observe federal laws against job dis-

crimination. The authority currently was distributed through some 11 federal agencies.

Carter Nov. 17, 1977 had urged federal officials to seek "aggressively and creatively" to promote career opportunities for women in the Civil Service.

Noting a 1967 executive order issued by President Johnson against sexual discrimination in federal employment, Carter said it was "an appropriate time to reaffirm the executive order, assess the progress we have made and evaluate our current efforts to be a truly equal opportunity employer."

Carter recommended an effort to develop, "within merit principles, innovative programs to recruit and hire qualified women" and to provide "satisfying career development" for them. He urged officials to be "especially sensitive to the concerns of older women and women from minority groups."

Carter's message was in a memorandum sent to the heads of federal departments and agencies.

The White House said June 15, 1978 that of the 1,140 appointments made by Carter, 10% went to blacks, 4% to Hispanic Americans and 18% to women. The percentages of blacks and Hispanic Americans were the same as, or just slightly less than, their proportion of the U.S. population. The percentage of women in proportion to the population was appreciably less.

Congressmen Liable on Sex Bias. The Supreme Court ruled, 5–4, June 5, 1979 that Congressmen could be sued for sex discrimination under the Constitution. The case was *Davis v. Passman.*

The case concerned a suit by Shirley Davis, a former deputy administrative assistant to former Rep. Otto E. Passman (D, La.). Passman had fired Davis in 1974, explaining in a letter that it was "essential" that her duties be performed by a man.

Davis brought suit under the equal protection component of the due process clause of the Fifth Amendment. She sought back pay and reinstatement.

The suit was dismissed by two lower federal courts before it reached the Supreme Court. One of the courts, the

U.S. 5th Circuit Court of Appeals, had held that Passman was immune from damages on two grounds: that the "speech or debate" clause of the Constitution made members of Congress accountable only to the House and Senate for their legislative actions, and the the 1964 Civil Rights Act—which banned sex bias in federal government employment—did not apply to the houses of Congress. The appeals court further held that Davis had no right to sue under the Fifth Amendment.

The Supreme Court reversed the lower courts and ruled that Davis' suit could proceed. Justice William J. Brennan Jr.'s majority opinion cited two past high court decisions that advanced the doctrine that federal officials did not enjoy absolute immunity from damage suits. The cases were *Bivens v. Federal Narcotics Agents* (1971) and *Butz v. Economou* (1978).

However, the majority in *Davis v. Passman* failed to address the issue of whether the "speech or debate" clause protected congressional employment practices from civil rights complaints.

Justice Lewis F. Powell Jr. and Chief Justice Warren E. Burger issued unusually sharp dissents.

Powell called the majority holding "a blind exercise of judicial power without regard to . . . constitutional principles."

Burger suggested that the ruling would allow federal courts to decide which staff members congressmen should hire and fire.

Justice Potter Stewart also dissented, criticizing the majority for neglecting to decide the legislative immunity issue. Justice William H. Rehnquist endorsed all three dissenting opinions.

Passman later settled.

The amount of the settlement was not disclosed. Passman said at a press conference Aug. 24 that he had reached the out-of-court settlement because he could not afford to continue fighting the suit.

Most Supreme Court Workers Are Male. The workforce of the Supreme Court was dominated by white males, particularly at the highest level, according to data made public June 11, 1979. The data had been released by the high court in response to reporters' queries following the decision in *Davis v. Passman.*

Most of the court's top staff positions were held by white men, including Michael Rodak, clerk of the court; Mark Cannon, administrative assistant to the chief justice, and Barrett McGurn, director of public information.

In the current term, there were 27 male law clerks and five female law clerks, all of whom were white. A total of 22 women had served as law clerks since 1972, about 13% of all the persons in that job. Only three blacks—William T. Coleman in 1948, Tyrone Brown in 1967 and Karen Hastie Williams in 1974—had ever worked as high court law clerks.

Alfred Wong, an oriental, was the highest-ranking nonwhite employed by the Supreme Court in the current term. Wong was the marshall of the court, or the chief of the tribunal's police force.

Nonwhites and women held many of the lower-level jobs at the court. For example, eight of the court's nine messengers were black, and the ninth was a native of Thailand. Similarly, of the eight courtroom attendants, or pages, three were black and three were women.

Black-White Wage Gap Narrowed. The difference in earnings between black and white male workers in the U.S. narrowed substantially from 1947 to 1975, and the gap almost disappeared between black and white women during the same years, according to a study released May 8, 1978 by the Rand Corp.

In 1947 black men earned on average only 50% as much as white men. In 1955 they earned 63% and by 1975 they earned 77%.

The gain was much greater for black women. In 1947 their earnings were 33% of that of white women. In 1975 they earned 98.6%.

The study dealt only with individual full-time workers (not families) and did not address the issue of unemployment.

The study attributed most of the improvement to the fact that "blacks and whites are becoming more alike in those attributes producing higher wages," most notably education.

In 1930, the black male began his working career with 3.7 fewer years of formal schooling than did the white male. By 1970 the difference had been reduced to 1.2 years. For women, the deficit in education was 2.6 years in 1930 and only four-tenths of a year in 1970.

The study suggested that "Among those with similar amounts of schooling, new job market entrants who are black will earn 90% to 95% as much as new white entrants and their earnings won't deteriorate (relative to similar whites) over their careers." It added, however, that it could be "30 to 40 years" before earnings matched those of whites because progress in overcoming inequalities becomes slower "the closer you get" to equal wage levels.

In addition to education, another important factor was the industrialization of the South, which opened up better-paying jobs to blacks. And much of the gain for black women was attributed to changing employment patterns away from low-paying domestic work.

The study concluded that there was some evidence that government affirmative action programs had had an impact, especially for women, but "our results suggest that the effect of government on the aggregate black-white wage ratio is quite small and that the popular notion that these recent changes are being driven by government pressure has little empirical support."

■ Carnegie Corp. reported April 10 in New York that blacks still held most of the low-level jobs and on the average made only 59% of the earnings of whites.

Urban League Challenges Reports—
The economic gap between black and whites was widening, according to a report by the National Urban League released Aug. 8 at the civil rights organization's annual conference in Los Angeles.

The report said that the proportion of upper-income black families, those with incomes of $24,000 or more, had steadily declined to 9% in 1976 from 12% in 1972. Middle income familes, with incomes of $16,200 or more, had remained at about 25% during the same time.

Because of economic recession, the study said, employment opportunities had declined sharply for male heads of families. The "proportion of black men heading families who were unemployed or not in the labor force jumped from 18% to 30%" in the years 1975 and 1976.

The study, titled *The Illusion of Black Progress,* concluded that "Much of the

increasing resistance among whites toward efforts to bring about racial equality is based on the popular misconception that the economic progress of blacks has been so great that the quality of opportunity has already been achieved."

Vernon E. Jordan, the league's president, said his organization's findings indicated that the nation was sitting on "social dynamite" and called on the movement to go back to the effective weapon of keeping report cards on the performance of elected officials. "Our friends will be rewarded and our enemies punished," he added.

Recourse against seniority bias limited. The Supreme Court, upholding the legality of collectively bargained seniority rights, ruled May 31, 1977 that minority members who had suffered discrimination prior to enactment of the Civil Rights Act of 1964 were not entitled to retroactive seniority.

The decision involved several cases consolidated for argument before the high court. *Teamsters v. U.S.* and *T.I.M.E-D.C. Inc. v. U.S.* concerned a Texas-based trucking firm accused of discrimination by its black and Hispanic workers. Two lower federal courts had found the company, T.I.M.E.-D.C. Inc of Lubbock, guilty of using separate seniority systems to trap minority drivers in lower-paying local runs, while lucrative long-haul assignments went to whites. Minority workers had been discouraged from becoming long-haul drivers because they would lose all seniority and benefits they had accumulated as local drivers.

The Supreme Court, too, found T.I.M.E.-D.C. in violation of the Civil Rights Act. The justices agreed that the regulation, which prevented the transference of seniority from one unit to another, was illegal. The justices also unanimously reaffirmed the landmark 1976 ruling that victims of job discrimination under Title VII of the 1964 rights act were entitled to retroactive seniority. The court took the ruling one step further to indicate that workers who could prove they had been discouraged by their employer's policies from applying for a better position might also be entitled to retroactive seniority.

The court divided, 7-2, on the ruling's effect on those who were victimized by biased seniority systems prior to the 1965 effective date of Title VII. The majority, led by Justice Potter Stewart, held that Congress had not intended Title VII to be used against any "bone fide seniority or merit system," even though that system had resulted in pre-act discrimination. Such an action, Stewart suggested, would "destroy or water down the vested seniority rights of employes simply because their employer had engaged in discrimination prior to the act."

In a sharp dissent endorsed by Justice William J. Brennan Jr., Justice Thurgood Marshall contended that this aspect of the ruling would have a "devastating impact" on minorities who, prior to 1965, had been "assigned the lowest paid, most menial jobs in many industries."

Marshall and Brennan also dissented from another May 31 decision involving seniority, *United Air Lines v. Evans*. This case concerned a stewardess who had left the airline in 1968 to be married in compliance with a regulation that prohibited married flight attendants. She had been rehired in 1972 after the airline had abandoned the regulation, but she had lost the seniority she had accumulated before 1968.

The Supreme Court, by a 7-2 vote, reversed a federal appeals court on the ground that she had failed to file a complaint within 90 days of her initial retirement, as prescribed by law. The high court also rejected her contention that the United seniority system constituted a continuing violation of her rights under Title VII.

Blacks awarded $1.8 million in bias case. A U.S. District Court judge in Oklahoma City Oct. 11, 1977 ordered Lee Way Motor Freight, Inc. to pay 46 blacks a total of $1.8 million in back pay. The compensation was reportedly the largest court-ordered amount the U.S. Justice Department had ever obtained on behalf of victims of illegal hiring and promotion practices. (There were larger out-of-court settlements on record.)

After a month-long trial in 1973 of the government's job bias suit filed against Lee Way in 1972, the court had found the trucking firm guilty of system-wide discrimination between 1965 and 1972 at each of its terminals in 10 states.

Under Judge Luther Eubanks' order, the largest individual award ever granted

in such a case, $138,150, went to Orville Wood. More than half of the awards exceeded $30,000. The judgment also required the company to offer jobs, with retroactive seniority, to most of those awarded back pay.

Quota Not Required. The Supreme Court ruled unanimously June 29, 1978 that affirmative action under the 1964 Civil Rights Act did not require a company to hire a maximum number of minority workers unless the firm had been found guilty of discrimination. The ruling in *Furnco Construction Corp. v. Waters* reversed a decision by the U.S. 7th Circuit Court of Appeals.

As an adjunct to the decision, the high court also held that a company accused of discrimination could defend itself by presenting statistics on the number of minorities in its work force. However, the court said, the statistics did not end the firm's liability for specific acts of bias. □

U.S. acts on job discrimination. In accordance with a 1965 executive order prohibiting federal contractors from employment discrimination, the Labor Department said Aug. 25, 1977 that Anastasi Brothers Corp., a major Philadelphia masonry firm, had been barred from doing business with the government.

Anastasi was cited for alleged violations on a federally funded hospital construction project in New Haven, Conn. from 1974 to 1976. The company's government contract had required the employment of 26.3%–36.3% minority bricklayers over the two-year period. The firm actually employed less than 16% minority workers.

The order against Anastasi was only the fourteenth such action in 12 years.

The Treasury Department Aug. 25 invoked the same executive order when it threatened the Harris Trust and Savings Bank of Chicago with loss of federal contracts. The government issued a show-cause notice to the bank, citing its "repeated failure to provide an adequate response" to findings that the bank's hiring and promotion practices were unfair to women.

Anastasi Brothers was reinstated as a federal contractor after making "sufficient efforts" to end job discrimination, it was reported Nov. 23. The Labor Department said the company had taken affirmative action aimed at compliance with federal minority hiring quotas and had also agreed to pay $13,605 in back wages to three workers who had suffered the effects of past discriminatory policy.

The Labor Department had reached an agreement with Prudential Insurance Co. of America whereby the firm undertook to increase its hiring of women and minorities for sales jobs, the Wall Street Journal reported Jan. 10. Prudential promised to more than triple the number of women on the sales force by 1979, the Labor Department said. For minorities, the goal would be to raise the proportion of sales agents in each local area to equality with the proportion of minority individuals with high school degrees or the equivalent in the area. Currently, the 25,000-person Prudential sales force had about 2,000 minority individuals and 750 women. Prudential also said it would conduct "availability studies" to determine what hiring goals would be appropriate for women after 1979.

City Service Oil Co. had agreed to pay $1,750,000 to 374 black workers for economic losses suffered because of racial discrimination, the Wall Street Journal reported March 2. The company, a unit of City Service Co., also promised to actively recruit minority workers and to drop, as hiring requirements, high school diplomas and certain aptitude tests that had not been certified as job related by the Equal Employment Opportunity Commission. The agreement, in the form of a consent decree signed by federal Judge Edwin F. Hunter Jr., came on a suit originally brought by the NAACP Legal Defense and Education Fund; the EEOC subsequently joined in the action.

■ The Labor Department announced that Avondale Shipyards Inc.—a unit of Ogden Corp.—had agreed to pay $275,000 to 1,125 current and former black employes who were victims of discrimination, the Wall Street Journal reported March 21. The New Orleans shipyard also promised to set up a $500,000 fund to train minority employes for higher-level positions.

The Labor Department said Oct. 6, 1978 that it was assuming sole responsibility for enforcement of equal employment opportunity rules involving federal contractors. The consolidation of compliance programs formerly handled by 11 different agencies into one office, the Office of Federal Contract Compliance Programs (OFCCP), was made effective by an executive order signed by President Carter Oct. 4.

The department had said May 30 that its Office of Federal Contract Compliance Programs would require 153 mining employers to show that they had affirmative action programs. The purpose was to ensure that women and minorities would get a reasonable share of the 200,000 new jobs that were expected to develop in the industry within the next decade.

Government reports indicated that nearly 98% of all industry employees, including clerical and office workers, were men. Men held 99.8% of the actual mining jobs, down from 100% with the advent of mechanization that reduced some requirements for physical strength.

The Labor Department announced Dec. 26 that it had approved an agreement under which Consolidation Coal Co., a unit of Continental Oil Co., agreed to pay $370,000 in back pay to 78 women the government said were discriminated against in the hiring of miners between 1972 and 1976. The company did not admit to any acts of discrimination or violations of federal law. The agreement included a promise by Consolidation Coal to fill 20% of its miner trainee jobs with women each year.

The department said June 26, 1979 that Merck & Co. had voluntarily agreed to develop affirmative action programs for its female and minority employees.

The pharmaceuticals company, based in Rahway, N.J., planned to spend $3.2 million over the next 3½ years on the effort. Most of the funds would be for job-training programs for female and minority workers and for training programs to make supervisors aware of the equal employment opportunities.

The agreement grew out of issues raised by the department with the company concerning a federal executive order requiring government contractors to take "affirmative action" to hire and promote women and minority employees. Merck was a supplier to Veterans Administraton hospitals.

Women's Construction Work Expanded. The Labor Department put new affirmative action rules into effect May 7, 1978 for construction projects where federal contracts or subcontracts valued at more than $10,000 were concerned.

By mid-1979, 3.1% of the industry's hard-hat jobs would have to be designated for women or contractors would lose their government business. The rules called for increases to 5% by mid-1980 and to 6.9% by mid-1981.

Many contractors expressed fears that there were not enough qualified women available. They also objected that with unemployment among construction workers running high, the women would be displacing experienced construction laborers.

Study charges bias in TV industry. The television industry was guilty of job discrimination and of perpetuating racial and sexual stereotypes in programming, according to a study Aug. 15, 1977 by the U.S. Commission on Civil Rights. The report, entitled "Window Dressing on the Set: Women and Minorities in Television," was based on employment data obtained from 40 commercial and public television stations, programs broadcast between 1969 and 1974 and on news shows broadcast between March 1974 and February 1975.

Local stations, the report said, had "misrepresented" their employment practices to the Federal Communications Commission (FCC), the agency charged with overseeing the industry. These stations were accused of placing women and minorities "in highly visible positions on the air," while leaving them "without comparable representation in decision-making positions."

The study said the FCC appeared "willing to accept little more than a paper commitment" by the industry to end the alleged job bias. (The FCC had no direct authority over television employment practices.) The report urged Congress to give the FCC the power to regulate broadcasting hiring and advancement policies.

White males, according to the study, dominated both entertainment programs and news shows. In the former, white males were said to have appeared in 65.3% of all major and minor roles, compared to the 23.8% of all roles played by white females. The report claimed that, while men were portrayed as older, serious, independent and the holders of prestige jobs, women were portrayed as younger, "family bound," usually unemployed and

were more often found in comic roles. Those women portrayed as employed, the commission said, "were in stereotyped and sometimes subservient occupations."

The study asserted that only 10.9% of all roles were played by members of minority groups (8.6% by nonwhite males, 2.3% by nonwhite females). Minority actors were said to appear primarily in ethnic settings or as tokens in all-white shows.

Network news shows were criticized for giving "minimal coverage" to national events dealing with minority and women's rights. White male "newsmakers," the commission said, were the focus of 78.7% of all network news stories.

The study called the current FCC policy of letting the industry regulate itself as much as possible a "failure." It suggested that the agency adopt "a variety of regulatory alternatives" to correct the alleged program bias.

Commenting on the report, FCC Chairman Richard E. Wiley Aug. 15 said it was "difficult to conceive" how his agency could "deal with stereotyping without becoming inevitably drawn into the role of a censor."

A spokesman for American Broadcasting Cos. Inc. said ABC's "policy and practice of nondiscrimination in employment" were in "full compliance" with federal laws. He said ABC had achieved "significant progress" in recent years "in the positive portrayal and treatment of minorities and women" in his network's news and entertainment programming. He expressed reservations about "the commission's suggestion of interjecting the government into questions of program and news content."

A National Broadcasting Co. Inc. statement said "some of the commission's broad-brush charges" appeared to be based on "out-of-date data" not in accord with the facts as seen by NBC.

NBC in out-of-court settlement—The National Broadcasting Co. unit of RCA Corp. agreed Aug. 31 to pay 2,600 past and present women employes a total of more than $1.75 million in settlement of a four-and-a-half-year-old sex discrimination lawsuit. The so-called consent decree, which ended litigation without requiring an admission of wrongdoing, called for estimated cash payments of $500 to $1,000 to women employed by NBC between December 1972 and December 1976. In the decree, NBC also agreed to an affirmative action program that would hire and train more women for diverse managerial and technical jobs.

Racism in News Media Condemned. Speakers at a meeting April 7–8, 1978 of the National Conference on Minori ties & the News condemned what they described as discrimination in the employment practices by the print and broadcasting media and called for extensive programs to remedy the situation.

The Rev. Jesse L. Jackson, civil rights activist and founder of People United to Save Humanity, April 8 told the conference that the news media had a "knack of keeping us busy looking at everybody else's sins but their own." Jackson urged a timetable for the "elimination of racism" in the hiring practices of the news industry.

Robert Maynard, a black former Washington Post reporter and chairman of the Institute for Journalism Education, April 7 outlined an 11-point program for the recruitment and training of minority members seeking a journalism career.

A survey showing that two-thirds of U.S. daily papers had no minority employees was presented April 13 to the annual meeting of the American Society of Newspaper Editors in Washington. The survey was conducted by the F. E. Gannett Urban Journalism Center at the Medill School of Journalism at Northwestern University.

The survey said that only 4% of the reporters and editors of the 1,762 daily newspapers in the U.S. were members of minority groups. In 1968 the proportion had been 1%. Minority employment was found to be closely linked to circulation. All newspapers with circulations of 250,000 and more employed minority journalists. Only 12% of newspapers with circulations of under 10,000 had minority reporters.

N.Y. Times Settles Sex Bias Suit. A class action suit charging the New York Times with discrimination on the basis of

sex was settled Sept. 28, 1978, an hour before the case was scheduled to go to trial in federal court in New York. The draft of the final terms, subject to the court's approval, was made public Oct. 6.

The agreement provided for the Times to pay $233,500 in annuities to its women employees and to modify an existing affirmative action plan.

The annuities were to range from $100 for female employees with less than five years service to $1,000 for those with 20 or more years. The 560 women covered by the suit could hold the annuities until maturity at age 60 or cash them at face value immediately.

The Times also agreed to pay $1,000 each to 15 women who gave depositions in the suit, and up to $100,000 for the women's legal fees and other costs.

The settlement provided that women would hold 25% of the top editorial jobs at the Times and occupy one out of every eight of the top 22 executive jobs within four years.

The women contended that the annuities offered were "camouflaged back pay." The Times denied the charge.

Reader's Digest Settles. The Reader's Digest Association, Inc. had agreed Nov. 4, 1977 to pay 2,600 former and current female employes nearly $1.6 million to avoid what it said would be "lengthy litigation" of a 1973 sex discrimination lawsuit.

The class-action suit brought by eight women had charged discrimination in hiring, promotion, work assignments, pay and other conditions. Of the cash settlement, $200,000 would go toward salary increases for 142 women presently on the magazine's staff. A company spokesman said that "while in no way conceding that there have been any discriminatory practices," the agreement represented "an amicable compromise among all parties."

Coors signs antibias pact. A 1975 job bias suit filed by the Equal Employment Opportunity Commission against Adolph Coors Co. was dropped May 9, 1977 when the Golden, Colo. brewer agreed to hire more women and minority employes. Coors signed the antibias pact without admitting that it and three of its unions had discriminated against women, blacks and Mexican-Americans.

Included in the agreement was the provision that the company would spend about $50,000 annually to train women and minorities and would counsel them on promotional opportunities.

Earlier, the U.S. Justice Department's Community Relations Service announced April 8 that various Mexican American rights groups had agreed to end their nine-year boycott against Coors. The boycott, organized to protest alleged job discrimination, was suspended after Coors agreed to develop employment, education and economic programs to aid Chicanos.

The federal suit had been brought by eight community school boards that opposed the racial assignment process as a step toward imposing racial quotas in the schools.

In a related development, the board of community School District 26 in Queens had been suspended by School Chancellor Irving Anker for a month, beginning March 10, for refusing to supply ethnic data on its students and faculty members.

The information was required to obtain federal and state aid. The district board, as well as several other community boards in the city, objected to the collection of ethnic data as a violation of individual rights.

New York Ends Assignment by Race. The New York City education board dropped its controversial system of assigning teachers on the basis of race. The decision, made April 5, 1978, went into effect April 7.

The system, designed to integrate the teaching staffs of the city's 1,000 schools, had been instituted in September 1977 as part of an agreement with the Federal Office for Civil Rights, an agency of the U.S. Health, Education and Welfare Department.

A "random selection" procedure was to replace the procedure used in September 1977, when teachers from minority groups had picked their assignments from one box and other teachers from another box.

Although supported by civil rights groups as a way to avoid discrimination, the "black box/white box" assignment process was denounced by numerous critics, including Sen. Daniel Moynihan (D, N.Y.). Moynihan called it a "prescription for division and hostility."

Actually, the agreement between the board and the federal civil rights agency had been declared invalid March 7 by U.S. District Court Judge Jack B. Weinstein in Brooklyn. The ruling was made on procedural grounds, that required public hearings had not been held before the matter was decided.

Not wanting to disrupt the system, Weinstein delayed any change in the assignment process for 30 days and did not nullify assignments already made.

Police & Fire Department Quotas. Twenty-three Louisiana cities and parishes June 29, 1977 signed consent decrees pledging them to hire more blacks and women for their police and fire departments. The agreements were in response to a U.S. Justice Department class action suit, filed in U.S. District Court in New Orleans, alleging that 39 cities and six parishes statewide (all with populations over 7,000) had refused to recruit, hire and promote blacks and women on an equal basis with white men.

It was the first time the Justice Department had filed such a vast, statewide suit. The U.S. action was made possible by Louisiana's system under which one state examiner administered civil service tests for all municipal fire and police departments.

Under the quota plan, the defendants were required to hire black and female police officers and firefighters until the black-white and male-female worker ratios reflected those of the particular city's overall labor force.

The cities, charged with violating the Civil Rights Act of 1964, among other laws, had been threatened with the loss of federal funds. New Orleans, governed by separate civil service laws, was exempt from the suit.

An association of police officers in Detroit filed suit Jan. 4, charging that promotions in the city police department had been made on the basis of race rather than performance on competitive exams. The suit, filed in Wayne County Circuit Court, named Detroit Mayor Coleman Young and Police Chief William Hart as defendants. An attorney for the officers' association charged that the city officials had "set up a quota system where they promote one black for every white, no matter where the black officer appears on the list." In the latest list of 38 officers eligible for promotion to lieutenant, there were 16 white and 16 black men, and 3 white and 3 black women.

The California Court of Appeal in San Francisco Dec. 26, 1978 reversed a lower-court ruling that had approved the Oakland Fire Department's ratio plan for hiring and promoting minority members. The appeals court ruled on the basis of the 14th Amendment and the 1964 Civil Rights Act.

The appeals court agreed that there had been discrimination in the fire department but added that Oakland had for .more than a decade in good faith engaged in a "well-funded and monumental effort to recruit minority persons as fire fighters."

Women's Job Status Reported. About 80% of all working women were employed in low-paying, low-status jobs, such as typists, salesclerks and waitresses, according to a June 4, 1978 report of the National Commission on Working Women.

The report also said that the 1976 median earnings of women with full-time jobs was 40% less than the median earnings of men who worked full time.

Another study, reported May 22, suggested that women's traditional concentration in the less desirable jobs could change "significantly" if they continued to make advances into management jobs.

The report, by the Conference Board, a business research group, said that the number of women managers in corporations rose 22% from 1970 to 1975, when men made 8% gains as managers.

(Women were 19% of all managers in 1975, compared with 16% in 1970.)

The number of women in professional and technical jobs increased 24% from 1970 to 1975, compared with a 1% gain for men.

The greatest advances by women managers were made in so-called female intensive industries (where at least 31% of the employees were female), such as publishing, finance and retail trade.

Most of the gains made by women managers were in the "very large" companies, according to the study.

The corporate world continued to be male-dominated—68% of working men were employed in the private sector, compared with 50% of working women, the report said.

The report said the chief factors behind the gains made by women in management were federal anti-discrimination laws and the 1973 consent decree signed by American Telephone & Telegraph Co. providing more employment opportunities for women.

Minority construction quota challenged. A provision of the 1977 Public Works Act requiring that 10% of the federal government's construction projects be contracted to minority-owned businesses was ruled unconstitutional Oct. 31, 1977 by U.S. District Judge A. Andrew Hauk in Los Angeles. The minority-hiring requirement had been attached to a $4-billion program to stimulate the nation's economy with federally funded jobs.

Hauk's ruling would not prohibit the use of $58 million already allocated to the city and county of Los Angeles, but it would bar the future use of any government funds that imposed a racial quota.

Associated General Contractors of California, a branch of the trade association representing some 8,000 general contractors nationwide, had filed suit charging that the 10% requirement was a form of reverse discrimination that barred nonminority businesses from competitive bidding.

The U.S. Justice Department argued that the provision was a necessary measure to compensate for the past effects of discrimination. Minority-owned businesses currently accounted for about 1% of the construction industry's gross receipts. Department officials noted that the quota could be waived on federal projects when no qualified minority concern showed interest.

Similar lawsuits challenging the provision's constitutionality had been filed by local chapters of the Associated General Contractors in Pittsburgh, Cincinnati and Butte, Mont. Federal judges in those states had variously upheld and blocked the government's program and court decisions were being appealed. Extended litigation would delay the start of construction, thus defeating the purpose of the legislation, which was aimed at reviving the construction industry.

Racial Poll Optimistic. A recent survey of racial attitudes in the U.S. found that whites were more tolerant of integration than in the 1960s, but blacks felt that discrimination remained strongly entrenched.

The study was conducted by Louis Harris and Associates for the National Conference of Christians and Jews. The study, issued Feb. 20, 1979, was a new version of polling Harris had first conducted for Newsweek magazine in 1963.

Among the major findings were that whites were less given to racial stereotyping than in 1963 and that whites were ready to accept affirmative-action programs.

"White attitudes toward blacks and toward real progress for blacks in this country are not more hardened than ever before," the study concluded. "Indeed, the conditions appear to be ripe for blacks ... to strike out for an acceleration of progress on many fronts."

In reporting the most recent survey, Newsweek magazine Feb. 26 pointed out that the results were susceptible to dispute. "Such surveys may measure what people are willing to say publicly, rather than what they really feel," the magazine said.

The article quoted Eleanor Holmes Norton, head of the Equal Employment Opportunity Commission, as saying, "If you look beyond what is respectable to say to what people do, you find backlash."

Among the results of the survey (a polling of a nationwide sample of 1,673 whites and 732 blacks in October and November of 1978):

■ 35% of the whites said they favored full racial integration, another 42% favored integration in "some areas." Only 14% said they would be upset "a lot" if blacks moved into their neighborhoods, compared with 33% in 1963. Fifty-four percent said they would not mind at all.

■ 85% of whites opposed busing. So did 43% of blacks. But 56% of white parents whose children had been bused considered the experience "very satisfactory." Forty-nine percent of the white parents felt that black children would do better in integrated schools, and 67% denied that their own children would suffer in the process.

The study pointed out the apparent "irony" in the situation, that "rarely has there been a case where so many have been opposed to an idea [busing] which appears not to work badly at all when put into practice."

■ 70% of whites thought special training and advice for minorities was a good idea.

■ 74% of blacks surveyed said they felt discriminated against in getting white-collar jobs, 68% in obtaining skilled-labor positions, 58% in acquiring decent housing and 61% in the wages they were paid.

■ While only 39% of the blacks thought the government was committed to equality, 71% of the whites thought so. Forty-three percent of the blacks listed unemployment as their most pressing concern, but 93% of the whites felt that blacks were "getting a better break in getting jobs than they did ten years ago."

Index

CARNEGIE Corp.—174
CARNEGIE Council on Policy Studies
  in Higher Education—118
CARROLL, Gov. Julian M. (Ky.)—120
CARTER, Jimmy—171–2
CARTER, Robert—9–10
CASSIBRY, Judge Fred J.—132
CATHOLICS, Roman—48, 110–3
CAUCUS of Women Biophysicists—109
CELEBREEZE, Judge Anthony—62
CELLER, Rep. Emanuel (D, N.Y.)—92
CENSUS Bureau—13–4, 114–5, 141–2
CENTER for National Policy Review—
  124, 137
CHARLOTTE, N.C.—50–4, 80, 162
CHATTANOOGA, Tenn.—63, 98
CHEMISTS—16, 18
CHESTERFIELD County, Va.—66–7
CHICAGO—15, 21, 30, 105, 112–3,
  139, 162, 164–7
CHISHOLM. Rep. Shirley (D, N.Y.)—
  5–6, 8, 15, 92
CINCINNATI—15, 33, 180–1
CITIES & States: College admissions &
  desegregation—157–8. Employment
  discrimination—20–5, 29–30, 32–3,
  103, 130–40, 174–5. School integra-
  tion—15, 37–8, 124–30; busing contro-
  versy—47–67, 70–7, 97–102, 162–7.
  See also specific city or state by name
CITY Service Oil Co.—176
CITY Stores, Inc.—32
CIVIL Aeronautics, Board (CAB)—131
CIVIL Rights Commission (U.S.)—69–
  70, 106, 124–5, 130–2, 147, 162
CIVIL Service Commission (CSC)—17,
  19, 34, 106, 108–9, 133
CLARK, Dr. Kenneth B.—46
CLEMON, U.W.—51, 73
CLERGY—16, 18
CLEVELAND—15, 111, 164
COFFIN, Chief Judge Frank M.—77
COLEMAN, James S.—45–6, 120, 126–
  7
COLEMAN, William T.—173
COLLEGES & Universities—16, 18,
  103, 115–8, 125, 128–30, 145–62
COLLINS, Rep. Cardiss (D, Ill.)—8
COLORADO—15, 65, 98, 101, 178–9
COLUMBIA, District of—23–4, 80, 101,
  137
COLUMBIA, S.C.—39–40
COLUMBIA Broadcasting System
  (CBS)—26
COLUMBIA Pictures Industries—26
COLUMBIA University—115–6
COLUMBUS, Ohio—33, 164
COLUMBUS Board of Education v. Pe-
  nick—164

COLVIN, Reynold H.—147–8
COMMUNICATIONS Industry—108
CONGRESS: Employment bias policy—
  2, 4–9, 103–4, 136–7. House of Representatives—137, 162; Education & Labor Committee—15, 92; Judiciary
  Committee—92; school integration—2,
  4–9, 15; Rules Committee—97; busing
  controversy—40–1, 46, 80, 91–2, 94–7,
  119–23, 162–3, 166. Senate—136,
  162–3; Aeronautical & Space Sciences
  Committee—110; Finance Committee—
  120–1; Government Operations Sub-
  committee on Intergovernmental Rela-
  tions—137; Labor & Public Welfare
  Committee—68, 120–1; Operations
  Committee—135; Select Committee on
  Equal Educational Opportunity—46
CONGRESSIONAL Black Caucus—19,
  93, 147
CONNECTICUT—98, 111
CONSOLIDATED Freightways, Inc.
  (Menlo Park, Calif.)—83
CONSOLIDATION Coal Co.—176
CONSTRUCTION Industry—20–5, 29–
  30, 105, 133–4, 175–7, 180–1. See also
  specific occupation by name
CONTI, Judge Samuel B.—113
CONTINENTAL Can Co., Inc.—132
CONTINENTAL Oil Co.—176
CONTRACTORS Association of East-
  ern Pennsylvania—20–1, 29
COOK, Ed—64
COOPER, Julia P.—78
COORS Co., Adolph—178–9
CORPORATE Executives—17
COURT Actions: College-university ad-
  missions & desegregation—102–3,
  117–9, 145–58; Bakke case—145–56.
  Employment discrimination—20–1, 23,
  26–9, 31–3, 82–3, 87, 105–6, 108–9,
  111–3, 132–3, 137–40, 140, 142–4,
  167–75, 179–80; Weber case—167–9.
  Housing integration—130. School se-
  gregation—37, 117, 125, 128, 130;
  busing controversy—8–10, 38–9, 42–3,
  50–77, 97–102, 121–2; 163–6
COUNCIL of Economic Advisers—114
COX, Archibald—147–8
CRAMER, Dr. James A.—118
CRAVEN Jr., Judge James Braxton—
  66–7

D

DALLAS—15, 67, 97–8
DAVIS, Calif.—145–56